ROLLING WITH THE
6.57 CREW

Kevin Main

ROLLING WITH THE 6.57 CREW

The True Story of Pompey's Legendary Football Fans

CASS PENNANT
ROB SILVESTER

JOHN BLAKE

Published by John Blake Publishing Ltd,
3, Bramber Court, 2 Bramber Road,
London W14 9PB, England

www.blake.co.uk

First published in paperback in 2004

ISBN 978 1 84454 072 3

British Library Cataloguing-in-Publication Data:

A catalogue record for this book is available from the British Library.

Design by www.envydesign.co.uk

Printed in the UK by CPI Bookmarque, Croydon, CR0 4TD

5 7 9 10 8 6 4

Papers used by John Blake Publishing are natural, recyclable products made from
wood grown in sustainable forests. The manufacturing processes conform to the
environmental regulations of the country of origin.

'IF YOU WOULD TAKE THE PAINS BUT TO EXAMINE
THE WARS OF POMPEY THE GREAT, YOU SHALL FIND,
I WARRANT YOU, THAT THERE IS NO TIDDLE-TADDLE
NOR PIBBLE-PABBLE, IN POMPEY'S CAMP.'

Henry V, Act IV
William Shakespeare, 1599

THIS BOOK IS DEDICATED TO MY WIFE KAREN
FOR HER CONTINUED SUPPORT AND FOR MARRYING
ME WHERE I WANTED ... ALSO TO MY CHILDREN
BLAISE AND DEXTER 'SO BEAUTIFUL TO ME'.

Rob Silvester

Contents

Acknowledgements

The authors would like to thank the following for valuable assistance of many different kinds during the research and writing of this book. Its production would have been impossible without their help.

Special thanks to: Eddie C, Jim B, Ray G, Trev, Tay, George B, Pat, Jack, Mush, Doug, Tim & Chris (Fareham Loyal), Gingeman, Billy W Chalky, Stevie W, Fooksie, Rob Mc, Geoff L, Tim F, Stu (F'ham), Colin B. With a particular word of thanks to Dave & Loz, John Blake Publishing for their patience, and for contributing illustrations, Warmwork Photography plus AG. Special thanks also to Wendy Sanford and Charlotte Fitzpatrick.

And *Rolling Along*: Page Bros, AK, Gary H, Steve Rog, Giss, Ernie, Bidds, Wayne J, Woz, Micky B, Stocky Bros, Brian P, Richie B, Danny H, Jimmy W, Tommy B, Marty F, Ex, Ritchie Sex, Jeff Gallon, Perry L, Derek C, Lee T (Oz), Jeff R, Billy R, Emptifish, Mark A, Micky D-Tox, Jake, Brad M, Grant H, Storf, Andy B, Tony C, Isaac Day, Paul S and Danny, Stevie Y, Snoop, Johnny K,

Hewi, Birdz, Froggy, Van H, Aaron G, Stu W, Tony T, Zee, Tony Andrews, Kev Mayes, Fred Rob and the Chi Boys, Cookie, Rory, Daker Man, Paul & Jim Finnegan (F.U.G), Fareham Phil, Jez Warren, Coach, Aidey Fuller, Marco, Ross C, Steve R, Soz, Toosh, Walt, Tosh, CJ, Moss, Ikie, Sean, Mark & Rats (Salisbury Loyal), Big Dave, Chas, Ian Essery, FJ, Savage & Mrs, Chris Hall, Darren Vear, Dredger, Enge, Coxy Mayes, Kev, Limo, Lucky & Box (Leigh Park), SOSS, Steve L, Smeegel, Bill Haley, Micky Boyce, Devil's Child, Ray Smith, Macer, Ben Pompey Fookes, Will, Dorran, Strawbs, Lee George (Cuddles) C.N.E. Gas Squad, Lee & Jay C, Harry Gang & Porkies. Anyone know what's happened with Raffles?

Others: Big Kirky, Kenny, Sam, Lex, Ohm's Crew, Davie J, Darren W, Kev Courtney, Alan & Kenny (Belfast), Gilkicker, Martin Lee, Gary H, Parky, Soul Crew, Bruno, Raggsy, Wilko Bros, Tony Oakey, Jella, Shaksey, Jasper Naughty Forty, Dave Saif, Dolly, Paul Fen, *FHM*, Acarine. Also, Jen, Phil & Andy, and for no special reason other than he's Pompey's No.1 Fan, John Westwood.

RIP: Rob Porter, Rob Clark, Docker Hughes, we will remember them.

Finally, a message from Cass Pennant: this book is dedicated in friendship and gratitude to all the staunch loyal supporters of Pompey FC whose co-operation, advice and research assistance was invaluable, as was all the beers that came my way. Cheers, lads, I hope I've achieved your expectations with it as well as mine and Rob's.

Introduction

Portsea Island, which the city of Portsmouth sits on, is one of the most densely populated areas in Europe. Rows and rows of rabbit hutches were crammed closely together to provide the working class with cheap housing. In days gone by the city was a living hell as press gang fought press gang on the streets of Old Portsmouth, while vice and crime flourished among the impoverished. Many a conflict has been launched from Portsmouth: Agincourt, D-Day, the Falklands and Trafalgar have all used our city as a launch pad for famous and glorious battles. The city, on these historic occasions, has been awash with patriotism and pride.

After its pounding by the Luftwaffe in the forties, Portsmouth was re-built into a concrete jungle of council estates, re-housing ex-servicemen and their families who chose to settle here. After much neglect and a lack of investment, these areas of false hope quickly became downtrodden and breeding grounds for the hard-working labour class of the city. The mass of tower blocks that sprang up out of old bombsites spawned generations of kids who had nothing but a bleak future to look forward to.

There is no easy answer to why football violence was so prevalent in Portsmouth. Other cities with a higher population and just as many deprived areas have not had as many active thugs hell bent on causing trouble at games. People reading this book may ask, Why did they do it? What was the point? What prompted a bunch of mostly kids to roam the country looking for a fight? What end did it serve? It could be argued that it was one of the first generations of working-class men to be untouched by a major war. It could also be said that the parallels between the violence and the 'no society, start of individualism' philosophy of Thatcher contributed to it. Also, the growing number of unemployed in the ever-declining economy could not have helped. These factors may have contributed but for those who were there it was all about the buzz and the surge of adrenalin only felt when the familiar roar went up and the whites of the opposition's eyes were just a punch away.

The recollections in this book of the main faces of the 6.57 will take readers through these violent and sometimes humorous events. The government always had tough words for such 'terrible displays of violence', but would have used this aggression to its own advantage had a conflict where conscription was necessary presented itself. Who have always been at the forefront of every battle? The upper and middle classes have historically led from behind the front line. Well behind it. It's the working class who fight the battles, yet apparently they must have the permission of the ruling classes to vent this aggression. A case of you can only be violent if we want you to and it suits our needs, otherwise be passive and put up with being downtrodden. Aggression usually stems from a person's way of life and upbringing. It is the effect of a cause. If the government creates an underclass of people with low-paid jobs and no self-respect, then places them in cheap housing, it is obvious that the youth of these areas will revolt.

INTRODUCTION

The violence on the terraces spiralled across the country following the riots in most cities in 1981. The country's youth felt isolated and disenfranchised. The incidents of the eighties were widespread and frequent, with the violence of the era getting intense and out of hand. The numbers seemed to increase with every game and the authorities knew something had to be done to combat it. They had mistakenly thought that the 6.57 Crew had become organised, as rival mobs fought out battles dressed in fashionable sportswear and expensive clothing with pinpoint timing and military-style precision. As usual, they were way off the mark. The 6.57 Crew was about as organised as the proverbial brewery piss-up. The closest we got to organisation in the early days was 'see you in Punch and Judy's after the game' or 'meet you at Portsmouth and Southsea at half-six Saturday morning'.

Portsmouth is not a place of many shootings or organised crime. It is very contained and rather small for the number of people who live in it. The police were on top of most of the illegal activities that went on but football was one boil they just could not lance. And it really grated on them. The Old Bill like to drum up sinister and budget-justifying reasons to target certain groups and they used the 6.57 as a scapegoat for every fight in and around Portsmouth for years. Some justified. Some not. The 6.57 were even accused of having ranks and generals and soldiers. Absolute nonsense. Every group of human beings has people that take control and that the others listen to: born leaders who led from the front. But there were no ranks. The police spotters loved the name 6.57, from the days of King and Hiscock right up to the budget-wasting overkill of HOOF. The media love a sensation and cover soccer violence thoroughly. It makes good press to have these almost mythical type gangs with sinister overtones roaming our vulnerable streets picking off innocent football fans. As every thug across the country knows, this rarely happens. Like-minded people met like-minded people to have a fight. That's all.

ROLLING WITH THE 6.57 CREW

The 6.57am train to Waterloo is the earliest train you can catch to the capital and gives you the flexibility to be almost anywhere in the country by no later than one o'clock. This was great for us as it got us into enemy territory as early as possible and we could set about causing maximum mayhem. It has to be said, though, at the time when casual dressing and weekly rumbles were at their most active we did not really call ourselves any name. At the time, we just thought ourselves game fellas up for a row.

The name 6.57 has been slowly accepted and has gone into folklore status subconsciously and was never more prominent than when Docker Hughes was running for Parliament and the crew got national coverage. The branding of our gang was an eighties thing. It was all the rage in that decade to have a name and most of the top firms went by some moniker. But that is taking nothing away from the achievements around England of the original Pompey Skins and seventies-style boot boys. This book deals predominantly with the Air Balloon crew, one of the many and probably the largest firms in the city. They were into everything: football, fighting, the casual movement, thieving and drugs. All round anarchy. And all this at 100 miles an hour. Also the Eastney lot are covered. They were a more serious-minded crew but really tough with it and would always stand their ground. The boys from Somers Town and Paulsgrove and many others integrated well and could be usually found on a Friday night drinking in the Air Balloon with the Stamshaw boys.

The people who are categorised as the 6.57 are mainly town boys, but there are some from outside the city limits who ran with the top firm. But they were just as active. Some of their escapades are unbelievable. A book could be written about their exploits alone and it would make a cracking read. It was always a good blend of people and the amount of nutters on the firm were too numerous to mention. Solo attacks have been frequent. In one famous incident one of the chaps jumped into an end full of Boro on his own after scaling a huge fence, which they still talk about up there to this day. Another windmilled into a side full of Cardiff and two well-known faces were dragged out of the Leeds end before they were torn apart. We at Pompey have the same legendary moments to share that every major firm in the country has.

The times we had together and the feeling of camaraderie and unity are unparalleled by anything else those involved have ever felt. If you were a hardcore member of your particular firm you will know what I mean. To be in battle with your pals can be an uplifting thrill and highly addictive. The aftermath and buzz of a major punch-up was hard to beat as everyone swapped stories still rushing on the high. Feeling danger with someone else and knowing that you could count on their support should events go wrong forges strong and unbreakable bonds. Though obviously not at the same level, those involved in the violence can relate to the old war chums who still meet up every year and shed a tear for fallen comrades.

You will read about the country's major firms, also a few surprises will be thrown into the mix. We have played in all the divisions in the last 30 years and would pull 30,000 crowds in the old fourth division. But make no mistake about it we are THE football fans of the South. If you believe what you read on the internet you would think that the idiots up the road used to trade blows toe to toe with us, sometimes coming on top, sometimes not. It is pure fantasy. We do not respect them at all, and have never really had it properly with them. We would have loved to have had a major crew just up the road. We were hell bent on violence in those days and a Millwall or Cardiff, 16 miles away would have been heaven. This so-called rivalry is pure geography. If Bournemouth were closer they would be the team vilified. If Southampton had a major crew as active as ours then there should be countless stories of battles between us. There are none. They are not in our league as a football firm and everyone knows it. They never get mentioned in any book about football violence and they only get a mention in this one so we can put the record straight in print once and for all.

However, there is plenty of stuff to read on the top crews we have encountered, and also the nutty little firms at the likes of Lincoln and Hartlepool. We have been just about everywhere and had mixed results in battle, but it is from the lower divisions that some of the best memories come. The reader of this book will be taken on a rollercoaster ride of violence, adrenalin, laughter and excitement, with humour unearthed at the most unexpected of times.

Follow the journey through the golden era of the Original Skins of the Golden Bell Pub, where heady nights on Dexy's and mandrix were followed on by the next day's outing on the terraces. Then the crazy lawless days of the seventies and taking the opposition's end on match days decked out in three-star jumpers, Anco Skinners and knee-high Docs are covered in detail. Also the times when the Bovver and boot boys ran riot all over the country. Classic encounters like the storming of the Grange at Ninian Park in 1973, right through to Pompey Animals at Reading in '77 and then to the heady days of the 6.57 in the early eighties. There is also an in-depth chapter on how drugs invaded the top firms in the country, doing what no police tactic could do – quell the violence.

Forget all your current so-called firms, this is when it really went off and violence was proper. There were no surveillance cameras or technology dedicated to stopping it, the fighting was long and fierce and reputations were earned the hard way.

The first-hand accounts which follow are given by Pompey boys from all eras. You know who you are and which are your stories. Thanks for sharing them with me. For clarity, the fans' first-hand accounts are in italics.

This book is dedicated to all our boys, past, present and future. To the best days of our lives. Play Up Pompey.

Rob Silvester

Glossary

DIMLO	stupid person; wally
SCARFER	A supporter who feels he has to wear a club scarf to prove his allegience
SKATE	Sailor
NCIS	National Criminal Intelligence Service
HOOF	Hooligans Out Of Football
'KICK THE GRANNY'	To dish out or receive a servere kicking
DAIRY	The best; the cream of the crop
NECKED	To swallow or gulp down
POMPEY	Portsmouth Football Club
E	Ecstasy

Rob Silvester – 6.57 Crew

'THE NECESSITY OF LIVING IN THE MIDST OF THE DIABOLICAL CITIZENS OF PORTSMOUTH IS A REAL AND UNAVOIDABLE CALAMITY. IT IS A DOUBT TO ME IF THERE IS SUCH ANOTHER COLLECTION OF DEMONS UPON THE WHOLE EARTH. VICE, HOWEVER, WEARS SO UGLY A GARB THAT IT DISGUSTS RATHER THAN TEMPTS.'

GENERAL JAMES WOLFE (1758)

Far from flattering were Wolfe's comments on Portsmouth, in a letter he wrote to his mother, shortly before sailing from Portsmouth to Canada and his eventual death on the Heights of Abraham, in 1758.

I caught the London Waterloo train bound for Portsmouth, for a journey to Portsmouth Football Ground where I was to meet up with Rob Silvester. As I looked up at the departure board – Fratton, Portsmouth and Southsea, Portsmouth Harbour – I remembered Rob had said Fratton. Fratton Park was their ground and I just couldn't believe I had never been there in my football-going days of travelling around with the West Ham boys. Never ever remember playing them, but Rob was to pick me up on that point later. I said something about it couldn't have been a row game. Rob said one word – Swallow. I said, 'You're kidding, I don't remember much said on that.' 'No, it was mainly Under 5s, all them. It's not a problem, Cass, there's never been no real animosity between us. We later got to know some of them well

1

from the rave scene, Downham Tavern and Centreforce and all that.' Suddenly, I remember there's a lad they won't hear a bad word against who's been coming to West Ham for a number of years, but they only ever call him Pompey. And I can go back further, right back to the seventies. Whenever we came down to Southampton, a few Portsmouth would wait at the station and would want to join us. At first we were a bit surprised as back then, away from London, West Ham only ever had a small travelling firm, nothing like the firm that went away in the eighties. Even then we were used to being hated by all. You had this Pompey geezer that acted like one of those loners, but he was bit of a hard-nut kitted out like those dudes in *A Clockwork Orange*. He would join our escort, making these grunting and growling noises. People didn't take kindly to it and thought he should know. When a few decided to challenge the loon, a few of us had to step in. Even though the kid looked ready to defend himself, it became obvious he was a deaf and dumb mute – it would have been a liberty. No sooner had we befriended him, shouts went up that Southampton have made their showing. Fuck me, he was gone, out the escort, through the Old Bill and straight into them. People like to say we're mad, but he was proper mad. He didn't give a fuck. Later, we thought we had lost him, but in that shit ground they called the Dell, back then you could have the odd row in that Milton Road end, where they had solid concrete parts of the ground that reminded you of the old war-time pill boxes placed along Dymchurch and St Mary's Bay. Anyway, believe it or not, in those early times you could get a little off going with the Southampton lot and you would have to be showing your age to remember that. But only when you first went into the ground, mind, when no one's really mobbed up fully. Once everyone got together it would only be the Old Bill's dividing human wall before they had fences that would save them, but that wouldn't deter matey. You looked up at the other end, and it would be full of Southampton. I remember you see a small gap on the terraces appear, not big enough to register a mob going in. You wonder what West Ham are up there and then you see Old Bill pull him out and 'cause he's deaf and dumb the Old Bill don't know quite what to do with him yet he seemed well known to them, all right.

As we marched through the seventies he became a familiar face for a few seasons. People would tell others that hadn't made the trip before that a band of Pompey would be waiting to join us and to look out for the deaf, dumb, mute, he's OK, well mad, certainly in his hate for Southampton and he wasn't alone. Another trip we had a proper firm of Pompey meet us unannounced as usual. Now this was pushing it. For a start we didn't need anyone and by now this was bigger than any Southampton crew we were likely to find. To us, Southampton was a nothing day, just one of those away trips you had to make. Then someone spotted that they all had brand new West Ham silk scarves on the wrist. Now that gives the game away on what period we're talking here, but with them going as far as wearing brand spanking new West Ham scarves, any thoughts of hostility between the two groups went right out the window. Whatever anyone in the know thinks of Southampton fans, there's something far more going down with the Portsmouth lot when it comes to their local rivals. Other London clubs that went there told similar stories and of the period no doubt it was the same Pompey crew. And coming out of the seventies into the casual-era eighties. During which times you couldn't give Southampton a mention, those that bothered going only ever found what can only be regarded as a family club.

Rob just shrugged his broad shoulders. I had gone past the amusement stage and it seemed to be me mentioning Southampton that was doing it. We were round by the ground now and his blue eyes seemed to sparkle and now he would do the talking, but first by way of polite explanation he tells me quite warmly nobody says the word Southampton round here. 'Nobody can bring themselves to say it, Cass, and I ain't just talking about football supporters.

It's Scum – we call them Scummers, Cass. That's what they were called before me and it will be the same after me.'

Silvester is taking me an away supporter's route around his home team's ground. As we walk and talk I notice Rob's leather Burberry bomber-style jacket, he raises his builder's arms silently pointing to graffiti further along some turnstile wall as we momentarily pause in this alleyway. 'FUCK OFF SCUMMERS' is written in classic Rolf Harris paint style.

'They're your nearest rivals, aren't they?'

'Yeah, 18 miles away. Anyone in between, Aldershot?'

'Yeah, but with Aldershot, Portsmouth outnumber them five to one.'

'How far away is Aldershot?'

'About 45–50 miles. You've got Bournemouth one side, 50 miles; Brighton the other, 50 miles; Southampton, 18 miles; and you've also got Reading. But as you'll find out later when you see the headlines after Portsmouth played Reading, the first time was *Pompey animals*. Run up there, pitch invasions, fucking chaos. These fucking square terraced houses are almost backing on to the ground. Some big games you get people getting on their roofs where the scaffolding is. Another good game I can remember getting thrown out, against Huddersfield, Spring 1980. That one I had actually been working on the roof of one of these houses, so I gets thrown out and I tries to get up this wall adjacent to the away end, when I see this bloke come round the alley with a Crombie on, dragging two crates full of empty milk bottles, sees me and puts them down right there. "Here y'are, have one each." Straight over the back there is where you've got the away support gathered and totally exposed in an open end. And it's these alleyways where the away supporters used to come in. But further along and over where that big yellow building is, that's where the coaches came in and there's plenty of places round here for just heads down walking, and just appearing, not in an ambush but frontal attacks. Or you could just mingle in with 'em like you was

Joe Nobody ... Then smack, or you just spanked. You can have this away end sort of surrounded, 'cause the away end backs on to an alleyway.'

'What was it called, the away end?'

'The Milton End. It's sort of surrounded by the North Stand one side and the South Stand the other. I think it holds about four and a half thousand.'

'When the away supporters come unstuck here, I bet there's a few jumping over them gardens, then?'

'Well, they've been sort of run – what's the word when you can't escape – you run the gauntlet. Anyway, they run. If they run that way, they'll be coming out with all the Portsmouth fans emptying out. They'll all make their way round this way, and at the same time you had the other half of the Fratton End emptying – ambush. And in the old days, if you never went round the away end, you could still wait at train stations.'

'So what was it like when the Jocks came?' I asked.

'It was a money-raising game,' came Silvester's reply. 'Celtic lot weren't up for aggro. The police were there and just let them get on with it, stand in our end singing their songs. There wasn't many, but they still brought a good 800–1,000. Just walked straight into the Fratton End. I think it was '76. At the time, Pompey nearly went out of existence. They did the normal things like sell bits of turf, anything to keep them going, really. They just about survived. That was in the mid-seventies. Somehow they just survived it. Portsmouth is an island, isn't it? The actual city is Portsea Island. It's not man-made, it's an actual island which is why there's no major crime down here, just sort of three roads. Any bank robberies or big bits of work like that, they just stick their roads up and that's it, you can't get off.'

'Has Portsmouth got a major criminal community?'

'No, it's got its fair share of drug problems, thefts, you know. It's nothing like London. In the *South London Press* there's probably more crime in that than there is for like a year here.

Portsmouth I always associate with being a hard area, probably the sailors and the docks ... the way it's laid out, it's well dodgy. Everyone's in the same area, full of alleyways and side streets?

'Yeah, it is really, very run down. It was blitzed in the war, flattened. That's the roads where the away coaches would always park, even today. They would have had to leave the coaches, come down here and walk up past sort of two roads and then into the alleyways, even though there was a police escort. As for the main route in, any minibuses, vans, people making their own way, they all come down and then they found out there's two main pubs full of Pompey always waiting there. You'd get exceptions. Preston turned up here last season, about five-to-three, and fucking done a few straggling Pompey. Coachload pulled up here somewhere.

'Like any, we have a couple of main pubs, strongholds of Pompey lads, the main two really being the Brewers and the Milton Arms. The Milton's got a little extension on it, which is called the Barn. Match days you'd have the Old Bill there with the camera, videoing everyone. The pubs are only about five minutes from the ground, so they're ideally placed for everyone to meet up. I only live a bit further back where you can actually hear the roar when they play at Pompey on a match day.

'This is the pub the lads ambushed Leicester in the play-offs. Riotous game ... 2–1 up there and we drew down here, which wasn't enough. All Leicester give it, they came flying out of the away end and run into Pompey right here, and Portsmouth was all over the place, run them back down into Carisbrooke Road where they were just getting ambushed by everyone that had come up from all the alleyways and cut them off from the park across Priory Crescent.'

'In the annals of the terraces, who had the big name? Any leaders who stood out?'

'There was never really a guv'nor over there, it was a bit independent, always had been down here, never been one person who's the main man or something. It was always sort of, on the day, everyone together. One name that always sticks out, and they said he was hard – Bob F. I don't know him myself personally, but one of the best stories about him was, in the days of them taking places ... Portsmouth fans were in the rival's end. He couldn't get at them, so he climbed up, went across the girders at the top of the roof of the stand and got down behind them. Just done it solo, on his own, and he was well renowned for it. He was a character and we had a few of those – the legend Fish, Ray G, even in what you could call ordinary supporters we had some mad support. People like Westwood with his flaming bugle who would never miss a game, home or away, become a landmark to Pompey fans when travelling away. There was the legend of Fooksie's coaches; back then he was the first to book our own train travel, before the club saw money to be made and took it over from him.'

Fooksie was the older generation of Pompey lads and a must to interview 'cause he remembered the early lads. When I met up with Fooksie, I asked the same question, his reply was,

All right, there was Ginger Howard from Paulsgrove. When Millwall came down the first time they tried to drown him in an ornamental fishpond at the station along Goldsmith Avenue. Big mop of ginger hair he had, from Paulsgrove, and, personally, the way I look at it, the way the City Council treated them people from Paulsgrove and Leigh Park was politically disgusting. The City Council let those people down terrible. It's one of the biggest housing estates in Europe and is just outside Portsmouth, that's also where you've got Paulsgrove which is on the hill that overlooks it. This is where the hardness of the city comes in. They got bombed out and they stuck them up there as a short-term thing and they're still there. The war finished in '45 and they're still there. The same as those Leigh Parkers, which is further out. It was only put up in 1946 for all the sailors who lived in prefab houses after the Second World War. You've still got them people up there. It was meant to be a brand new thing that's going to be a sensational way to develop, house 'em, get people out into the country, fresh air. Stuck them there with no amenities at all. They're council tenants living at Leigh Park, so they've got an attitude an' all. They feel nothing has gone forwards for them.

Fooksie has a point, suggests Silvester and reflects some more. 'I guess we have this feeling we're on our own down here, no one's going to help us ... Take Paulsgrove, that's where they had those paedophile riots, that estate up there. That's some estate. Fucking mad screaming women coming out and wanting to kill you, but that's a hard place. Dads know the dads and kids know the kids, it's very close up there. So think about it, if you're a Grov'ner, if you're brought up on Paulsgrove, you've immediately got the chip on the shoulder. You've got the chip and you've got the Grov'ner walk and you're anti-everything, and you take that to football. The Portsmouth area is bit of a hard place and it weren't the only place to be blitzed in the Second World War. If you take it, Coventry got whacked in the war and it got all rebuilt up lovely. But this city of ours never got rebuilt. It still had bombsites on it up until 1980. It's taken Portsmouth years and years. It's the last to be rebuilt. It sort of gives you an inner toughness.

'Relating it to football, especially when we played away, we was never afraid. We'd go Millwall, we'd go Newcastle, we'd go Birmingham, we'd go anywhere, we weren't scared. We didn't have a fear even if we were a bit naïve as a firm. We didn't used to question whether or not these teams we were playing had a firm, and whether they would be waiting for us and that, that didn't come into it. It was, "C'mon then, let's get up there, and we'll sort that out when we get there", you know, if there's aggro to be had and whatever's going to be done.'

According to Silvester, the other characteristic, which was not the norm when it comes to the elite of any top hoolie firms, is something Fooksie picked up on in the days he'd put on the travel arrangements – the fact Pompey never used to go tooled up on their travels. Fooksie recalls:

> *Something I used to find in some ways frustrating, never a little 2lb hammer in the top pocket or a little Stanley. They never ever went with that in mind, even though we'd be going away and there would be thousands of 'em. I could never work that one out with our boys. They would come back to me saying they'd got into a rumble, bit heavy [and then the shattering equation] – 'They was all tooled up, Fooksie' – I'd say, well, you know I can't help you. If that's what they are doing, that's what they'll do and you've got to make your own mind up about it now. But they never did it.*

'We had to be the most disorganised, organised firm ever. There was no leaders but we had a firm, always had a firm, often firms within firms, 'cause the firms would be pubs. I was from Stamshaw and we would leave Stamshaw and come and associate with the Air Balloon mob, that was our pub, that was our firm. The Eastney boys would go in the Milton Arms, that was their local and the Somers Town lot would come from the Sir Robert Peel pub. There was the Fox over on Leigh Park. Years ago, all these pubs ran one coach to the away games, which was the Fox. This became legendary as it was famous for going straight into our rival's end. We've come unstuck, we've had little firms and gone and done some right big firms, but we've had big firms come unstuck with little firms. I remember being in Chesterfield's end, about 1981. We were being stupid. Had a few beers before we went to the ground, got split up from the rest of the firm. There was about four of us left. We'd gone straight in their end thinking, We'll have a go, see what's what, just take the piss and if it comes on top, we'll just fuck off. Well, within two minutes, and the funny thing is, I was with three boys who all had ginger hair, and a geezer comes up and looked at me. "What, you all fucking ginger round your way?" I said, "Well, it looks that way, don't it?" But we was round their end and you know when the old bottle goes a little bit, you're thinking, Fucking hell. And I think the Old Bill knew we was Portsmouth and they let the crowd get close to us and it's not a nice sight when you've got 50 or 60 geezers wanting to fucking hurt you as well. You've got your backs to the wall and you're thinking, Do I turn and do a bolt – or what's the next move? But the adrenalin buzz and the feeling that goes through it is, I mean, it's second to none. You know it's probably how them First World War soldiers felt: Do I go over? Well, it's a case of having to, the only difference is they had the orders to go over the trench and steam in, where when it was us we had our own choice, and there were some hairy moments, coming across geezers and that. But, as someone young, free and single, it took you on a journey and the crack in going football with your mates was like no other.

'The first time I started going regularly to football I was about 16 and you know all the home games were obviously easy to get to, and the odd away game, you could always jump in a minibus or one of Fooksie's coaches from the now defunct pub called the Monkton in Copner Road, which is situated two miles north of Fratton Park. There'd always been big turnouts from Pompey fans and the main firms in the town at the time were from Stamshaw, North End, the Eastney boys always had a minibus going, maybe two. There were firms from Somers Town, Portsea, Landport and these were all the sort of areas that largely consisted of council estates or rows upon rows of houses, you know, like the opening scene of *Coronation Street*-fucking houses, because Portsmouth is one of the most densely populated cities for its size. The main pubs round this time – the Landport Boys had the Havelock, which is on a housing estate. The Somers Town Boys, they used the Peel or various pubs on their estate, the Robert Peel later became famous as a meeting point for the 6.57. Just north of Portsmouth out of the city is a place called Cosham – their firm incorporated the Paulsgrove Boys and a lot of these boys were really game. Their main pub at the time was called the Clacton or the Beacon or whatever one they were allowed in at the time because various pubs used to bar a lot of people for the sake of barring them and the rest of the crowd used to follow to another pub.

'In this season, '79–'80, when I started going away, Pompey had always been renowned for violence at away grounds, even going back to the sixties, you know, they were famous for having skinheads and Blackpool seafront in the '69–'70 season, which you'll read about in the book. But, anyway, the '79–'80 season kicked off with what had sort of become a regular thing – Swindon Town – home and away in the Football League Cup. Anyway, I can remember being 16 getting a train up there. I met some boys from Fareham, which is another place just outside Portsmouth, and they always had a good firm turning up, and we got the train. We arrived at Swindon – normal thing, straight into the nearest boozer. It was already full of Pompey, mainly from Cosham, Leigh Park – and sort of dribs and drabs of, you know, official supporters' coaches and people who'd made their own independent way up there. As normal – well, it wasn't normal at the time – this football-going era was just losing the old routine of taking people's ends, but Swindon looked like an easy touch. I think Pompey had been there the year before and cleared it out, so it was just sort of carrying on the tradition of going in and taking Swindon's end. Got in there and there must have been about 150 of us from all the firms that I've mentioned and within 10 minutes of getting in there, it had kicked off. Swindon just sort of backed off. Because they had a big old end in them days and they sort of backed off. There was a little bit of fighting, mainly scuffles. The Old Bill came in and broke it up and marched us to the opposing end. This was the first time I'd been involved in anything like this, but I sort of just carried on with the crowd I was in and ended up in their end.

'That season saw away violence: at Hartlepool away and, bearing in mind how far that is from Portsmouth, you know, to go up there and kick off wasn't a bad thing. I think there was Wigan away that season. Bournemouth away on a Friday night – that's 50 miles up the coast for us. Bit of a liberty getting in their end, 50-handed. Same thing – within 10 minutes, clearing it out, the Old Bill separating people. Even though there wasn't really anyone firm-wise at Bournemouth to get separated from. There was a few big games that year and at home games Pompey were capable of pulling in 15,000 which in '79–'80 was good for Div 4 status and wherever they went they had good turnouts. But there wasn't any really big teams in the Division 4 as you can imagine at that time. Portsmouth's got Southsea seafront and with its clubs and nightlife, etc., so everyone at the time used to meet up there weekends. If we were going away the next day or if we were at home, people used to talk, you know, about what the firm was like that was coming down. But, as I said, in Div 4 '79–'80 there wasn't a lot of teams with organised firms to come down and even nearly have a go.

'That year, the '80–'81 season, we were promoted to Division 3. Now this turned out funny because we ended up again in the League Cup First Round, first leg away to Plymouth. Now Portsmouth hadn't played there for a while so that was something to look forward to. I think we left Friday night and we had a boy called Guffer to take us in his Mark III – a yellow Mark III Cortina. And it was always boys from the Air Balloon pub. It'd be me, Trev, Mayley, Fish, Guffer driving and always one other, but it'd always be from the Air Balloon Pub, good Stamshaw Boys. It was summer, 9 August, this away game and we got into Plymouth early, as you do when you're at a new place, you go round the town centre looking to see if there's any firms about. Outside Plymouth's ground they had a big park. So, after we'd had a look around the towns and seen that there was nothing about for us, we all decided that everyone would meet back at the park, you know, the various groups you'd seen in the town. When we got to this park, there must have been a good 300–400 Pompey already there, all turned out in minibuses, the same firms again who I've mentioned, all there, all deciding what to do. Some people went back into the town, and there was a normal carry on of – Plymouth must have had a firm of about 50–100, but it was the same old thing. Bit of aggro during the day.

When we all got back to this park before kick-off, everyone was sort of hanging around the cars and just waiting to see if Plymouth would turn up. I think they did turn up but only in twos and threes and got into their ground. When we got into the away end, it was a baking hot day. I can remember it must have been in the seventies which, you know, for British summer time that is warm. Everyone stripped down to shorts and what have you, just bare-chested. Plymouth's away end was behind the goal and on the right-hand side, and that's where their firm started getting all together and started the normal thing – bit of baiting, you know, a few hand gestures, them baiting us, us baiting them. Well, all of a sudden that was it. A hundred Pompey – same people, same faces – straight over the top of the advertising hoardings, straight into Plymouth's sides. I can remember someone – I think it was Fish – picked up the corner flag and he was one of the first straight in over the hoardings, straight into them, backed them all off, swinging this flagpole like Richard the Lionheart with his great big sword holding off about 15 of them, giving enough time for the rest of the boys to get over the hoardings – bang, straight into them. I give them their due, Plymouth tried to have a go and with the police's help we all backed off, back over the hoardings, which delayed play by about five or 10 minutes. A funny thing happened that day. When we were all up – we all got pushed back into the end and we had a mini Hillsborough. You know, they had so many Pompey trying to get into this corner to have a go again at the Plymouth, and all of a sudden the hoardings collapsed at the front. All right, being as there was only 50–100 of us, I don't want to compare it to Hillsborough because that was, you know, there were fatalities. But the same sort of thing happened, the crushing was only 10 deep which, believe me, if you were at the bottom of it, wasn't very nice. Same old thing as normal happened after the game. Police escorting everyone back to the cars and coaches that were in the car-park. And we made our way home along sunny coastal roads all the way back to Portsmouth.

'This was the '80–'81 season when we drew Liverpool, just coming out the 4th Division and only in the 3rd. It was like we're playing Liverpool and there was a real buzz for this game, you know, plenty nationally in the papers. Everywhere in Portsmouth, people would ask not if you were going, but how you were getting there. The football club laid on a couple of specials. There were untold coaches. Anyway the estimate at Anfield on that Tuesday night in October for a Football League Cup 4th round was a good 14,000 Portsmouth. Everywhere up from Portsmouth was heading north up the A34. Coaches and cars, minibuses, Luton vans, furniture removal lorries – any means of transport to be had – Portsmouth fans were on it. They even put a special edition of the *Portsmouth Evening News* halfway up at Birmingham or somewhere to pick it up en route, wishing the team good luck. Anyway, when we got there, you know it was the first time for Liverpool and, because there was so many Portsmouth there, the firm was all split up, you know, none of the firms were together. There was every firm you can imagine plus more because it was a big game, it was a one-off. Portsmouth was in the 3rd Division and we're playing mighty Liverpool, so by any means people were getting up there. Anyway, we didn't know what was in store for us up there. So many people got picked off by those Scousers. I mean, we all know what they're like and what they're capable of. But on a cold northern night up there a lot of Portsmouth fans got picked off. I think even the specials got raided by the Scousers – cleaned it out, picked up all the fags, drinks and crisps. Everything they could get their thieving hands on, they took. Anyway, a big thing at Portsmouth at the time, when the Portsmouth team came out, was a tickertape reception, you know, I think a few clubs did it but no one ever did as good as Portsmouth. So, with these 14,000 fans in the crowd at the Anfield Road End, when they came out, the whole Anfield Road End – there's photographs of this – the whole Anfield Road was just one mass of tickertape. Anyway, predictably, we got done 4–1, but, you know, we scored a goal which was good enough up there. And we all had a good laugh. Scousers as normal took liberties on a lot of people. I think one boy got concussed and was taken off the special halfway home with a serious head injury.

'As well, '80–'81 was the first time we came across Millwall. The first time we played them was the day after Boxing Day. We – as normal for a London game – would always take a minimum of 3,000 – a minimum. And it's a lot of people who don't normally go to games, but for the casual fan it's easy to get to, you know, if you're driving or if it's the coach it's straight up the A3, or if it's the train it's Portsmouth to Southsea, one line straight up to Waterloo. We knew the way to get to New Cross where the ground was. We all got off the train. We all met – Portsmouth and Southsea, all the firms were there, normal boys. No one was ever in charge of Portsmouth's hooligan element. There was never one person up front – you know, a lot of people have said who was Portsmouth's main man. But on the day, like at this game, whoever was first off the train at Waterloo, you know, it was follow them and, you know, if there was Millwall waiting for us, let's have it with them, which was a common occurrence going to Waterloo. The Millwall game – I give them their due, we were all in that side bit penned in at the Den, penned in that sort of corner bit, surrounded, with them in the seats and the others in the side at the away end, but it was all fenced off. And I give Millwall their due, they had about three or four boys who actually got in with Portsmouth. There was probably about 1,500 Portsmouth in this corner bit. All the fans, it wasn't just the hooligan element. It was everyone – every fan, season tickets, supporters' club, everyone was in this away section at the old Den. And these Millwall started giving it, but within seconds they were just overpowered, pinned up against fences and had the shit kicked out of them. The police came in, chucked them out and that was the end of that. After the game, normal thing, Millwall trying to get at you, but I don't think they just had the numbers that day and it was a shock to them seeing as it was the first time we'd played them for a couple of years and seeing the numbers we had up there, I think they were impressed with what we had and what we were capable of, which led to a lot of later confrontations.

'It was the same thing this particular season. We'd been promoted from Division Four to Three and there still weren't any teams with big firms. Portsmouth were virtually untouchable at home and at a lot of away games there were more than average support turning up.

'And this was at the same time when the clothes were adjusting. Now people had come out of the trendy fashion of big collars and paisley pattern shirts, people were now starting to take note of what was being worn at football. Even people wearing cords and sweatshirts and training shoes, which was unheard of a couple of years previous. All the pubs were still the same. You still had all the boys in town meeting at certain places, their local pubs all on their estates. All up the seafront on a Friday night, Saturday night, to the discos and clubs. And there was a general sort of bravado and comradeship that we stuck together and there was very little internal fighting, even though it did go on and it escalated years later over the drugs scene and that. Portsmouth people always got on together at football, and the planning and the organisation was always there. Even from the people outside the city, you know, you got from Fareham, Salisbury, Leigh Park, Havant, even Bognor, Hayling – Portsmouth supporters, you know, virtually right across the south coast, as far as Chichester, Hayling Island. And there was some good boys come out – and they were always welcome in certain area pubs, like the boys from Fareham could go down the Air Balloon or the boys from Leigh Park were welcome down the Havelock, you know, it was a good sort of bonding and everyone got on.

It was about this time as well that the skinheads had come – arrived back on the scene, when a lot of people were mods, skinheads. I mean, the Havelock was famous for its skinheads. It became the number one skinhead pub in Portsmouth at the time. Some of the boys in there used to go and watch when Madness, Specials and Selector were all on tour together, and there was even a picture in the *Melody Maker* of Pompey boys and the legend Fish giving it his stuff. At the time Portsmouth was quite run down because the dockyard was closing down and that was a major employment place. You know, a lot of places in England in the early eighties were sort of run down. Portsmouth was no different. At the same time, everyone was going out, everyone was into the music, the ska bands and what have you, The Jam and they were all the main bands at the time. The fashion sort of coincided with the music, which coincided with the football. You know, people were sort of going to football as mods, you know, with the Fred Perry gear on or they were going as skinheads, rude boys, you know, it was a big fashion at the time with the parkas and the Harringtons, tonics, everyone used to get from Shirt King. Everyone used to think they looked the bollocks and that. Then Madness kept changing their fashions with their box jackets and, you know, Pompey was getting on the scene of what the Millwall fashion was, Lois jeans, Adidas kick trainers, the leather jackets you used to get up Carnaby Street for 30 quid, with the bomber jacket with the vertical pocket, or the safari jackets. Portsmouth was up there with it, with what they used to wear. They always looked smart at games. I think there was a thing in *The Face* magazine later on or in a lot of these magazines, whenever football fashions in the early eighties began starting to take a hold, Portsmouth was always mentioned one way or another. As I say, the dockyard was slowly closing down. There wasn't a lot of work about. Apprenticeships were coming to an end. But people were still going out, you know, beer was cheaper then. You could earn yourself a couple of quid doing some casual work or whatever – some people took that road, but we were all still there. Always out, always turning up for football, always looking smart and always giving it to any team that came down here.

I missed the '82–'83 season because of my Borstal training. I missed the whole season, but I remember receiving a lot of letters from fans, even ones saying that in early '83 there'd been a letter written to *The Face* magazine or one of those saying that we were now the 6.57 crew and infamously named ourselves as that. Being that the 6.57 is the first train you can get to London if you're going to a far-off northern place, which we did. Like I say, I missed the whole season but there was a lot of carry on that season. We had Millwall again home and away. I think there was trouble at quite a few games of this season, the main one being Plymouth away with another big turn-out by Pompey – last game of the season. Had to win the game to win the 3rd Division championship, which we did, and of a crowd of 14,000 there must have been 10,000 Portsmouth up there. And they'd left Friday night again, for Plymouth, and just caused a trail of destruction from Portsmouth. This included Stonehenge being sprayed up with "PFC – KICK TO KILL" and sheep being sprayed blue and white. People making their way down there were buying cars for £25–£30, driving them down there and leaving them there, knowing full well they'd get on a coach or train back because the police, as it worked out, were just glad to see the back of Pompey that day.

'As I say, Portsmouth won it that year – '82–'83 – so that put them into Division Two. Not forgetting, a lot of people know of the 6.57 firm, you know, because being a genuine football fan, whatever you're going to call it, there's people who've had aggro from Pompey because basically they've been and played in almost every division in the last 15 years, except the Premier League. They've been in the old First Division. So somewhere along the line we've had it with you.

'Season '83–'84 – now this was the season when Pompey were clued up. We had a big season in front of us. We had big teams – for once we had a few big names, you know, teams above us had been demoted from Division One or due to money problems or whatever, they were still in Division Two. And there was some big clubs in there. And looking through the season, we had the mouth-watering fixture list in front of us, and we were looking at teams like Middlesbrough, Man City, Cardiff again, Palace, Newcastle, Brighton, Sheffield Wednesday, Blackburn were on their way up, Huddersfield, Derby, Swansea, Chelsea. Now all these games that people spoke about, there was aggro there and this is when it was established that there was a 6.57 crew. I think even the police were stamping down on it and the power that the Portsmouth magistrates' court had was that anyone caught and being convicted of any football hooliganism was going to prison and that was it. Which they did enforce.

'The first game of the season was a big 'un – Middlesbrough at home. Now we lived in Stamshaw, and our main pub was the Air Balloon. It's right at the end of the motorway that comes into Portsmouth. I had a phone call about half-past nine in the morning saying, "You won't believe this, but there's a minibus full of Middlesbrough at the top of the motorway." They must have come down and they're all crashed out on it. So everyone on the manor's got the phone call. About 10–15 of us have gone up to see what's going on. By the time I'd got there, the minibus had been totalled, every window had been put through, every

Middlesbrough geezer had been dragged out that hadn't run away, and was given a severe beating and told to fuck off, which was a bit hard considering they had no windows and windscreen left on their van. They thought themselves clever, they'd come down, they were well out the way, but they didn't know they were on one of the worst manors they could have ever fucking thought of. Two of the boys received 12-month sentences for this affray, which they served at Guysmarsh Youth Custody Centre down in Dorset.

'Pompey was looking good at the time as well. More and more fashion was available and they would try to be seen out with the Armani stuff and the Pringle jumpers and everything everyone else had. Every main bit of fashion used to end up in London and it was only an hour and a half up the road for us to go and get gear and everyone started looking smarter and smarter, more and more colourful, you know, the Burberry, Aquascutum gear, that all came out, you know. We was all well aware of it and who wore what and who done what.

'One of the big games after Middlesbrough at home was Man City at home. Now we always thought Man City was big and they'd have a big firm and they'd do something when they were down here, but I think they sneaked in under the cover of darkness, 'cause all of a sudden we went to the game and the whole away end was full up with them. And that's the first I'd seen of them the whole weekend and the last. I think they were escorted back out – escorted in, escorted out, and that was it. I don't know if anyone's got anything to say about that, but I can't remember a lot of aggro that game.

'Just after that, we went to Cardiff away – it was the first time for me. We went down there and I think there was 60-odd arrested. Didn't get the 6.57 because that train only went north and we were going west. I think there'd been a few bits of trouble the year before, but this year we went down for it again – we got straight off the train, same firms were there. The 6.57 then was well established and people knew what the score was, everyone knew what time we were leaving and there were enough pubs round town to find out who was going where and when, which, you know, if it was a 10 o'clock train, everyone would be meeting at half-nine or whatever. And when we went to Cardiff, there must have been about 350 – 400 on the train firm-wise and, when we got there, I think there'd already been a bit of trouble the night before. I know there'd been a stabbing – someone, a Cardiff fan, had been stabbed with a screwdriver. A couple of boys were already nicked. There'd been the normal thing, I think the Paulsgrove boys were up there early in their van and Cardiff was all plotted out in their pub, which got turned over. There were 60 arrests that day.

'The next big 'un – Newcastle United away, 1 October. The 6.57 had about 250 – same lot, well, the 6.57 consisted of everyone who was about at the time. If you were on that train, that was it, you were, you know, like it or not, you were 6.57. And not a lot of people make the numbers up but there was a good hardcore of 100 there. And going to Newcastle, you know, Portsmouth again, were a bit naïve, didn't know the score. Heard they had a firm up there. Well, fuck it, let's get up there and have it with them then, innit. Silly Geordie bastards. I'd seen in the papers a couple of weeks before that some of them wear kilts, so it says a lot for an Englishman. We got the 6.57, and got to Waterloo twenty to nine. Normal thing, I expected Millwall waiting for us. Might have been a bit early for them, they might have been somewhere else anyway. We didn't see anyone. All on the Underground. Northern Line 'cause we're going to King's Cross. Straight to Newcastle. When we got to King's Cross, there was a big mob of Chelsea waiting for us. I think they were going to Leeds or Sheffield it could have been. All I can remember is, well, they're Chelsea, we're Portsmouth, we get it on with them but we've got a train to catch. Come on, we've got to make this connection. Don't forget we're going to Newcastle. We'd already come two hours up the road, do we have it with them or not.

Then, unbeknown to us, another mob of about 50 Pompey came out the tube station, so we're sandwiching Chelsea, so we just went straight into them, give it to them. All they could do was fucking leg it, and they were gone. Someone shouted, "Quick, hurry up, hurry up," and we've run through the station to see the other half of the Pompey on the train already going to Newcastle. So we're just shouting to them, "Hang on up there, we'll be there soon, don't panic. Just hold your own at the station. We'll be on the next train behind," which was 20 minutes or half an hour later. Anyway, I think Chelsea tried to give it the fucking large one again because we'd lost half our men on to the train going to Newcastle to have it with who we were originally going to have it with. It was like something out the film *The Warriors* trying to get back to Coney Island, you know, there was just people waiting for Portsmouth everywhere. And, knowing that we hadn't even got to Newcastle yet and we'd already had a ruck, we knew that coming back Chelsea would be waiting for us. And so would Millwall, they always made a show, 'cause they knew we were coming down back in the south, and they'd always be at Waterloo 'cause they knew we'd always have a firm on the train.

'We finally get to Newcastle and there's 250 Pompey at the station. The Old Bill were there saying, "There's two ways to the ground – town centre or that way. Don't go through the town centre 'cause they're waiting for you." "Oh, are they? Well, let's go to the town centre then." So we've all marched down there, all running. Got to the town centre, first pub we see, straight into the pub, held them off, done their pub. Unbeknown to us there's another pub opposite. As we came out of the pub they steamed us, so we're having aggro with every fucking pub in Newcastle High Street, running up and down. A couple of boys nicked. Anyway, they didn't do us, we had the better of them. The Old Bill came in, normal lairy Geordie bastards. "You're not in fucking Portsmouth now" is how they said it and, you know, kicking you in the back of the heels and smacking you round the head. They escorted us to the ground. Portsmouth got fucking smashed 4–2. Time to come home. Herded to the train station, rounded up together, put on a train. "Fuck off, don't come back." Normal thing from Geordie policemen. They don't like us, we don't like them.

'Anyway, when we're flying back down south, we get off at Doncaster, and who do we bump into? Chelsea, who were waiting for a connection at Doncaster. One man first off the train Portsmouth 6.57's Derek steamed straight into them. He had them on their toes on his own, but by then we're all getting out the doors, big bottleneck trying to get off the train – fucking running everywhere. "Fuck off, Chelsea, you're nothing." Jump back on the train, down to King's Cross. Chelsea were back before us and waiting – here we go again. The Old Bill marched us back on the tube. "Fuck off back to Waterloo." When we get back to Waterloo, Millwall's waiting for us, but not enough Millwall. They had a little scouting firm, but they were not going to touch 150–200 battle-weary troops. We'd had aggro all day long and when you get to Waterloo sometimes all you do is have beer – Casey Jones (at that time), get on that train, wake up and you're home.

'That season when Newcastle played the return game at Portsmouth, we did the same as normal. When we thought a firm would be turning up, everyone met down the shopping precincts or the town centre waiting for them. And for some reason those Geordies stick out, don't they, because they wear their black and white football shirts and you can just see them everywhere. Apart from that, we had a lot of naval personnel in the city at the time and a lot of them were obviously from the north-east and a few of them were hanging about. There's like a precinct, you cross over the road – Edinburgh Road – but, as I crossed, we got fronted up by about five or six Geordies and they were already pissed and it was only about half-past ten. Told them to fuck off, we'd go and get a proper ruck, not taking it out on you fat bastards. And one's punched me in the head, so I've had a go back at him. Straight away the Old Bill's on us. "You fuck off." Yeah, OK, I'm away. Go on, you go that way, we'll go that way. Which we did. So, anyway, half-past two, my mate's giving me a lift from the town centre to the football ground. About quarter to three, blue lights, police cars, motorbikes, vans, dogs, you fucking name it have pounced on our car and there's only four of us in there. Fuck me, what's going on here? They've done the normal, got the driver out, turned the car off, and then they arrested me. What for? Threatening behaviour. OK then. Arrested me, cautioned me, took me down the Central Police Station. And it's amazing what powers the police had at the time. Anyone found guilty of football hooliganism was automatically going to prison. Well, I thought, I'm in the cells for a couple of hours, let the game finish. Threatening behaviour. Fucking Mickey Mouse charge. I'll be out at 10 o'clock and see what happened in the game, what the result was. Anyway, because of the seriousness of the charge, as the police put it, "We're going to apply to have you remanded in custody." You know, I thought they were having a fucking joke. But no, this was the powers the police and the Portsmouth Magistrates had. You know, I don't think paedophiles and fucking rapists get this treatment and it's not on a par with what goes on now. And I've ended up in Portsmouth magistrates' court on Monday morning, half-past ten. Looked in the gallery, there's a few of my pals there, and everyone's stunned, they can't believe it. What they're going to try and do is remand me in custody for threatening behaviour. It doesn't make sense. So the Magistrate says, "Stand up." Name – all that bollocks. "Well, Mr Silvester, we're remanding you in custody for seven days." Seven-day remand. Anyone who knows the law knows that's what they do. You get remanded in custody for the first week, seven-day remand, and then it gives you time to sort out all your legal team and see what the fuck's going on and at least have a chance to talk to a few people 'cause I'd had no visits, nothing, over the weekend.

'The following Monday, going back to court, I thought it was just a production of seven-day remand to see how my case was getting on, bearing in mind I hadn't spoken to a solicitor, hadn't seen any witnesses, hadn't spoken to any witnesses. The only letter I'd had was off my mum and dad and a couple of mates in that week. I go up in front of the magistrate and the magistrate says, "We're going ahead with the case today." I said, "What do you mean?" He said, "Well, last week you were remanded in custody for a week just to see what's going on," and it's another stitch-up by the Old Bill/magistrates' court with this football hooliganism thing. So I've had to get a duty solicitor on the day and this is not easy. Don't forget, I'm being produced by the prison and thought, All I'm looking at is another seven-day remand, have a chance to have a chat with a solicitor and get my head round things. No, they're going ahead with it that day. I said, "Well, how am I going to get hold of my witnesses?" And they gave me a duty solicitor who gives it the normal, "Why don't you just plead guilty, get that lot over and done with? Portsmouth sees it as a good act." And I said, "No, no, if you can get a message to my mum, she should have my phone book with a couple of names in it. The boys who were with me at the time when I was assaulted first by this Geordie might come up and say their bit in the court." Which they did do. But nevertheless I was found guilty in the normal course of magistrates' kangaroo courts and sentenced to 90 days in prison, which I'm still stunned by even to this day. The only good thing – well, nothing good about going to prison, but the only decent thing that happened was, the week before, Portsmouth had played Southampton in the fourth round of the FA Cup and there was something like 90 arrests at this game. I think three or four of them ended up in the jails, so I knew a couple of the boys already up there. And the same thing happened the next week and the following week with Leeds United. All of a sudden, four or five Leeds boys turned up on remand, shitting themselves, miles from home, wondering what the fuck's going on. I've only gone to football and got involved in a bit of pushing and shoving and now I'm on remand. You know, and there's rapists and monsters getting bail all the time. I've served 60 days out of the 90, so as you can imagine, I missed a few games. There were a few big 'uns involved in it. Leeds United at home, and Sheffield Wednesday away was a big one where Pompey turned out in force. We ran them all up and down them seven hills.

'This was also the season that we played Cambridge away. And it's funny as you see in Cambridge or any sort of university place like Oxford, everyone's flying about on bikes. So what do Portsmouth do? Everyone who gets on the 6.57 makes sure they've got a pushbike with them. And we show them how to ride a bike. Anyway, that was the scene at Cambridge everyone – about 50 of them – all on pushbikes. They were taking them from Waterloo, Liverpool Street, that'd do me. You'd never seen anything like it according to the photographs – it was one of them funny ones where you've got 50–60 Pompey all pissed and pedalling pushbikes. It was just for a laugh, never been done by anyone else, I shouldn't think.

'First game back when I got out was away to Charlton. And, with Charlton, sometimes they got a mob, but sometimes they haven't, but I think on this day they did. It's easy to say that someone said there was Millwall with them, Chelsea, this and that, but I don't give a fuck, at the end of the day, you know, you don't turn up for another club. We've never done it and I don't see why anyone should. But anyway the battle's raged on all day, we got in their end. Same thing again when Portsmouth's playing in London, you're looking at 3,000 minimum and there was probably about that amount for this game. But before we got to Charlton, we turned up at Stamford Bridge, about 100 of us. All right, it was half-past one and there weren't much Chelsea about, but at least we made a point that we will turn up places even if we ain't playing you. Oh, we just give them a little show, I think a couple of Pompey boys got nicked, but we just let them know that we're about. And someone from Chelsea opened his big mouth saying if Chelsea hooligans are so bad, why did a team who are playing Charlton 20-odd miles away turn up at Stamford Bridge. Well, I think the answer was in the paper that we got on the wrong tube and somehow we ended up paying you a visit.

'Also in the summer of 1984, it was Ritchie's – one of the Somers Town boys – 21st birthday so he hired a coach and it was decided we'd go to Brighton for a peaceful Saturday night out. Well, we've all got on the 52-seater coach and I think there was about 72 of us, so obviously the driver lost his bottle and decided that some had to get off, which – lucky bastards – they did. I wish I was one of them because what was in store for the rest of us was fucking mental. Anyway you're talking about 60 6.57 geezers on this coach going to Brighton for this 21st birthday. Everyone's having a laugh, taking the piss, everyone's got mad clobber on. It was a fucking giggle as far as we was concerned. We'd go down to Brighton, surprise them one night. I was sitting at the front and, when the coach pulled up along the seafront somewhere, I was one of the first off. And as a geezer two or three behind me got off, he just went and chinned the nearest geezer to him, a Brighton geezer. He said, "What you do that for?" He said, "'Cause we're Portsmouth, and we're here." And that was it.

'There were a few minibuses followed up as well, vans and cars, so we're looking about 85–90 in total. Anyway, we'd got off and the idea was that we'd all split up, go our own way, have a couple of beers, meet up again later and try and get in a nightclub somewhere. Well, it never happened because all that happened was just full-scale fighting all night long, with geezers coming out of pubs, coming at Portsmouth because we were all split up, you know, we were having bundles all over with this lot. The Old Bill turned up, and we were running all through the narrow streets and alleyways, and bumping into other Pompey lots who'd just had aggro with other geezers. So they were going up the road having the aggro with the lot we'd just had it with, and we were going to have it with the geezers they'd just had it with.

'One of the funniest stories was a bit later on in the night. We didn't last that long, but about 10 o'clock there was about eight or 10 of the Paulsgrove contingent and all these bouncers came out of a doorway and this bird said, "Here y'are, they're Kung Fu experts. Now you're in trouble." Well, at the end of the fight, two of them had broken legs and what was left of them was smashed to fucking bits. You don't mess with them Paulsgrove boys because they're a fucking evil bunch. Anyway, no matter, there was just aggro everywhere. We couldn't go anywhere. People were trying to steam us. We were having fights with everyone and more people were trying to attack us, from young kids to older people, and people who probably weren't even Brighton fans, they were all just trying to fucking get at us. And so the police must have got hold of the coach driver and said, "Look, tell them all to meet here, get them on the coach and fuck off out of it." Well, this is Saturday at about half ten. We're all outside one of the clubs on the corner of the road. All sat down against the wall, all had enough; everyone's got fucking lumps and swollen hands, teeth missing. It just resembled a battle zone. The coach pulled up and the police got us all on it and said, "Right, we'll escort you out the town." The only place they escorted us to was Brighton Central and one by one we were all taken off the coach. So what everyone did was start getting to the back of the coach, so you had the police going, "Right, next." Shouts were coming from the back: "Come and fucking get me then, you cunts," and abusing them, everyone having a laugh, taking the piss, laughing at them. But it never paid, because whoever were the last 10 off, they got a severe hiding from the Old Bill, as they do. Anyway, I think there were about 70 people arrested that evening and I think about three people got charged in the end. We were all locked up and some were sort of slowly let out in groups 24 hours later. What a horrible weekend that was.

'The Cardiff game next year in '84 was another first done by any firm. The 6.57 decided that we would all wear our blazers, 'cause everyone had Daks, Burberry blazers or just cashmere blazers, anyone who had one, wear it and we'd say to the Old Bill on the train that we were going to a wedding at Bristol so they'd leave us alone. So that was the plan. So we got firmed up, all having our photos done, everyone looked the bollocks in their Crombies and smart in Aquascutum ties and cashmere blazers, Farrahs, you know, imitation croc shoes and loafers. Everyone looked the bit. We got off the train at Bristol as we said we'd do, about 20 of us. Said to the Old Bill we were going to a wedding anyway, so they left us alone. Went and had a couple of beers, got back on the train. No one on there, just us lot, the blazer firm, and we got left alone. Got to Cardiff but funnily enough the Old Bill were waiting for us. And they seemed to say we had out-foxed them a bit and they put in their little police newspaper that we all hired morning suits. Well, being dressed in a blazer and Farrahs and shoes compared to a morning suit, you know, that's how the police get confused easy because they don't know what they're talking about half the time. And I think there was a lot of police on duty this year because the year before in October '83 there was something like 60 arrests at the Cardiff game when we steamed their pub.

'The '83–'84 season saw Bognor Regis Town, one of Pompey's junior teams, do well, I think it was in the Ryland League and they had a good Pompey support and a few Pompey supporters actually played for Bognor. Bognor played Swansea in an FA Cup 3rd round and police intelligence said there'd be no connection between Portsmouth and Bognor – I don't know why 'cause 90 per cent of Bognor will regard themselves as Portsmouth fans. The police had no idea that the 6.57 would be turning up on behalf of Bognor at Swansea, which they did. This caused the Swansea Police some enormous problems. The match was drawn and so the replay was at Bognor and with the carry-on at Swansea there was sort of violent scuffles on the terraces and Swansea couldn't believe that Bognor would have a firm as good as it did. There was a coachload of about 60 6.57 turned up at the game and give it to them. But Bognor drew some of their support from a place called Littlehampton and so a bit later on in the game, what was left of the Bognor fans who didn't support Pompey sort of joined up with these Littlehampton, and some might have been Brighton fans, and they started turning on the 6.57, so there was a bit of a battle again. Portsmouth had to have it with two different fucking firms in one day again. But it was nothing new to us really.

Hallo, hallo,
Play up Pompey
Kaiser must go
Offside is he

Sung in the trenches, 1914 – 1918 and possible origins of *Play Up Pompey*.

The Original Portsmouth Skinheads

'THE ACCUSED WERE IN THE LARGE GROUP OF PORTSMOUTH
SUPPORTERS WHO ADOPTED A PECULIAR STYLE OF DRESS,
SIMILAR TO THE ROYAL NAVY'S FATIGUE WEAR. MOST OF
THEM HAD CLOSE CROPPED HAIR, WORE THIN BRACES
SUPPORTING JEANS WHICH WERE IN A HALF-MAST POSITION
AND ALL HAD HEAVY BROWN BOOTS.'
CHIEF INSPECTOR CHEATHAM, FOR THE PROSECUTION.

To fill you in on those real early years, we've enlisted the knowledge of old skin Pat who in 1967 moved up to London from Hayling Island to seek work, but still followed his beloved Pompey around the country bringing his new-found London experiences with him. Pat and Robbie Mc, another older lad, tell with accuracy how the skinhead scene took off in Pompey. Here's their account.

> 1966, the year England were to win the World Cup, I went to my first game, Manchester City at home. I was a school kid, a typical 14, 15 year old. Some of the lads had got me to go. I wasn't particularly interested in Pompey in any way but I was keen on football, keen on playing it and I thought Manchester City was a big name. So I went along to the game and I can remember walking into Fratton Park. I actually remember the moment I walked in there. You know

what it's like the first time ... you see the crowd, you see the Fratton End. A lot of the lads I'd been going with, they'd been going to football every Saturday. We walked in the Fratton End and there's all these Manchester City fans, right, they're all little blokes with leather jackets and scruffy, greasy hair. But we'd been inundated with the info that the hard people were Manchester United, Liverpool ... because up until that point the only football violence was them smashing trains up. This is when it was first coming in. And I thought, God, they are going to be dead hard, their fans. So, anyway, I get to the ground, and I had no thought of seeing violence or fighting at football, but, of course, everybody starts chanting and I could feel, you know, you're getting carried away with it. I suddenly cottoned on that Pompey was going to be as hard as, or even do, Manchester. And then the next thing is I turn up and I see one bloke with wild ginger hair, glasses that thick and, to look at him, you wouldn't think for one second he was going to be hard, you never connected people with glasses as hard. And then I saw Ginger go in on them and the next thing I know is this mad feeling of excitement – Manchester City are running. I'm suddenly clocking that – and everyone says this – you suddenly realise you're not watching the football very much. And then in the second half the trouble died, Manchester City had moved, they tried us, no joy, so they moved. This is very small ... it's not like the pitch battles you see later on. Basically Pompey then had a group of fans, people like Dinksy, Dave Dwaine and that, who I could see were older than me. It's obvious, they've got the nice clothes, obviously got girls and when you're young you think,

I'll never do all this, you know how it is, and so you have that sort of lot. Every football crew had older blokes, might have a suit on, looked a bit like Jimmy Tarbuck, a right mixture. We'd even have Teddy boys, it was like that, but you were Pompey.

After that I started to go to a few of the home games, the next one was Southampton, this was the same year. That was good because I'm standing outside the ground and about 200 or 300 Southampton fans come up. I still didn't know the score and I see this lot and think, Blimey, and then they're all there giving it gob, but it's still very low key, not how you would have felt in the seventies … frightening. Then they go in the Fratton End and within 10 minutes Pompey had had them off and they were burning their scarves on the terrace and I said,' This is wonderful'. I'm 15, I'm terrified, don't get me wrong, I'd have been the first to move. You're little kids and you're on the periphery of it, you're not right in the centre, and then you're starting to recognise faces. I started to recognise an older kid and I used to watch and see how stylish he was … and that was Dinksy.

The big style and the big thing at the time was that you had a scarf, always tied in a knot and you had the metal football badges. We all had those, well, Dinksy had loads, he also had a Levi white denim jacket that he'd wear, he'd have Levis on and the most important thing was he tended to cut the bottoms off and have the white rim about half an inch done like that, that was very, very important. We were called Moddy boys, but this was very sort of low key. You still had all mixtures. You had the guy of 25 with a suit, you had all sorts of mixtures. Generally the music we liked was in the top ten and we'd have a chart record as a football song in 10 minutes. So this is all still fairly low-key stuff.

Season '67–'68, we went to see Chelsea play West Ham and I think you ought to hear about this one, because this was an amazing sight. We get outside the ground and we're kids, and we're like, 'Who you going to follow? Chelsea? West Ham?' Next moment, we hear this noise coming like a train and this fucking mob of West Ham come up, the whole of West Ham came in one go, hundreds of them. There's skinheads, there's men who look like the Kray brothers, there's men who look absolutely evil with scars up and down them and they are IT. They've all got a little badge on: 'North Bank, West Ham'. They come in and I've never seen a mob like it, I remember thinking, How the hell are Chelsea going to do anything about this? So anyway, gates open, West Ham pile in, the push surges from top to bottom, you're going flying, it's unbelievable, slowly but surely Chelsea are coming in chanting, 'Chelsea, Chelsea'. They're getting more and more together. I look to Chelsea and I give them their due, they give as good as they get. The end was shared, the result was shared, although outside it was basically a West Ham rout. I could see these London mobs are scared of nothing. So, you know, they both have huge mobs, West Ham, Chelsea. Spurs are getting established. Of course, Millwall always had the name and the reputation.

The first time Millwall came to Fratton Park in '66, they'd just come up through the divisions. Now Millwall were getting a reputation on the news. In one particular incident, they'd not lost at home for about two years and they lost to Plymouth Argyle. It was an absolute riot and Millwall were getting a name. So we had them at Fratton Park for the first time. They all came in one group and it was led by men of about 40 years of age. They were massive. They came in the Fratton End and for about 10–15 minutes there's a gap between the two sets of supporters, and then the fight's going to start. A bloke started sizing up to Ginger. There's Ginger and one other bloke who has a go. Ginger came out of that with his shirt off and his vest hanging on by one thread. I can remember he turned to us and said, 'I'm not having any more of that.' Ginger had more guts than the rest of us put together, he'd had a go, and, of course, you're thinking, Well, if he can't do it ... So Millwall routed the end and absolutely took it. We were all gobsmacked – this is taking it to another level. We're all mainly youngsters, of the same age. But this Millwall thing, I can remember an incident where I saw 14-year-old kids laying into a bloke of about 20, no fear whatsoever. They were coming up to you, they were looking for it. It was murder. It was a complete and utter rout, no two ways about it. There's no use pretending otherwise, they routed us. That was the first time we had Millwall up there. But over the years there were to be plenty more Millwall stories.

In season '67–'68 we're doing well. I'm thinking I'm it, we're all thinking we're all it, and then came my wake-up call. I started going to my first away games because Pompey are flying that season. So I go to Crystal Palace away, season '67, Boxing Day game. Now when I get to Crystal Palace, we went up the other end. There still weren't any real fight ethics going on at that time. Not a lot of madness is happening because you've still got the World Cup fever and that. Things are still peaceful. But this

*Palace game is a very important moment. Nothing
happened at Crystal Palace. It was an 11 o'clock kick-
off, something like that. So, after the game, me and
my mate and all the Pompey fans split up. Some sad
bastards went to Charlton versus Millwall, something
crazy like that. We went to Spurs versus Fulham.
Spurs were always a big popular team amongst
Portsmouth fans. West Ham were number one, Spurs
were second. So we go to that, you know, good game,
big crowd and all of that. Here's the funny bit, you
see, Pompey had gone to Spurs in the FA Cup the year
before and near on 20,000 Pompey fans had taken
White Hart Lane with ease. The reason being that
Spurs hadn't formed as a mob in '67. Now if you want
to clarify that, read the Chelsea book by Martin King,
which was his first away game, at that particular time.
So Spurs were getting turned over at the time. Pompey
had gone and turned them over without any fighting,
just with weight of numbers. So I went up to Spurs
thinking it wasn't a very dangerous, hard place,
because I knew Pompey had turned it over the year
before. Coming out the ground, we got on the
underground station, basically in dimlo clothes, I had
a combat jacket on with Pompey on the back,
absolute dimlo. I've got a blue and white scarf
showing, and all of a sudden there's loads of kids
around me, aged 14 to 20, and it's Spurs and they're
around me and they've clocked the blue and white
scarf. Straight away they come up to me and said,
'You fucking Chelsea?' Basically me and my mate
thought, What's best? Shall we just go to pieces? They
might leave us alone. We're still kids, you know what
I mean? I looked at this bloke and he's like, 'Ah, no
leave them alone, they're only kids,' and this bloke sat*

down. We're sitting down with Spurs all around us, and he starts talking to us, one of the nicer sort of blokes. I started asking him about his clothes, I couldn't get over it, looking at their clothes. They all had black army boots on – that was the first boot, the black army boot. They all had little checked shirts, they weren't the Ben Sherman, you know, the old man's shirt, they had that later. They had either navy blue or green sleeveless jumpers, they've all got the Levis rolled up, got scarves down the front, the suede clipper jackets, things like this are coming in, I'm starting to see, they've all got braces. I'm starting to ask where they've bought all their clothes and I'm getting clued up, I'm learning fast. Eventually the train pulls in somewhere and there's about 30 Norwich fans they spot. So the whole lot just goes off and starts kicking ... and me and my mate sat there thanking our lucky stars we weren't the unfortunate ones. It was more the fact that we were country bumpkins and looked hicks – if we'd have been dressed as skinheads, we'd have been beaten to pulp. But they probably thought, Leave them alone.

And this is where Pompey are wising up, straight away you start seeing the emergence of the first serious group, the Southsea boys as they were known, some good people. I'm beginning to grow up and they're all 15, 16, but they're beginning to know me as coming from Hayling. I'm beginning to get in. I'm getting very friendly with Dinksy, I'm meeting people like Pete Harris, Dave Dwaine, now these to me were style kings. Now all of a sudden I'm getting to be a bit of a style king, I've moved up London for a job.

Season '68–'69, and football hooliganism now is getting into full flow, it's becoming the purpose now of going to football. I don't like the word hooliganism, I mean, just the whole thing of you're young and that's where it's at and that's what you're doing, that's what you did, if you were with the in-crowd. The thrill, the excitement, everything was on the terrace, and every football book I've ever read will say that. It's part of you growing up and becoming what you think is a man, at the time. You start off down the front, two, three years later you're standing in the middle, one day you might even start a song off. It's all a process.

So come this particular season I'm talking about, this is when we're starting to move into the serious business. Because I've moved up London at the time, I'm on the streets and this is when the skinhead fashion was getting immaculate. Now the big clothes of the time, believe it or not, the traditional Burberry flyfront mac, the classic one. They weren't cheap and you could have navy blue or you could have cream. V-neck jumpers, you always had maroon or navy blue; cardigans were coming in and then jungle greens. Now to get jungle greens there was a shop down Southwark I used to go to. Jungle greens suddenly became the in thing, you'd get them, little rim again and you'd press them and they'd be high up. Then the boots started coming in, you had cherry red Commando boots, you'd have Monkey boots, you'd have long brown ones that came up high. Now you're starting to get with the cult skinhead thing. Trilby hats are coming in, sheepskins are starting to make their appearance which was a big cult thing – to have a sheepskin you had to have a lot of money as well. Now the whole of London is buzzing on this, nowhere else in the country is, don't get me wrong, this is a

London thing. I don't care what Manchester and the rest of them say, 'cause I went up there and we just laughed at their attempts. So the London thing's moving fast now and I'm going to Spurs games.

Now I'm wising up fast, and I'm learning the real great days were the thrill of the underground, the thrill of the chase. First game I went to was Spurs versus Man United. They were great moments. The first thing I learned is that London crews at a game like that would tend to attract supporters from other London clubs if they weren't involved with each other. So there were West Ham and other people there, in that sense, 'cause it was north, it was Manchester. So I'm looking at Man U who are meant to be it and I'm looking at them and they are making me physically sick – they've all got moustaches, they've all got this dodgy sort of hair. They're absolute dimlos with about 30 scarves round them, they are dimlos. Lesser people think that it was Man U running the show back then, they make me laugh. Anyway, the Spurs crew are getting smart now, they are really geared up and they've got this look that no one else had. I can remember in the game, I'm standing outside the ground with some Spurs lads I know, and a young black kid, about 16, comes up, and says, 'I've been in there and I've been thrown out. I'm going back in, it's fucking great.' I got to talk to him and that was Sammy Skyves. At that time it meant nothing, but Sammy later went on to become the big Spurs leader. He was just a little black kid of 16. He had no fear, he just ploughed in there time and time again.

Spurs and Man U, up to half-time I can see Man U are getting the worst of this. Half-time, we go underneath the Tottenham stand and we're picking off

Manchester mercilessly, absolutely mercilessly, they're getting murdered. All of a sudden I see a strange sight. I see about four or five blokes and they're going 'Arsenal', like, and they're going to these Spurs fans, and these Spurs fans, you know, they're dead hard, yet these four of five Arsenal are barging their way through, and I find out later that one of these blokes was Johnny Hoy who's another big, big name of those times. At the time, '68–'69, everybody seemed to think that Arsenal was it, they had a deadly reputation, but the overall cream of the crop, the people who ran it were West Ham. There was no doubt about it, you knew that West Ham were the ones.

So I'm up London now and the skinhead thing is kicking off big, although the reggae and the music thing hadn't come so much then, and the main music was the soul things of the time. You tended to find if skinheads went out in the evening they'd be extremely smartly dressed, expensive suits and things like that. With the second stage of skinhead basically came tonic suits, the cropped hair, the Ben Shermans, the shoes – you had tasselled loafers, you had weave wear, you had Royals, that was a very big shoe. It's taking off big, the real smart look's coming in now and obviously the Crombie's coming in. Not only that, the reggae thing's coming in. I started going to all-nighters. And the main thing about all-nighters was East-End lads who were skinheads, rock-steady and reggae, I use the generic term reggae, it was more rock-steady. This is the music of the streets; this is when you get the big explosion, the 'Tighten Up' albums starting to come out. The music started coming down here and you started getting a whole *thing now where you've got a working-class, young people thing, the football fan. There was Motown, reggae, ska, that's where you were. If you weren't there, maybe you were a hippie, or you could be a biker, but you were a no one. So the football thing now has really taken off in a big way.*

I'd take our first end when we knew we had something. The year '67–'68 was the year we nearly went out. An important day was 28 February, Rotherham away. To the best of my knowledge that was the first time Dinksy organised a coach away. Up to then you would have got on the specials or whatever, but Dinksy organised a coach for us specially. So that's Rotherham away, but I didn't actually go to that one. It was 30 bob, one pound fifty, and it left at midnight from the Crystal Palace pub which is now defunct. All the lads came back and told me the good times they had, so I went on the next one to Hull. This is the first time we are free, we can do what we want and we are away in a mob. One coach and about 50 people. Hull City was a stroll 'cause they didn't have a recognised end or a recognised football crew, simple as that.

The next game we went to was Blackpool away. Now Blackpool's getting good. I hitchhiked up there and I met the Pompey lot as they came in. At the time we were wearing our scarves. It's about Easter time now. We're wearing scarves linked and hanging through our Levis and if you nicked anyone's scarf from the other end you'd have it. So we'd be walking about like Christmas trees, with a thousand scarves. To me it's an important moment. We're up north, we're over 200 miles away and we suddenly realise we do have a talent for what we were about to do, because quite frankly we ran Blackpool out their end and out the flaming town. Fifty of us. Going up north, it's all the same – they're all bikers, they're all rockers and greasers and stuff. So that was that season, Blackpool away and that would have been about it that season.

So the next season things are getting serious now. The first away game, Birmingham City, we all got on a train and we all went up there, I would say about 250 of us. So we all start marching down the streets down to Birmingham's ground and this is a story that's repeated itself two or three times with me after a trip to Birmingham. We're standing on the sidelines and we can see their mob coming around. Their mob gets near us, we chase them, and they go flying. This is what happens at Birmingham. Ten minutes later there's twice as many. We chase them and they go flying. They come back 10 minutes later and in the end we're totally and utterly outnumbered. But I didn't rate Birmingham or Villa or any of those crews at all. They always seemed to need vast numbers. So basically nobody got hurt but we didn't win that one, we had to split up and go away. But we were learning then, and it's a long walk back to the station – if you walk down one road, they come up another. With two sides to everything it can be a nasty experience. We all got home safely. I was living in London at the time and I got the Chelsea train back from either Leicester or Forest, I think it was. And there was hundreds of Chelsea and I knew some of them. I think it was Forest 'cause they took Forest apparently, and not many people did at the time.

So after Birmingham, it's Millwall that will be the next decent home game. Yeah, Millwall, oh my God.

At the time, we know what's coming, we've got Millwall. So we all go down to the game. I can remember from half-eleven, 12 o'clock, the whole thing was getting nasty. I went to get off at Fratton station and if I remember correctly there was Millwall all around. We went to Portsmouth Harbour station and their mob were backed down to the platform. Now Millwall had a superb crew, which at the time would have been a sort of mod-skinhead look, guys in suits, you know, that sort of look. Almost Ronnie and Reggie in a way, that sort of general look, well groomed, cropped hair. They looked the part; they looked like they could be a bouncer in a nightclub. They came down and they've got the Fratton End basically. They infiltrate, they're very clever, and you don't know where they are. And then, two minutes before the kick-off, you suddenly realise they're standing next to you. They say, 'Come on then, come on' – it's all of this and they've infiltrated you and they've got you, and they're round you. And we had to move, we got the worst of it, simple as that. Then, coming outside the ground, we all got up together and we got up to Fratton station where that bus shelter is and Millwall turned: 'Come on then, if you want it.' And they ran us, it's as simple as that, I can remember running for my life, hiding in a garage with two other blokes 'cause these Millwall blokes, about eight of them, are outside, going, 'Bastards are somewhere here.' We were going to get killed ... madness. So that's another time we've met Millwall and we're two–nil down by now. They have routed us again, that's all I can say. I know the stories later in the eighties, but I can only put it in perspective. At the time we were not in the league of a West Ham,

Chelsea ... we were not in the league of the things even the 6.57 were to do in the eighties. I could see that we had something, definitely, but we didn't have the big numbers. Millwall away was a no-no. We went the first year in '67 and nobody bothered going again after that. I'd go Millwall away but I'd go incognito. I went twice and I kept very quiet and low, it's as simple as that. I don't even know why I went but I did.

Millwall's near neighbours, Charlton, they had a go. People laugh now but I'll give them their due. Charlton came up and I always had a slight respect for Charlton because it's a hard club to follow if you've got West Ham and all the rest around you. They had a go and we turned them over, simple as that. I can remember Cardiff, they always strike me as not so much wanting trouble, but if someone hit them they'd always hit back, there's no doubt about it.

For me, the season Pompey came of age was the year that we had Blackburn Rovers away in the FA Cup. This is one of Pompey's finest glory moments. At this period, '68, '69, '70, you may find this hard to believe, but we were getting warned, the only two northern teams we were getting warned about apart from anything obvious – I'm not going to say Man United away – were Nottingham Forest away and Blackburn Rovers. Man United fans had told us about Blackburn Rovers and West Ham also told us about a nightmare trip they had up there in the FA Cup back in '66. So anyway we all go to Blackburn, this is the FA Cup '69 year, and the day starts off badly. The simple reason being that, at the home game that year, about the second game on the Tuesday night which I didn't go to, there's three or four Blackburn blokes down, big leather jackets, big blokes and what had happened was, after the game, some Pompey had spotted them and had followed them out, and apparently this Blackburn bloke turns round and says, 'Come on then, if you're going to do it, do it.' And they got a kicking. So we get to Blackburn, right outside the ground, and I'm standing with Dave Dwaine and all that lot. Then someone said, 'Oh, Christ, it's that bloke.' And it was this bloke with his mate and we knew straight away they'd spotted us. Blackburn's the same, all filthy Hell's-Angels types, big, big, big. So anyway we get in the ground, and there's only two coaches of us doing this because the special was delayed until half-time. The coaches were Dinksy's again, and they both left from the Crystal Palace pub. In fact, Dinksy had only the one coach. For Dinksy's coach, you had to be one of the 40 or 50 people to get invited on it, simple as that. You had to be one of the people. And by this time we had a pretty hard sort of crew of all good lads I grew up with, mainly known as the Southsea boys. And Gosport always supplied some very, very tasty boys, Dave Dwaine, people like that, very important early people and a solid sort of Gosport crew of about eight or nine used to come over too.

So Blackburn away. This is before the game's even begun, we're up the other end and all Blackburn are up their own popular end. This is a good half-hour or hour before the kick-off, I would say, because the terraces at each side are fairly empty of people and, as you know, in those days you could move round the football ground. The whole thing was about taking an end. The whole thing was the battle of an end; that was the most important thing. So Blackburn start to move round our end, so they get to about halfway round the side terrace to the left and the whole lot of us just went to them and scattered them. During these early preliminaries I can remember one guy, Ian McKay – he lives in Australia now – who lived on Hayling, and I can never forget him – he had his boots on and his braces and that, and he carried on walking, and he walked right into the Blackburn end, took a few punches, like that, like the hero everyone thinks is mad ... there's always a madman somewhere, you think he's going to stop in a minute.

We're up our end now, we're bolstered, but you can see more and more Blackburn, right, and I'm looking at this and I'm thinking there's a hell of a lot of them. Football has started, you can forget the football – after 20 minutes we're 4–0 down, something like that. So what's new, this is typical Pompey, isn't it? So now the fun starts. The back of the end we've got is like Arsenal's old North Bank with stairs up the back, wooden stairs, and Blackburn come piling through. All big blokes, they're piling through; they've got the old pennies and they're chucking them at us like hell. There's some strange liquid coming over. I've heard rumours, although I can't say for definite, that they were chucking ammonia. So, anyway, they're all around us now. It was one of those efforts, to me, where Pompey was standing against overwhelming odds and they were standing their own to the last. I was very, very bloody proud of us that day, it was a different story. This has gone from us being 15-year-old kids to this now becoming a serious business. And I can remember coming out of the ground and there was Pete Harris and me walking and there's Blackburn about 200 yards behind us. I'm looking at them and I think it was Pete that said, 'Just walk slowly,' and I was thinking, Well, why don't we all just bloody well leg it to stay alive to be honest. He said, 'Just walk slowly,' and we just walked and these Blackburn walked behind us and I have a sneaking suspicion that maybe this was because of the way things were at the time about 1969, 1970. They could have given us a good hiding, but I had the feeling they didn't because there were only a few of us. It wasn't the type of thing that happened later, I mean, three or four years later you would be dead, wouldn't you? Fifty of them would kick you. But I still don't think it'd got to that stage.

Anyway, we get back to the coach and on the way it stopped at Manchester at about seven in the evening. The express purpose for me and Dinksy was to go and see the Twisted Wheel club. That may not mean a lot to some of you today, but it's a big Northern Soul club, right. It had finished and closed, and me and Dinksy said we wanted to go along and see it. We went and saw it, and we get back to the coach. This is about nine or 10 o'clock at night and we're just hanging about by our coach. All of a sudden four or five Manchester City blokes come for us. They were the skinhead type, but quite frankly they didn't have the clothes. They didn't have white Sta Press up there. They used to wear cook's trousers, right. These Man City blokes had been to Chelsea the week before and Manchester City had taken a bitter hammering from Chelsea fans. Really, really bad. I know that because I'm living in London so I'm getting the gossip. They'd been slaughtered.

So they come up and our man Dave Dwaine had a pair of Jungle Greens on. And this Manchester City

*fan goes up to him and says, 'They're fucking Chelsea
trousers,' and throws a kick at him. He throws a bit
of a kick where it's an antagonistic thing but not in the
definite sense that he was offering him out. So Dave
goes on to the coach and gets a bloody great big rattle
that used to travel with us to away games. It was a
bloody great big thing with metal pieces, right. So I
see Dave Dwaine getting off the coach, this is a bit like
the scene in* Goodfellas *where he sees him walking. So
I see Dave Dwaine walk up to the bloke and he gets
the rattle and he goes bang, and the bloke's head splits
and there's blood all over. The bloke staggers like that
and he goes, 'You haven't fucking put me down, have
you?' And we're looking at him going, 'Oh my God.
If it was anybody else they'd have been in hospital.
The next minute, it's about 10 o'clock and Man City
have just come back from Newcastle for the FA Cup,
fifth round, and about 200 Man City fans dive on the
fucking coach. They're all around it, the back window
goes through, but by a miracle the police turn up and
get us out. We'd already had a fight; we'd bumped
into a mob of about 50 or 60 Man United and we just
chased them to the middle of Manchester. Also I
remember Pompey fans went into a club – and I'm not
proud of this – and long leather coats were very much
in vogue, and they cleared out the bloody cloakroom,
which ain't nice, but there you go. We're suddenly
realising we can go to away games and we've got a
crew, simple as that. We'd gone, we'd had a go at Man
City, had a go at Man United, had a go at Blackburn,
and that's not a bad day's work for any of your
football mobs.*

*At that time I was the only person from Hayling into
football in that sense, right, so you were still an*

unusual figure; it was still a cult thing, a skinhead-type thing. We were getting more influences now because we'd got London boys working in the holiday camp. They were coming up and they were wearing some beautiful clothes, everything was changing now. Mustard-coloured cardigans; Fred Perrys are appearing, although that was a big mod thing in the sixties, right; three-button granddad vests, though I never rated them and never saw much of them anyway. Now that same year of 1969 in the following season was when the skinhead explosion was taking off big time. This also coincided with me having another big culture change in a way. Funnily enough this was the first time I ever took speed. I bought five Dexys off someone. I introduced them to another part of the culture, the clubs up Farnborough, the Blue Moon and that and the marina all-nighters were kicking off and a lot of us were starting to get into that. So we were starting to take all that. And now reggae was coming through the boards and all of a sudden the riots started going off at Easter, the skinhead riots.

Just before the start of the '69–'70 football season, the Daily Mirror *printed a report on the Isle of Wight pop festival. It was the usual crap about Dylan, about hippies stoned out of their heads on acid, the old peace and love bit. However, the article ended with a report on a 'strange youth cult', which had sprung up in East London. The youths, said the article, had severely battered several Pakistanis. As the days went by, various newspapers printed reports on strangely dressed, short-haired youths involved in punch-ups in various cities around the country. As usual the press didn't know what the fuck was going on. The skinheads had arrived – peace and love died; hate and war was born.*

And the next thing you know is everyone's a skinhead. This is the big thing. The next season everybody had cropped hair and you suddenly realised that people who'd maybe had long hair for a long time had suddenly gone and had it cropped to the point you didn't even recognise them on first look. Obviously the movement, the whole scene, was getting diluted, it was bound to. So let's have a look at the games that season, because it's a serious business now. Everyone's fighting now.

The Portsmouth skins first made their presence felt at the Pompey versus Leicester pre-season 'friendly'. They steamed the Leicester mob, most of whom still had long hair. The boots went in fast and furious up the Milton End before the game had even started! Then a week later Pompey opened the season away to Blackpool. The Pompey skins made more headlines than the team. They ran riot across Blackpool seafront, smashing the place up. Then they pulverised the Blackpool mob at the match.

I didn't go to Blackpool personally, which is the greatest regret of my life. The reason being that, at the time, I'd got so into the sort of club culture, reggae and pills, that I was a bit of a sick case for a while. I was dropping out of things. I missed Blackpool away, like I say, but I've heard so many good stories.

The word went round, who fancies going to Blackpool for the crack? There would be many who would heed the call, as Blackpool football ground was the least of its attractions. Three coaches were put on with everyone meeting and leaving from the Crystal Palace pub situated at the top end of Goldsmith

Avenue, a big boozer close to nearby Fratton station.

Leaving after closing time on a Friday night was a sure-fire sign high jinks would occur somewhere en route. This turned out to be in Oxford where one of the coaches broke down. The delay, leaving a coach load of boozed-up Pompey supporters hanging around to amuse themselves, had the local police called out, as things began to get naughty. It was only the start, as further on the coaches pulled into a service station meeting up with Chelsea supporters on the way to Liverpool. No problems, as both sets of fans took to talking and chatting with each other, catching up on all the football stories of the day and it was all very jovial until a coach load of Man United going to a match the other way pulled in. Immediately, a few Chelsea and a few of our boys decided they wanted to have a go at them. Over they all went, routing the United fans almost as soon as a few punches were let go. With that being over quick, the Pompey coaches ploughed on, eventually reaching Blackpool just before nine on the Saturday morning. The coach that had broken down arrived as well, so we all met up and went about the town. Some went drinking, some went down to the funfair, and generally it was a good day.

We had all arranged to meet again before we went into the ground, and a half-hour or so before kick-off we went into Blackpool's ground en masse, straight in their end, everyone from the three coaches. Straight away we made for the middle of their end behind the goal, and there must have been 200 mobbed-up Blackpool who broke off and ran. With no opposition, everyone stood about enjoying themselves, singing and generally having a laugh.

Their end began filling up quite quickly and Blackpool's boys started having a go back, by mobbing up and coming in from different angles. It was going off all game. But never once did they shift us because never once did they stand. They just kept running away. The Old Bill never tried to shift us from their end, even they could see nothing was going to happen here as there was only one mob. With the other lot running off, no one was getting hurt. We lost the game and went outside and waited for them but they wouldn't come out of the ground. After what seemed about half an hour the police just moved us on, because the Blackpool fans just stood in the ground and would not come out.

So now we all split up into various little groups, and then everyone converged on to the seafront where it went off with various incidents going on all along the Blackpool mile. I was in a little group of 10 when a knife was pulled on us. One of the boys from Leigh Park just went for the geezer and chased him down the road as he took off, running down the road still with the knife in his hand. Things were just happening along that seafront but there was no suggestion that this could be Blackpool's mob, they could have been locals, day-trippers, anything. But the main thing about the day was that our appearance, and our hair in particular, seemed to really shock people. Ninety per cent of us had cropped hair. A few arrests were made and the police just appeared to be amazed. They would ask questions like, 'Why do you have your hair like that?' and get a response of 'So you can't grab us by the hair.' They had not seen anything like this before – it was all new to Blackpool. They had obviously not played Millwall and seen the big boots and rolled-up jeans, because for the next three days it was in all the national press. Papers like The Mirror *ran articles about the trouble and all the arrests, but the focus was all about the Portsmouth skins and skinheads.*

If you were there that day and of the age, as a Pompey fan you would never forget. To go to the other end of the country, have a laugh and read about yourself in the papers for the next few days over this skinhead business. It was a first for Pompey and it was one of the games that even today people say, 'Did you go to Blackpool away?' Blackpool away was a big talking point and it still is. You had to be there to appreciate it. It gave Pompey fans a name long before the exploits of the later 6.57 crew. To be part of that first skinhead explosion was a real happening time. We never left Blackpool until midnight and incredibly it could have gone off with Millwall that day. We had stayed around the funfair, our three-coach mob, when about the same number of Millwall came in. They had played away to Bolton and decided to drop in. You can imagine a real nasty situation here. There was a bit of banter between the two rival groups but, after a few calls of 'Let's leave it, we're both here to enjoy ourselves' – there also seemed to be mutual admiration with us both sporting the skinhead look – both groups just walked away. It was that kind of weekend, it really was.

The week after Pompey's 5–1 home defeat at the hands of Sheffield Utd the front cover of the Football Mail *was dominated by an article on the skinhead menace and showed a picture of a skin outside the Fratton End being frisked for weapons, but the remainder of that season continued without the*

*sensation of Pompey fans making all the headlines. So
basically looking at the 1969–70 season, apart from
the obvious boring facts that Millwall came down and
took us again, there wasn't a lot happening aggro-
wise. That is, until Norwich away. Now Norwich
away was well planned. The moment we knew it was
an away game everybody's getting excited. So it's the
same thing again, Dinksy's coaches. Now everybody is
in their full skinhead glory. It's August and I'm
wearing a bloody knee-length sheepskin because you
know what fashion's like – you don't care if you're
sweating or not. Everybody had a Ben Sherman and a
porkpie hat; we've now got a solid Pompey crew. We
all tended to be the same age. The older blokes – a lot
of people who'd been Teds or whatever – they've
gone, their time had gone. It was the early seventies.
So we go to Norwich away and I'll never forget it. We
always travelled up in the night, Norwich, Torquay
anywhere. So we got there about five in the morning
and straight away we're wandering the streets with
not a lot to do. About 10 o'clock we start hitting the
pubs and all that. We start drinking and so now
you've got a drunken mob of Pompey absolutely up
for it. We make our way to the ground, we get in the
ground first and then Norwich start to come in. They
didn't like this one little bit, I mean, who would?
We're on their end and then the serious business of
fighting goes on for about three-quarters of an hour
and Norwich quite simply lost their end, they lost it
and they got pissed off. They probably outnumbered
us about three to one. When you look back we
probably had about 150. The coaches were always the
vanguard, we did the fighting, then the trains or other
people might pull in. They'd be on the periphery but*

they'd join in. It was the same in the seventies and the eighties, wasn't it?

So we've come out the ground and they've all regrouped. And I shall never forget this, we start to march back to the town centre. But we confronted Norwich. I can remember, for some crazy reason, in between us and the Norwich mob there was a wedding going off and I can remember, for some reason from somewhere, 'Tears of a Clown' by The Miracles was playing dead loudly. There's Norwich there and there's us there and that's it, we charged at them. And I can remember – and this is terrible – but I can remember the bride and bridegroom ducking down like this and all this wedding party goes flying. It's not funny and we're flattening anybody and everybody. This is the town centre and we just cleared it, just a full-scale riot. I can remember standing there and the next moment a brick went smack into my chin and I sort of fell back right and then I saw a Pompey fan – I can't remember who – picked up, you know, like the Coca-Cola swinging sign. He picks that up and he chucks it straight into these blokes. We've wiped it and have run Norwich everywhere. I notice when this happens that the town hate it, the whole town, everyone hates you. This is bad news. Right now this brought us a lot of bad publicity, the newspapers were full of it and it made the Sunday papers, just like before with the Blackpool riot.

One word sums up the football scene of the 1968–71 year – skinhead! As the months and seasons passed, the number of skins in Pompey grew and grew. It wasn't long before gang warfare ensued.

The hardest mob in Pompey were the Bell Boys, who took their name from the now disused Golden Bell pub under the tricorn where they used to gather in force on match days. Besides the Bell Boys, there was the Eastney mob, who were constantly at war with the Pier Boys from Southsea, led by Robbie Jones. North End had a tough crew of skins with the Page brothers, Ritchie Blake and Stef Kurder in their ranks. Portsea had a big mob, as did Portchester and Fareham, who were always kicking fuck out of each other.

Besides battering each other, the skins indulged in Paki-bashing, skate-bashing, and hippy bashing. They were also at war with the local Hell's Angels. The main gathering place for all the Angels was a café in Palmerston Road called the Milano. The skins used to hang out at the Marina discotheque in Goldsmith Avenue, or the Crystal Bar in Southsea. I can remember sitting outside there on the steps, watching the older skins and their birds going in and wishing to fuck that I was 18 instead of 13.

The skinhead cult was at its height in 1970. The bank holidays that year saw skinheads on the rampage in Brighton at Easter. Holidaymakers dived for cover as skins and Hell's Angels battered each other on the seafront. By August, the coppers had got wise to the skins. They were rounded up as soon as they arrived in Southend on Bank Holiday Monday. Besides confiscating knives, coshes, steel combs, etc., the coppers took their braces and bootlaces, which made it extremely difficult for them to run riot. The media, as usual, was going over the top with hysterical reports on any incidents of violence involving skins. The skinheads, of course, loved it.

As 1970 came to a close, a lot of the skins began to dress in a suedehead style. Their hair was cut about an inch all over and they wore a Crombie overcoat, carried a brolly, usually with a sharpened point, and wore heavy brogue shoes or loafers rather than bovver boots.

The clobber may have changed but the violence went on unabated through 1971. In the autumn of that year a mass ruck took place between skins and greasers in the Gilded Cage bar at Queen's Hotel. Billy Madden and Phil Hansford were both stabbed as the place erupted. The skins and suedeheads, however, were dying out, as the Smoothies came in wearing Rupert-checked trousers, round collared shirts, tank tops and interlace shoes. By late 1972 the skins had completely died out in Pompey. The original skins of '69–'71 were some of the hardest geezers ever to follow Pompey.

Pompey
Animals

'I DO WHAT I LIKE AND I LIKE WHAT I DO
(ORGANISED GANGS TAKE THE LAW INTO THEIR HANDS)
HOOLIE CULTURE, HOOLIE PASSION, HOOLIE
OUTLOOK, HOOLIE FASHION'
LYRICS TO 'STONE ISLAND WARRIOR': ACARINE

READING AWAY '77

I just went on a sort of normal coach, we had supporters' club coaches. We got up there and couldn't get a drink, as the pubs were all cordoned off. The ground their end was on the side opposite the tunnel and we went in that bit. We got there half-one, two o'clock. In the ground and in the away section there was a load of Reading fans, they were like Teddy boys or something. Not many, I don't know, about 20 or 30 I suppose, and there's a little punch-up in the away section. Pompey were all on the side and quite heavily packed out. Probably a couple of thousand Portsmouth, something like that. You know, they wore blue and white and we wore blue and white but I don't think there was any opposition from Reading, it was just like us lot up there messing around. It was an important game because we were in a relegation battle.

All of a sudden we went 2–0 down and I think that's when everyone just started getting on the pitch. There was no pre-planned thing of attempting to get the game stopped. You know the way it is, you're just sort of pissing around and you end up on the pitch. There wasn't a Reading firm anywhere so there was no one to run. So you're on the pitch and you start poncing about, and from there I run behind the goal at the opposite end to where the trouble had been earlier. I was about 18 at the time and I run behind the goal the other end and that's when some big trouble occurred. There's old boys of about sort of 30–40 grabbing us and holding us for the Old Bill. You know, the 'We've got one here' sort of thing, we'll give them a few clips round the ear. And that's where I think that Reading geezer came a cropper. 'Cause a few of the old boys had some of our young lads, had them head-locked and that, I got the feeling that's what happened with that fan. A few people took exception and there's a couple of rucks over it. You know, they weren't football fans, they were like members of the public and that bloke nearly died for it. I don't know whether he had hold of a Pompey fan but that's where that sort of went wrong, and he got hurt. People took exception and that's maybe why one was under the floodlights on a stretcher, obviously quite bad. And I remember, like, the referee Clive Thomas. He was running round, saying, 'I'm not calling it off, I'm not calling off,' while we're all on the pitch.

* * *

I remember the first away game I went to on my own was Reading, I think about '77, when everyone was wearing Dr Martens and faded jeanwear, the sort of skinhead look but you didn't have the haircut, it was sort of before the Fred Perrys and Harringtons had just came back in again. There was a real load of trouble at that Reading match and it was all in the paper on the Monday, 'Pompey Animals' and everything. I remember coming out after the game and Pompey just going down the road smashing windows, overturning cars and hitting anything really. When I got home my mum was waiting for me, and she said, 'That's the last time you're going to an away game'. But you get the buzz off something like that. I didn't see Pompey smash things up much, but they were putting windows through and everything there.

***

I don't think people went down there thinking, Let's smash up Reading. I think it was just a case of high spirits. You know there was this thing about '75–'76, of Pompey fans going places, just turning cars upside down and the name 'Pompey Animal' just stuck with the media. A friend of mine, from Hayling Island, actually made up T-shirts with 'I'm a Pompey Animal' on them, but he wasn't that clever, 'cause he actually got nicked for fighting at Fratton Park and he had an 'I'm a Pompey Animal' T-shirt on. Rather than turning it inside out or not wearing it at all, he wore it in court.

It's sort of funny if you look back at an era – and Man United were probably famous for it as well – of just going to places and wrecking things. I don't know whether it's through being naïve, or just being fucking mad. Pompey's just a violent place, a mad place, you just grew up with it and that's all I've ever experienced watching Pompey, whether there's five of you or 500 of you, you're just Pompey and you just don't give a fuck.

PLYMOUTH AWAY '81

We'd played them a few times but the first time I can remember was the 1981 season, '80–'81 season, division three, 21 March. Thousands went down there, well, I'll quote you a headline from a newspaper cutting, Monday, 23 March 1981, 'Pompey Animals Caged, gate torn from hinges as fans go into battle'. It starts: 'Honours may elude Pompey this season, but according to the Plymouth police, their fans have retained one title, they are the worst behaved supporters in the land. Their unruly behaviour at Plymouth on Saturday frightened locals and shocked West Country Police. We've branded them animals. They now have the worst reputation in the country and, according to a senior police officer on duty at Home Park, Portsmouth fans are 100 times worse than the once-feared Manchester United fans'. That is actually written in the local Evening News.

For that game with Plymouth I travelled down by car, we went down in my mate Guffer's Mark III Cortina. In fact, there was me, Rob, Ainser and Fish – God rest his soul. There was a shit train service so we just thought we'd go in the car. We left about 2 o'clock in the morning, all pissed up 'cause we had a mad night out before. So we travelled down there, got down to Plymouth about 5, 6 o'clock in the morning. I think it was Rob suggested we all go for a swim to wake ourselves up. We went and had a look around the shops, did a little bit of shopping, as you do, to get some money for the day. Pubs opened, straight in the pubs, just drinking. We met up with a few of the lads who had made their own way down there – some had hitchhiked, some had come down in the vans, some had got the trains down, but they'd all made it. In the end there was about 500 of us. It was just coming to the end of the skinhead era, everyone had cropped hair, flight jackets and baseball boots. We had a few little bits, but Plymouth didn't want to know. They weren't out that day, so we had a little run about. Saw a few of them, chased them up the road, usual stuff. This was all before dinnertime. I mean, we'd been there since about 5, 6 o'clock in the morning. We were just hanging out having a laugh. It was just a joke, Plymouth, we were running around like we ruled the place. Every pub you went there were just 10, 15 groups of Pompey. I remember seeing the Paulsgrove lot there, the Eastneys, and all the old Landport skinheads were down there too. This was when I can remember it all starting to go. This was pre-6.57. We did have a good old mob starting to happen for Portsmouth. There wasn't any sort of leadership, everyone was just into it, everyone was in their own little firms, everyone just wanted to go somewhere, wreck somewhere, smash someone up. It didn't matter whether you were Landport, Portsea, Stamshaw – you were just all Pompey and you were just all off your heads, just mad, everyone. You just didn't give a fuck who you were with, you just had no respect for no one, no respect for property, no respect for the Old Bill, no respect for the locals, you just went there, smashed the place up, abused everyone, and if you were lucky you'd end up having a fight as well. But, as I say, Plymouth didn't really want to know.

We got to the game eventually. We were in there, usual things, I think there was a few Nazi salutes *being thrown out. The Old Bill didn't like that. Then we started throwing things at the Old Bill: a couple of golf balls, things like that, few rocks, stones, anything you could break off the terracing, spitting at them, all the usual stuff. So they'd come through a gate in their specially erected fence. I'll go back to the newspaper: 'Fans were put behind a specially constructed Home Park cage which cost the Plymouth club £800' – and I mean, we're talking 1981 – 'to erect this fence just for the away fans, and that was money well spent according to the Plymouth Argyle secretary.'*

The police came into that section and tried to grab a couple of the blokes they thought had been throwing missiles and everyone just pushed forward. A couple of people smacked the coppers and the old hats fell off. The police were outnumbered. They were pushed back against the fence and we all started trying to pull the fence down. Everyone was climbing up the fences, swinging on it, all going mad. There was only a few of us there really, there was probably only about 800 fans of which there was a couple of hundred hardcore Pompey loons. They were climbing the fences, shaking them, trying to pull them down. We were trying to go on the pitch, trying to have it with the Old Bill and that. And the Old Bill came back in and we were just pushing against them, spitting at them, smacking them, punching them, and trying to get on the pitch.

The Plymouth fans didn't want to know. They weren't trying to get on the pitch or nothing and they had to call in extra Old Bill. All the police that were in the ground all came to that end of the ground to try and keep us under control. This was during the game, and throughout the game we were trying to get on the pitch, trying to pull the fence down. I mean it was a strong fence, and it stopped us. If the fence had gone we would have gone on the pitch but it did its job. But in the end, obviously, they drafted in loads of extra police officers, and nothing much really happened after that, we just stood there. But as we were standing in the terracing, I think some Plymouth geezers had left the ground and they were throwing things over the back. I think a couple of Pompey got a couple of Coke cans, lemonade bottles, silly little things, smack on their heads. So we turned round, and we've gone mad at that. There was some fencing behind us with a metal gate, so we've all gone mad and started ripping and pulling the fences. In the end the gate gave way and we just piled out through the gate. A few of them stood, but they were no match for us, we were just like chasing them, they were battered. I saw a couple of Plymouth trying to run, just tripped them up, and they fell on the floor. They got a right good kicking. There's a big old park next to the ground. We chased them all through that, through the cars, straight across the park. Just running them everywhere. A few of them stood, but we were just kicking fuck out of them all over the place. It took the Old Bill a while to get there. They managed to get it under control after about 15 minutes or so and a few people got nicked.

PLYMOUTH, THE LEAGUE CUP TIES '80–'81

In the same season but the year before, the League Cup was the main trouble at Plymouth. We had them in the League Cup over two legs in '80–'81. Loads of Pompey went down there and about five minutes before the game, a couple of Pompey lads went in their side and there was a bit of trouble and they got run out. With that, Pompey had gone on to the pitch.

It started off on the fence; everyone was rocking the fence, and there was fighting, a few on top just punching down and that, and then after that a few got on to the pitch by the corner flag and suddenly the whole end just went on to the pitch, Pompey's end. If you can imagine: they had the sides, we ran them at one point virtually back to the halfway line. But they were pretty game, Plymouth, and about 40 Pompey actually got on to their side, the rest was going on the pitch. There was real trouble at that first-leg match. Fish had the corner flag, didn't he? Threw it into their end. That got quite a bit of coverage in the papers. He picked the corner flag up and charged at their end with it. I went to Plymouth a couple of times after that and it only got better.

What I always remember is that they had a skinhead girl at the game when we had them on the Tuesday night at Fratton Park in the second leg. She had a proper shaved head, boots, Sta Press on and everything, and she was as game as they come. And I remember that she came in the Fratton End with a bloke and got marched out round the pitch. Never forget it, it was the first time I'd seen a girl at football getting stuck in.

PLYMOUTH AWAY '83

The best time was the afternoon Portsmouth clinched the third division championship and Pompey hadn't won anything for years, so obviously everyone was up for that. It was a West Coast invasion. Big game this one, our mate even cancelled his wedding 'cause it was on the same day. Something in the region of 10,000 went down there. I think everyone who was anyone in Pompey, every thug, every criminal, every loon, everyone's loon dad who was just as mad, everyone was just down there, their aunts, their nans, everyone. There were thousands of them and everyone was down there just having a good time. An invasion. They didn't know what hit them.

Plymouth weren't really known for having a mob – we went up there to have a giggle, you know, lots of people there, not just the usual football lot, not just the dressers. They were making their own different ways down there, coaches, cars, it was a big day out. Thursday night, Friday morning, as soon as they finished work everyone was down there. Some had gone down the night before and stayed in Torquay, others, Torbay, all the guesthouses were booked up. There was trouble there, with people getting pissed up and getting nicked, everyone just getting a bit boisterous. It was going to be a mad weekend, one massive celebration … the West Coast invading.

We had heard about it on the way down, the stories were already filtering back. There had been trouble in Torquay with the local Scousers. Just the normal night out – going out getting pissed, smashing the place up. It was just gangs of Pompey fans everywhere, drunk, hell-bent on violence and abusing everyone. There were obviously no locals about, everyone had gone into hiding or gone home, so there was no one to have it with apart from the Old Bill. Before we got to Plymouth we passed this field because there were no motorways down to Plymouth then. Driving along we saw this sheep and it had PFC sprayed on its back in a field of sheep. Yeah, just sprayed on it. Somebody had obviously got there in the morning and sprayed it. We weren't Welsh fans, otherwise we'd probably have shagged them.

We arrived in Plymouth early that morning, and Pompey were everywhere. We've come down the road looking for a pub, and the first pub we've come to some Pompey fan's come out, pissed out of his head, walked to the side of the road, smashed his glass on the side of a milk float and walked back into the pub totally out of it. This was still the morning. It was unbelievable and so were some of the things we were hearing. We'd got a local paper and it had said all about the trouble. On the way down some had stopped off at Stonehenge and sprayed that up with Pompey slogans. Yeah, it was 'PFC KICKED TO KILL' and Pompey slogans were sprayed in large letters all over the Stonehenge monument. People were up in arms about it and this made all the national papers as well.

Everywhere you went there were Pompey. There was no sort of organisation, as you can imagine with so many boys. There were just so many it was difficult to be organised. There was never going to be any trouble in the town centre 'cause there were that many of us, so we had a couple of drinks there. There were little mobs of Plymouth but they came out, had a little go, but Pompey just run them. We walked round the town. There were a couple of shops selling Lacoste. We had a look in there, people robbing shops, fags from newsagents – petty stuff and you knew you weren't going to get touched because the Old Bill were occupied. You could have done a lot more – there were times when you could have really taken advantage but then you stand a chance of getting nicked on the way home.

It was at that time that the designer labels were all the rage. Pompey were one of the sharpest dressed firms at that time. Everyone was dressed up, tracksuits, Tachini tracksuits, FILA tracksuits, Ellesse shirts, Pringle jumpers, training shoes. We looked like a real smart mob. As the day wore on a lot of fans made their way to the ground and that left maybe about 30 of us having a beer and then about 100 of them came out of all sorts of cubbyholes. We were thinking, Where have they all come from? Obviously they weren't going to show their faces completely outnumbered. They came at us, and we stood our ground. There were helicopters above our heads in all my years of going to football, I've never seen a police helicopter. I couldn't believe it. You know, they had already said that we were the worst fans in the country that they had known since Manchester United. Anyway, there we are and it should be coming on top with this mob of Plymouth, but they just backed off. West Country nature – they haven't got that nastiness about them. Basically they shit themselves – they should have done us really but the fact that we didn't run and that we were just there for a ruck, seemed to make them back off. As we were having it on the underpass with a dual carriageway above I remember this coach stopping and all these scarfers jumping out to help us. But Plymouth didn't want to know even when they outnumbered us.

Now out of the pub, we were on our way to the game and across the road there was a wedding ceremony going on and – I mean this was a bit naughty 'cause I'm married and I wouldn't like it happening to me – being young, we were having a laugh. Anyway this bread van pulled up with trays and trays of eggs at the back of the van. I think it was one of the older lot, believe it or not, who got into the back of the van and started passing out trays of eggs to everyone. 'Ready, aim, fire' was the command. Then everyone just bombarded them with eggs. They were having their wedding photos done outside the church and we just covered them. And, you know, at the time you can pay money to have a laugh or whatever you want to call it. But, looking back, that was a pretty sad thing to do. It was one of them silly things again.

In total, there were over 10,000 fans down in Plymouth that day. Pompey had both ends behind the goal, we were in the main stand and the terraces under the seats there, and Plymouth had a few seats and occupied the terrace to our left. There weren't many of them, certainly not as obvious as the mob they had in the past when we played them in the old League Cup. Pompey was fighting on the pitch and giving it to the locals whilst dancing about to the old Tom Hark 'Piranhas' tune. Plymouth didn't have an end – they had a side and all their boys used to go on the side. We got in there and, as we were getting in, about 20–30 of us who were down the bottom just ran up the steps, ran straight into Plymouth, fighting. Once we were in their end, Plymouth all turned round. They had a good go for a bit, came charging at us, and I remember big Spagsy was just knocking everyone out who came anywhere near him. There were various scuffles breaking out and it was quite amusing to see the different mobs of Pompey going into the Plymouth terrace to have a crack at them. At one stage Plymouth were all huddled at the back of their own terrace. They were to-and-fro fighting, police joining in and all that. But it was no good – Pompey had about three-quarters of the ground. And the one *part that was Plymouth – they were getting battered.*

This was the year Brighton got to Wembley. I'll never forget it because there was Jimmy Melia wigs about, you know, the funny-haired football manager that took Brighton to Wembley. Being the end of the season, May time, I think this match was the week after the FA Cup final or the week before, and one incident that sticks out again in my mind was this older chap who was with us – a generation above us and a well-known face in Portsmouth – who got into the ground, and paid straight away to get into the Plymouth side. He had a confrontation with a policeman, punched him and ended up laying this policeman out cold. He's actually knocked him spark out. Within seconds there were police and people all round, and out the corner of my eye I could see people were trying to change his coat so they couldn't get him. He put a Jimmy Melia wig on. Once he'd got this wig on and taken his coat off, he looked a completely different person. Now this copper's just come round on the ground and the bloke's had the audacity to go up to him and ask him if he was in need of a hand, after knocking him out.

The fighting carried on. The Old Bill kept getting Pompey out then at half-time another mob would come across from the other side of the pitch, get in there and kick it all off again. And then, with about 10 minutes to go until the end of the game, Alan Biley scored – 1–0. When Pompey scored there was a pitch invasion. We had the fences down and everyone turned round and went on the pitch and headed straight for the Plymouth. Half the Pompey support – it must have been about 5,000 at one time – were on the pitch, all loons, everyone was pissed out of their heads, everyone got smacked, anyone who was anyone, just anyone who was male was getting smacked. We didn't know who their boys were so everyone was just getting hit. We went into every stand, smacking anyone that wanted it. A few Plymouth came on the pitch but when they realised that they weren't going to stay, that they didn't stand a chance, they just bolted out the ground, just ran out.

Then we were having it with the Old Bill. It was mad, a mad day. The place got wrecked. Pompey were just smacking the Old Bill. I saw loads get nicked. At one stage even the police were running. They had no control over it. Everyone going potty celebrating winning the division three championship. John Deacon – who was chairman of Portsmouth Football Club at the time – actually got on the microphone and asked all the Pompey supporters to simmer down. The reply was just seat covers and bits of seats being thrown everywhere. There was no way anyone was going to simmer down. Bobby Campbell, the team's manager, had to come out and ask the fans to get off the pitch. It was quite funny 'cause Plymouth had just been run out of their own ground and it was just Pompey everywhere, it was fantastic, and as the final whistle went the pitch was lost under a sea of blue and white. Brilliant.

Leaving the ground, everyone headed for Torquay. We drank three or four pubs dry that night. They ran out of beer, lager, wine, everything you could drink, they ran out of it. There were just so many Portsmouth there. There were cars abandoned there by Portsmouth who just got a car for the day and left them up there. There were arrests, nickings – it was just one really mental day in Portsmouth's history.

Millwall Was Our Main Foe

'YOU KNOW HOW IT IS, I DO NOT LIKE PORTSMOUTH FANS AND THEY DO NOT LIKE US.'
MILLWALL FAN'S WORDS TO MAGISTRATES COURT, BEFORE BEING SENTENCED TO 42 DAYS

The Millwall boys used to come down to Portsmouth with a vengeance because they knew Pompey had a bit of a hardcore. After all, it was a dock town. They took a few liberties and were the only team to completely take the Fratton End in the mid-seventies. Millwall were a London firm with a pedigree and history long before the era referred to as the football violence days, which really took off nationwide around the time of the first mod youth cult phasing out, not long after we won the World Cup as a nation in 1966.

Even so, many clubs' supporters never really got organised until the early seventies when the boots really went in on the terraces. But where the name of Millwall is concerned this outbreak of a bit of bovver around the country's grounds just played into their hands, or rather to their strengths. Even though a relatively small club, their support had proved a handful for the authorities for years. No other club had calls to have their ground closed on so many occasions as the dockland club.

We've heard accounts from men that can recall the period of the original Pompey skins, who had their adventures and had their time but who were never going to have the organisation and numbers of a serious firm. That came much later on towards those heyday eighties. We hadn't played each other since the season Millwall got relegated in '75. Now, with both of us back in the old Third Division, the old rivalries and hostilities could be renewed.

In the eyes of any Pompey, Millwall were the best opposition we ever faced in the peak years of the 6.57 crew. Things got so violent that a two-year ban on travelling to each other's ground was given to both set of fans after numerous incidents between 1981 and 1983. The FA even made Millwall play Bristol Rovers at Fratton Park in '78 after the ban they received for Millwall fans attacking Ipswich players in a 6–1 FA Cup defeat at the Old Den. Whoever made that decision must have been mad as 400 Pompey turned out and defended the Fratton End for all they were worth.

The next season three coachloads of Pompey fans turned up at the Dell for an FA Cup tie between Southampton and Millwall after Pompey's game at Swindon was called off. Mayhem ensued in the Archers Road End between the three sets of fans. In 1981 deerstalkers and walking sticks were the dress code as 250 bushwhackers poured out of Portsmouth and Southsea station at 11am. Fighting ensued throughout the city all day. Charing Cross McDonalds, the Wellington, The Hole In The Wall and London Bridge are just some of the battles we had with them in the good old days. None of these places, however, saw the action that Waterloo station did in May '82 when hundreds and hundreds of rival fans fought in and around the station. It was only quelled when scores of police on duty for the Bobby Sands demo were called in to help.

The next year, to Millwall's annoyance, we parked up 300-strong in their seats on a Sunday morning game (we had earlier taken them by surprise at London Bridge while they all sat around reading papers and drinking tea). I must admit that it was quite early and it wasn't a real result in the ground. All the same, no one else ever did it. The police had a hell of a job shifting us as Millwall were mobbing up going mad. Though they did do the business against us outside the Star and Garter at New Cross. You could always rely on Millwall to try and get it on around Waterloo even if we weren't playing them. And, a decade later, in '93, the last time we ever played them, they pursued us with such vigour, it was a compliment to us all that south London's finest would want it so badly. We are, after all, only a small city in Hampshire. Everything from pool balls to sledgehammers, scaffold poles and concrete slabs have been used when it's gone off between us. We considered Millwall our main foe in this era, as you were guaranteed major fun when we met. They are without doubt a top mob and everyone around the country knows it. We like to think they feel the same way about us too, and we should be thanked for filling a big slice of the void they had in the barren years of the early eighties when they didn't play West Ham and the likes.

To sum up: where else would you hear of a baseball-cap-wearing 56 year old drop-kicking a police horse?

I first saw Millwall come down early '68 and it was probably the first bit of aggro I ever saw down at Pompey. You know a lot, in them days, would try and take the end. But you've got to realise then Pompey still had a big following and a hardcore mob and it was only the likes of Millwall that would come down. They were one of the few mobs that would go and stand in the Fratton End – a lot of the mobs that would come down wouldn't go in there. They would go and stand somewhere else in Fratton Park and normally, by the time the game ended, Pompey had gone round and piled into them.

Millwall were unlike any mob I had seen – it was

trainloads, they'd all come on football specials. It was brilliant and even though I was only a youngster I can still remember we had a sort of ringleader, a well-known lad then and my hero – a bloke called Ginger, probably the first Pompey leader. They'd have about the same numbers as us. You'd have the top of the Fratton End with the old blue doors, that whole top section, half Millwall, half Pompey, with a row of coppers. There was aggro all the way through the game. You see there wasn't any of that 'C'mon' nonsense then. If you had a punch-up you were ejected. The coppers would only ever throw you out, and some would come back in again. The whole game just going off, even at the back of the Fratton End, behind the stand – running battles all the time.

After that, Millwall would always come to Pompey. Pompey and Millwall would always steam into each other but Pompey have never been run out of the Fratton End. Don't forget, these were the days when we could go in any part of the ground and with the big crowds you would get away supporters in any part of the ground.

In the '70–'71 season it was Arsenal in the FA Cup and we had a 40,000 crowd there, with pockets of Arsenal in the Fratton End. That same season, Leicester came down and won promotion and, aside from Millwall, they were the biggest other mob I'd ever seen in the Fratton End. But with Leicester, although they were in the Fratton End, they were all down the front part and Pompey were up the back where they always stood. Whoever tried to have a go at the Fratton End, which was very few mobs they might have stayed in there for a while, but Pompey were in there as well.

MILLWALL AWAY '80–'83

Any fan will tell you once you've decided you're going to go Millwall away, you will go through an incredible experience that would prey on the mind and have your stomach in knots the whole week prior. Come the game, you would be so charged and psyched up. Then if you come through that game with anything like a bit of credit, even if it was just to show up, then the high and the memory of the day will always remain with you. And you would forever find yourself talking about the time we went to Millwall, remembering every detail like it was only yesterday.

The first major game I went to where I got involved with trouble, aggro, whatever you want to call it, was Millwall away, Boxing Day, 1980 season. I went up on a special train that was probably organised by Fooksie. It was a cheap way of travelling and as I was only 15 or 16 at the time it was a good way for me to get there. I've never ever known the number of Pompey that day, but it was jam packed. There must have been 1,200 geezers and boys on the train who were there for trouble.

It was over the Christmas period I actually got my ticket, and I'll never forget it because I was in approved school at the time, just on the outskirts of Southampton. One of the officers in there took a shine to me, being a Pompey boy, like. Fisher, his name was and we really got on. A week before I was due to go home he'd asked what I'd like for Christmas. At the time they were allowed to spend £5 on you. It doesn't sound a lot but back then it was enough money, and all I wanted was to go with my mates on this train to Millwall. It was £5 for the train ticket and the ticket to get in the ground combined. All my mates were living at home with their parents. They all had their tickets.

As I say I was in special school. The day before I went to go home, he came up to me, winked at me, put something in my pocket and said, 'Enjoy yourself. Don't get in trouble.' It was the ticket to go to the game on the train. I couldn't wait to get home to tell all my mates from round Landport that I was coming.

Obviously, being allowed home at weekends and being like 15 or 16, I'd just started drinking in pubs and the main pub in Landport where I was brought up was the Havelock. You used to get 20 to 30 from the pub who used to go to every away game and meet up with other areas of Portsmouth. You had the Milton Arms, the Stamshaw lot and the Air Balloon, which the Paulsgrove boys that came down would use too. That was your main contingent, those three pubs, to go to football with.

It was standing room only on the train that day. I can remember pulling into London, and the adrenalin started pumping. My heart was going. We got off at Waterloo, and then we had to walk across and join another train to Waterloo East. Once I got on the Waterloo East train, that was when the adrenalin started really kicking in. I'd heard a lot about Millwall, but I'd never been there before. It was the first time Pompey had played them for years, that's why everyone was there.

We got down to Millwall, got off at New Cross Gate and taken down to the ground by the Old Bill. Then they put us through the turnstiles and I remember Fooksie went, 'Here they are'. We turned round and Millwall were in the road, just as lots of Pompey were going into the ground. A few turned round and there was a bit of a punch-up. Then the Old Bill got there and split it up.

"Your Head Has Just Been Rolled" by the

P.S.P.

PORTSMOUTH SKULL PATROL

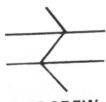

P.F.C

POMPEY 6.57

the new number one.......

PORTSMOUTH F.C.

Business as Usual

6.57 CREW

THE NEW NUMBER ONE

A selection of our firm's chilling calling cards.

Docker Hughes, a Pompey legend. *This page*: Docker's campaign, including his official party battle bus. *Opposite, above*: The man himself, the people's champion. *Below*: R.I.P., Docker, you will not be forgotten.

PORTSMOUTH SOUTH

VOTE DOCKER HUGHES

JUNE 11th 1987

Summer 1987. *Above*: The last away game of the season at Palace.

Below: A break between the seasons. The boys relax in Majorca.

Above: Sheffield United at home. Division One, 'ere we come.

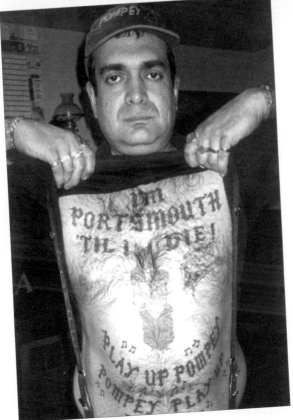

Left: The Pompey Bugler, the legend that is Westwood, shows how we all feel about Portsmouth Football Club.

Above: Rob Silvester on the set of *Hell To Pay*, Dave Courtney's film. It was an introduction by Kevin Courtney that led to Cass and Rob getting together to write the book.

Below: How it started. Kevin Courtney, third from left, Rob Silvester, third from right behind his son, Blaise and Cass standing behind Rob.

Then and now. *Above*: Bournemouth '82–'83. *Below*: The Portsmouth loyal today. From the despair of the Fourth Division to the verge of the Premiership, this is the heart and soul of the club.

From the World Cup to the European Championships, the Pompey contingent will be there in force.

MILLWALL WAS OUR MAIN FOE

We went into the ground and there was that corner piece, at Millwall, if you were the away support. A few of us stood on the floodlight part at the bottom there, the big concrete base which was a bit higher than the rest and we were stood in there when a few Millwall came into the ground, into the away pen. I remember Derek jumped down and drop-kicked one of them and it kicked off. There was about six or seven of them come in. They got split up and they got taken out. They must have been totally mad.

Not a great deal happened on the day and everyone just went after the game. But from then on Pompey got braver and braver every year they went there and in the end they just did what they wanted to do. This first day I was a bit wary. I think most people my age group were but we grew out of it and within time we went there and took the piss a couple of times.

MILLWALL AWAY 1983

It had been all the talk round our way for a while. All the time I had been growing up I had only ever heard tales of Pompey and Millwall rucking. Although I wasn't into football in a big way I'd got to know the young 6.57 from Pompey's pub and club scene.

That day we'd met at the City Arms then got ourselves over to Portsmouth and Southsea station. What a picture! There was just mob upon mob of Pompey, just hundreds milling along the platform which was an incredible turnout when you think this was a Sunday morning and the game was to kick off at 11am up in south London. Police had put this down as a high-risk fixture.

So there we were looking like the kids we were at the time, Pringle jumpers on and those three-striped

Adidas everyone used to wear. This, I remember, was the height of all that dressing period. Pompey, I can recall, before that had a big gang of skinheads until they all turned to the real casual wear. Guys going to football like that we used to call 'dressers'. It was expensive clothing and these guys were into it in a big way. Don't ask me how they got the money for all that gear. But people were doing different things, you know, tealeafing it in Europe or shoplifting it over here. All sorts of hooky business was going on in order to keep up or stay ahead.

It was probably the best ever time in going to football. I remember going to Millwall that day and looking around, like I say, in my Pringle and pressed 501s thinking, Cor, look at all this gear everyone is wearing. You could tell something was going on, there was just so many smart-looking people there. The other thing was these deerstalker hats, something I noticed when all these Salisbury boys came down to Pompey to meet up. They all had hats on. That was another thing about us Pompey: we had lots of little crews from all over the place. Later on, in '86 – '87, we even had a load of Brummies that used to come with us. Pompey's mob was really all different people with a real hardcore of top faces that came from three main pubs. Probably about 100 geezers would be the core, centred around these pubs, and that was the top firm. That was really how I got involved with that firm in regard to going to Millwall. Although I'd been going home and away nearly all that season, I really didn't become part of that 6.57 family until I actually went to Millwall.

When we got off at Waterloo that day, there were 500 geezers. Pompey always had a big mob that travelled away, but the numbers didn't matter, what mattered was that it had geezers, 'cause with geezers you know that they were never going to run. I look back to all the firms we had taken away to the big games we'd had – the Millwalls, the Chelsea, the Newcastles, the Leeds and the Birminghams – and we always had a hardcore. The firm we took over to Millwall that day was the same firm that was still going three years later and that firm just bonded together and we knew together no one was ever going to take us.

I'll say it again, the period of years I'm talking about was probably the best ever for footballing mobs. It was the height of the casual and top firms of which – without sounding biased – I would rate us top. All right, it might be us for a few months after a couple of good games, then it might be Chelsea or someone else. But, for a period, I thought we were number one or two in the country. My job takes me around the country and over the years I've spoken with many a lad from that casual era, and the one top ever firm was West Ham. It's a firm that we've always rated even though we never ever really came up against them – we only ever met them twice. Once when we played them and once in London when they were playing Norwich. West Ham were the top firm, but I always say that Pompey for me was in anyone's top five if not top three. You know, the top firms had to be West Ham, Millwall, Chelsea and Leeds maybe, but one firm I wouldn't forget – and this may surprise a few – Birmingham. I thought Birmingham as a crew were awesome, absolutely awesome.

But back to Millwall, we get to Waterloo and everyone is together and, as a 16-year-old kid, I'm just sort of caught up with it all. I'd been to Millwall a few years before on the special, and there was trouble, but nothing I got involved in – too young then. Now it would be different, I felt, as we all got the train from Waterloo East across to London Bridge. When we got to London Bridge it was all shouts of 'Everyone stay together', as with this firm we knew we weren't going to run.

At London Bridge we came down off the platform and there must have been about 100 Millwall there. They just weren't expecting us and we blitzed them. Everyone just went running straight down on to the platform and we battered them everywhere. A few tried to stand. The Millwall face Jacko got a touch-up. In a conversation years later, at the play-off in Cardiff, Jacko admitted that they never knew what hit them that day. They managed to regroup at the end of the platform. Then we ran them off the platform.

Next we all got on the train to go to New Cross, the stop for Millwall's ground. You should have been in the carriages at that moment. It was electric, everyone was full of themselves, did you see so and so, the big grins as that person relived the moment. You know, it was a train full of boisterous Pompey that had just done the famous Millwall. The train pulled in at New Cross and straight away a big mob of Old Bill surrounded us and walked alongside us to the ground. In them days, the London Old Bill were clueless. We had got there an hour earlier than they were expecting us to arrive. We seized on this confusion by telling the Old Bill we were Millwall and that we wanted to sit in our normal seats. So they put us in the Millwall seats on their side (halfway line). Some half-hour to 40 minutes before kick-off we've managed to get a firm of 150 to 200 Pompey in Millwall's seats. There we remained, waiting, but the game kicked off and Millwall still hadn't come. We're sat in their seats with a big gap around us. Then, all of a sudden, we heard this roar. I looked down and there was about 50 Millwall on the pitch. They had come down along the side. They were just so frustrated. We were on their territory, in their seats, they just couldn't handle it, so they tried to infiltrate us by just walking in twos and threes along the side of the pitch. A few boys in our side clocked this and started rucking with 'em. Then Millwall had run on to the pitch, and Pompey just got on the pitch with 'em to kick it off some more. There weren't enough of them there that day. The Old Bill took control easy and marched them up the other end. So we just kept our seats. Keeping them for the whole game, which is unheard of even to this day. I don't think any firm has ever done that.

After the game nothing happened, with us returning to New Cross. There were police all around us but we must have been 1,000-strong in this escort back to London Bridge. When we got back to London Bridge, there were about 50 of them waiting for us again. The one thing you can say about this Millwall lot is that they never had the numbers, yet they had unbelievable bottle and a good few older fellas that were really up for it. To make the point again they just stood in the middle of the platform. There's us, all 16, 17, 18, and these Millwall geezers about 45–50. A few young boys of ours just thought, What's the worst that can happen? So we just ran into them and kept backing and backing them off and battling them all along London Bridge. It only lasted a few minutes before the Old Bill came from everywhere and stopped it,

*rounding us up and taking us on to Waterloo. We got
the train home and I was back home by 4 o'clock. But
that was it for me. After that, I was up for everything
and there was a lot of other people who got that same
buzz in that same game.*

FA CUP '81

It's 21 November '81. We can't believe it and, to the dismay of the
City Council, we get Millwall at home, first round of the FA Cup.
We've gone from not playing them to can't keep away from 'em.

After the previous season, the police were more than ready for
any trouble and, before and during the game, they were generally
on top of it, after the game they ended up caught in a crossfire of
battling supporters. Millwall did the usual and went on a rampage
of destruction, walls kicked down, cars damaged, the Old Bill
bricked – usual story.

During the game there were plenty of Millwall up in the
South Stand, in the top bit. So, we thought we'd wait for them
to come down. There were only a handful of us, crazy really. As
they started to come down and round, one of us was on the
table, standing on it, and got the first one, sort of just jumped on
him and dragged him round. So what they've done, as it's all
kicked off now, Millwall have broken up this table and chased
us back upstairs trying to fucking get us with these table legs. As
we're going up we're running through more of them coming
down, all giving us side fists and we're getting it in the back of
the head and that.

The game goes to a replay after Hemmerman's first-half goal is
equalised by Millwall. That's fine because in the old FA Cup that
meant a Tuesday night – time to dust myself down and go again.

THE REPLAY

It was on the Tuesday, so we all decided to get the five o'clock
train from Pompey. Around 100 of us are going up on the normal

train. So we go off, get on the train and we turn up, get to Waterloo about quarter-past, half-past six. Across to Waterloo East, but instead of getting off at New Cross Gate, we got off at New Cross station.

We started walking. We didn't have an escort or anything. So we started walking down, 80–100 of us. We come up and there's a pub, the Rose. There's a few Millwall outside but as soon as we saw the pub we just charged across the road at them. Just took them by surprise, really. They were expecting us to come to New Cross Gate, and we'd come up from New Cross. It's gone off there and then; they'd come out, we'd gone in, scuffles going on, people bouncing in the road sort of thing. Then it all got split up, the Old Bill is right on it and one of ours gets nicked with a hammer which must have been part of a job lot. The Old Bill takes us up to the ground and I remember during the game a hammer's gone flying through the air and landed in their seats. Next thing, it's come back across. It was getting chucked backwards and forwards during the game. After the game we got taken back to New Cross Gate and they said they'd put a special on for us. We said we wanted to go on the normal train, but they made us get on it. We got back to Waterloo expecting them to turn up – and nothing happened.

MILLWALL HOME '80–'83

'80–'81: there weren't many big games that season apart from towards the end of the season. Millwall came down here and word had got back that obviously they'd be turning up on the train and Portsmouth's main station is in the town centre. So with the usual lot from the Air Balloon – we're north of the town centre, and we're coming down into the town centre 20-handed. By the time we got to the town centre we had to go through Landport. All the Landport boys were there. They were 20- or 30-handed. By the time we got into town all the other boys had met from all different parts of Portsmouth and there was a firm of about 100–150, 10 o'clock, waiting for Millwall to show.

As soon as the pubs opened we used the local boozer that was right near the ground called the City Arms and, just as we were getting to the pub, at about half-eleven, Millwall turned up on the train. Now at Portsmouth station there's a bridge that goes over the road. The pub's on one side; the station's on the other, and Millwall were on this bridge chucking everything they could off. Straight away, as soon as they got off the train they were on to the boys that were outside the pub. Millwall came off the station firm-handed, could have been 300 there and steamed straight across and had everyone backed off in the pub. Same thing again, the Old Bill turned up, dispersed Millwall, the Old Bill trying to keep Millwall all together. As they did just that, about 10 of us decided to make our way back into the town centre to see if there were any pockets of Millwall coming back down the road. And this was where I first encountered the infamous bushwhackers coming down with their walking sticks and umbrellas.

This was the first time I'd seen that at football: they were all smartly dressed. It was at the time when the leather jackets were coming out, the ones with the little vertical pocket on the left-hand side. Millwall were famous for the safari jackets in an ox-blood colour. Anyway, there were 10 of us and there must have been about 20 of them. They came steaming down Slindon Street, the road that runs alongside the station, leading back towards the post office. The 10 of us looked at each other and said, 'Well, come on. We've got to give it to them.' As they got close, I saw one had a walking stick. As he swung it at me, I kicked him. Well, I thought I'd kicked him and I'd fallen back into a flowerbed. My first natural instinct was to cover my head up with my hands, expecting this walking stick to smack me over the head. I could hear the geezer going, 'You fucking get up,' and my only way out was through him. But as I'd sort of looked to see where the geezer was, he was crouched down looking in pain with his hand on his bollocks going, 'Look what you've done, you cunt.' I'd kicked him straight in the nuts. Anyway, it stopped him getting me.

As for the game, we won that 2–1, but I don't think anyone watched. The atmosphere was evil, with tensions high and the Old Bill running around as policemen's helmets went flying from both ends. Both lots of fans tried to get on the pitch. Millwall did at their end, and play was held up until the Old Bill got hold of the situation.

Come the end of the game, the normal thing at Fratton Park was that the Fratton End emptied, or the South Stand emptied and you all got to the away end and waited for them to come out. When Portsmouth got round to the away end, there must have been around 1,000 Portsmouth all baiting the Millwall, because you could shout over into the old Milton End, and you could see them. And they were giving it the same back, going potty, smashing up the toilets, turnstiles and even the big wooden exit gates.

The police just escorted them out of the ground, straight up and attempted to get the Dockland club supporters straight on the train home. There were scuffles all over the place that day. Portsmouth's firm was spread from down Fratton Bridge to Milton Park, where all the Southsea and Eastney boys used to get, so it used to sort of split the groups up if you like and Portsmouth had to try and get at any opposing fans down the length of Goldsmith Avenue, which is the big long road as you get off the station that leads right down to the football ground.

Anyway, all day it was kicking off with groups breaking away. I believe there were a few arrests that day, both sides. Millwall had all split up. Portsmouth was all split up. And I think it was just on the day, groups of 10 to 20 having it with groups of 10 to 20. You know what to expect whenever you play them.

Whenever we now get round to talking about what was the best Millwall firm we'd come up against, it would probably be that day, but we met them so many times when we were 6.57. The thing that still sticks in the mind is the change of fashion the Millwall boys showed us that day.

Walking up towards the ground alongside the escort, loads of them had walking sticks. I remember they were taking the piss out of our clothes. They had sort of slouchy jumpers and Kicker boots, leather jackets with all the pockets, like hunting safari jackets. These safari jackets were just sort of coming in then. Just before this there were sort of pac-a-macs. We were still in flight jackets and 501s and that. I remember they went, 'You scruffy cunts. Spend some money on clothes,' and all that. I remember one of them actually had a pair of those sandals you used to wear down the beach, the plastic ones, Jelly Beans. He had a pair of them on and baggy trousers.

BATTLE FOR WATERLOO

I wouldn't usually travel away by train before the 6.57 got going. It was just too much of a problem. Nothing organised. I mean after that Reading game in '77, the club stopped running things – they didn't want any part of the trouble. They stopped running the club coaches and they wouldn't put any trains on. And that's when Fooksie started doing a bit of travel organising from the Monkton. Then there was Ted, with the premier coaches over Fareham, and they used to run everywhere. You know, we were still going, minibuses and all that, but on the train it was always a little bit iffy. The big bloke on the train that used to go everywhere on the old Persil tickets used to get ambushed every week. Travelling that way was plain madness back then. I remember seeing someone on a Monday who said they had been in a big ruck with Millwall at Waterloo on the Saturday. So the game that I'd been to up north, on the coach was the game that would be a turning point and make everyone to start to go by train again.

MILLWALL WAS OUR MAIN FOE

They said they got the earliest one out, which was the 6.57 and they went up there and waited for Millwall rather than Millwall waiting for them. They must have got up there sort of eight, half-eight. This was an early doors mob of Pompey because up to then they used to get any old train, you know, turn up across London sort of 9, 10 o'clock, all on different-time trains. That's when they were all getting picked off. I can't remember the exact game but I remember the big battle they had with Millwall at Waterloo, 'cause after that things sort of progressed. It was safer and safer to go on the train, 'cause there were more Pompey, the 6.57 crew.

* * *

We stopped at Forest Hill, just one of the stops back to Waterloo, coming back from the Palace game on an overground train with about 100, 6.57 mob on board. As we pulled away, a sledgehammer came crashing through one of the windows. As everyone jumped up, the train stopped. We were all looking out and we could see some Old Bill struggling to keep some really nasty-looking older fellas out of the station. They were in the car-park at the side of the station, jumping up and down on the platform fence screaming, 'Come on, Pompey. Come on, Pompey.'

We had an inkling that they would be Millwall because of their age and because of how keen they were to have a go with us. They were certainly not Palace fans. The Old Bill screamed at the train driver to go and as the train pulled away everyone was pulling the cord to stop, but to be honest everyone was looking at each other saying, 'Did you see that.

That was a fucking sledgehammer.' There was broken glass everywhere and everyone just piled out at the next station and set off on a mad jog back to the last station to have it with these fellas. There couldn't have been more than 30 or 40 of them. Even so, on the way back to this station everyone was picking up everything they could get their hands on 'cause we knew they would be well tooled up. By the time we got back, there wasn't anybody there, but the Old Bill rounded us up again and decided to put us on the next train back to Waterloo.

They were getting annoyed with us now and started walking along the train checking tickets. My mate Steve had tickets that took us on another route – I think it was via Victoria – so we shouldn't even have been on this line and I don't even know if it was my ticket.

They decided to chuck us off at the next station, which was the station we'd just jumped off at to come back and have a fight with 'em. So we pulled up at this station, which was an old derelict south London craphole, an old commuter station with a metal bridge. There wasn't a soul around, nobody on the platform, nothing. We were put off the train and everyone was hanging out of a couple of carriages giving us various signs and abuse and saying, 'See you back home, you pair of wankers.' As the train pulled away something rolled past my feet, and it was a pool ball. Not realising what was going on, I looked over my shoulder to my right, and over the metal bridge were the same fellas – our friends the sledgehammer gang, and they were just as keen as we were to get it on. Then another pool ball came flying through the air and I realised we were in trouble. I honestly thought

*if the train didn't stop I'd get killed and so did Steve –
we were running alongside the train screaming, 'Pull
the fucking cord.' The cord was pulled and luckily for
us the train stopped and everyone jumped out, some
hanging off doors. Everyone walked towards these
fellas and they backed off up towards the bridge. But
not in a way of backing out – they were calling us out
of the station. As we advanced up the stairs, a big
horrible-looking geezer with a bald head, who must
have been 40 years old, easy, just stood in the middle
of the steps, crossed his arms and said, 'I'm not going
anywhere.' Everyone stopped and looked at him. The
Old Bill came up and said, 'What's going on here?
What's going on?' As they pushed us back down the
stairs, we said we were from Bermondsey and we were
going for a drink with our friends, meaning the
Millwall lot at the top of the stairs. The Old Bill got
confused about who was who.*

*The Millwall geezers cottoned on to what was going
on and said, 'Yeah, come on. Let's go for a drink,' and
they looked well menacing. The three or four of them
at the front were in their forties, and they really
wanted it. The tension was electric and the Old Bill
quickly realised what was going on and pushed us
back down the stairs and back on to the train again.
We arrived back at Waterloo East after abusing the
Millwall fella at the top of those stairs, calling him
'Granddad', amongst other things, and shouting, 'Get
back to babysitting your grandchildren, you stupid
old fool.'*

*As we walked over to the main station at Waterloo
some Pompey came over shouting 'Millwall are here'
and stuff like that. The crew that ran down the hill
was top – pure 6.57 with 50 or so younger lot. Some*

Pompey were already engaged with them – the same fellas again, the sledgehammer 40-year-old pool-ball crew. They were Millwall's finest and it was really going off – we felt like the cavalry.

I'll give them Millwall boys 10 out of 10 for persistence 'cause they had landed at Waterloo before we had, but this Pompey firm weren't your average 18–25-year-olds and the fighting was mental. To be fair there was probably 100 Pompey and 50 of them. One of them crawled under a car to get away and people were jumping on the car to crush him. It was out of order really. His mates had gone and there was another one on the floor. They looked like they'd had a bucket of blood tipped over them. Me and Gary pulled the geezer out to save him, and took him over to a pub doorway to sit down because he was in a complete mess, but they were still trying to hit him with bits of wood and stuff. Yeah, it was a bad old row and I think people were putting down the old Skull Patrol calling cards. It was at the time Millwall were printing out calling cards saying that Pompey were never safe in London. He wasn't in too good shape this geezer. I remember someone saying to him, 'Are you all right, mate?' and he just replied, 'Don't worry, mate. I'd have done the same to you,' so he was all right. His mate had got a concrete breezeblock smashed down on his head whilst on the floor and he looked bad. It was really crazy.

We went back to the station and I had a bad cut on my hand where I had cut myself on the car trying to get him out. We were lined up and I couldn't hide the cut and got nicked. They nicked a few of us and I was put in a van on my own. Next an ambulance pulled up and the geezer who copped for the breezeblock was led out. He was covered in blood but he was conscious.

The Old Bill were saying things like 'You're getting remanded on Monday' and 'Malicious wounding', and stuff like that. I was a bit worried. They led him over to me and said, 'Is that one of them?' And he just shrugged his shoulders and said, 'I wouldn't fucking tell you if it was.' Much to my relief I was slung out of the van and no one else was charged with anything – no witnesses and everyone got off lightly. In the end, it was such a mad day I can't remember how I got back. I think I got a lift back in a car, but who cares. I was just relieved to get home that day.

***

We played Chelsea in the morning at Stamford Bridge, then someone had the bright idea that Millwall were playing at Wimbledon that afternoon. That was a 3 o'clock kick-off, and it was about half-one now, so we said, 'Right, let's all go over to Wimbledon.'

We jumped on the tube and went across to Wimbledon, about 50 of us, and we thought we'll show them that we were there. We got there about ten to three. We walked up by the ground and they were going, 'Who the fuck's this lot?' We got up at Millwall's end and there was a bit of trouble outside the gates and they had some big old lumps there. We had run down the road like a proper mob and we were going, 'Come on, Millwall. We're Pompey, who wants it?' and all this. They were mainly going through the turnstiles, but a few of their lads turned round and I remember Es facing the biggest geezer in the world. He said, 'How do you do this cunt?' I said,

'Well, you're going to have to hit him.' Then we got jumped on by the Old Bill. They rounded on us saying they were going to nick us all, but they just took us back to Waterloo and chucked us back on the train out of London.

***

There was a lot of Pompey out that day, a big, big mob. Being Boxing Day, a lot went back after the Chelsea game ended. Word was Wimbledon were playing Millwall that day, which would be a nothing game for Millwall as Wimbledon haven't got a mob. It was a normal 3 o'clock kick-off, so we said, 'Yeah, all right.' But the firm was too big 'cause the same thing happened again as had happened coming up in the morning. When we all went down to the tube station not everyone could get on the same train. We all got split up – 150 on one train, 200 on another.

I was in a mob of about 200-plus that went back to Covent Garden for a drink. I was with a different mob from the guys that carried on to Millwall's game. We never had a ruck, we just had a drink. But about 6 or 7 o'clock back at Waterloo we had a ruck with Millwall, a big ruck. And it went off again when they came back when the last trains were leaving out of London.

There were about 200 Millwall and about 150–200 of us. They ran on to the station through the exit, and they thought they were just going to whoop us. First of all we started going backwards and backwards, and then we grouped up and went into them and run them all down the road. But then, when we came round on to the front of Waterloo station, we met and it went *off for about 10 minutes, quarter of an hour. I mean they were getting us back, we were getting them back – it was even numbers, 150–200 each. That was their main mob. We had a good firm there though, and we held our own well. I don't say we won, I don't say they won. We were pushing them, but they were pushing us back.*

At about half-ten, 11 o'clock, just before closing time, we were already at Waterloo and, as the night went on, more and more Pompey that had been out in London all started to come back for the last train that went at about three minutes to twelve. In the end there was one hell of a mob of us. There was 500–600 of us when a firm of 80 Millwall came back and they just got slaughtered. I mean half the firm of Millwall came back when we were actually on the train station, but by then there was this mob of 500–600 Pompey, twice as many as the firm we'd had before and they only had what was left of theirs – about half of their firm.

Millwall's game plan, what they used to do, was come back for the pickings, and try and get 30 or 40 of us on our own against a mob of them, you know, to bushwhack you. They were always tooled up. Not that day though, that was one of the days when we just blitzed them, like the first ruck when there was 200 of us and 200 of them, it was like even stevens then. It was a different proposition for them 'cause what they were used to doing was waiting until your mob got on the train. Say the train pulled in at twenty past ten, 100 of you would get on that, then there was only 100 of you left; the next train would come and there'd only be 50 of you. Then they'd come back. Like vultures. But when there was a mob of you there, they wouldn't come out. By the end of the night there must have been 500–600 of us, and we weren't going to have a problem. I'm not saying they can't have the ruck, but that day there were no easy pickings, not this time.

***

Millwall were playing someone – and we went up on the train. We came back from Charlton and had it with them outside the Wellington in Waterloo. They were in the pub and we came back off the train at Waterloo East and I suppose there was about 30-a-side and both lots were up for it. It went on till the police broke it up. They were saying, 'We'll be fucking down next Saturday,' and all this. Yeah, so it was they'd had a night game of their own somewhere and they obviously came round to check what Pompey were up to.

But there's always been trouble between Pompey and Millwall. I remember we played at Fulham, I think it was, and they were there when we got back up to Waterloo. We were coming up the escalators and someone came down and said, 'Don't go up there, mate. It's full up with Millwall.' We said, 'So fucking what?' So we came up the escalator and they're all milling about under the clock. We flew up off the escalator straight into each other, all fighting and rowing each other. That was when H slashed some geezer.

So that was another off and a half. But we seemed to bump into them all over the place for a couple of years. I think both teams' firms respected each other, really. I mean, I see a few of their lads at England games and that, and they were all right with us. It's always, 'Oh, you've been a good mob to us, you know we can have a go.'

Chelsea
Give It

CHELSEA AWAY '83

The day after Boxing Day in the '83–'84 season was another fantastic day if you were a 6.57. I remember us all being down the station – never ever seen anything like it. It was unbelievable. I put it at anything from 700 to 1,000, but it was older people who'd done bits and pieces before us, it was younger boys up and coming, younger than me and I was only 20 at the time. Everyone who was on that train was there to be part of the firm and to do something. It was like the whole of Portsmouth turned out. There were carriages full to the brim. There were people sat on top of each other's heads. Every seat was gone, every standing place. They were sitting on the racks, where they keep the bikes, they were everywhere. There was every geezer, every boy, everyone you could imagine on the train. I've never seen so many people in my whole life get on, it really was some Pompey firm and a half that day.

I had a lovely jacket that I was wearing on the way up there. I thought the world of it. I looked the business in that, it was really tasty, and for some reason I was carrying a weapon, a lock knife, in the inside pocket of my leather jacket. I never really carry weapons. I wasn't intending to use it. I let a friend of mine wear my jacket and I completely forgot that this was in the pocket.

We got to Waterloo station and obviously word had gone ahead that there was a very large crowd of us and the police were there in force. They did the best they could, but there was just too many of us. They couldn't cope with us. They got us out of Waterloo. They didn't dictate to us where we were going, we were dictating where we were going. We wanted to be out on the streets causing havoc. We'd made for the main exit at Waterloo and they knew Chelsea. They had their scouts out and as soon as we got off, they was gone.

The friend who was wearing my jacket came running out as our train's pulled in and we all ran to get out into the main foyer of Waterloo to see who was waiting for us. We were disappointed it was only the police there and they grabbed hold of a few of us. They got my mate and wrestled him to the floor. He didn't know what was in the pocket – it was inside and it was zipped up. He got arrested, searched and a knife was found on him and he was swearing blind that he borrowed the jacket off his mate, he didn't know it was there. He went to court, and at the trial the jury believed his story. He's still cursing me for it today, my mate.

At Waterloo, we couldn't all get on the Underground, so we split up. There were three lots of 250, 300 here, 200 there, but we always kept in touch where we all were. The firm was just too big, you couldn't keep together and the firm I was with walked there, we actually walked from Waterloo to Chelsea's ground, right through London. It was absolutely brilliant, about 300 of us. The police were actually running alongside us to keep up with us. Now where it came from or how he had the time to do it I still don't know to this day. But he had a brick inside a sock, I believe, and as the police were running alongside us, he swung it and he hit this Old Bill full pelt in the face – KO'd, knocked him spark out.

It was shortly after we'd been attacked on the train by the Special Patrol Group and that was what we Pompey called our revenge against the police for what they did to us. One time, I can't remember the game, I think we had a bit with Millwall back at Waterloo. That all done, it was a burger in Casey Jones and the train home. Yeah, and they just got on the train, everyone inside there knew us Pompey had been taking liberties all day, and then it was their turn to take liberties on us. They were just beating everyone in sight, one had a truncheon in each hand – it was like watching England fans with the police abroad.

So we're down the King's Road now, I think we even went past the King's Head. There was nothing doing. We got to Fulham Broadway and went in a pub, or several pubs because obviously there's loads of pubs close by. We walked across a big massive common which separates Fulham from Chelsea and all you could see was masses and masses of geezers who wanted something to happen. I don't know what we wanted to happen, but we just wanted something to happen. That's what we were there for. We got to Chelsea's ground, and outside the ground there were a few scuffles going on, nothing major. We didn't see large numbers of them, just dribs and drabs, you know, mouthing off. We were behind the police lines, so there was the usual banter throwing. Chelsea always have a lot to say, especially with Pompey supporters everywhere. A couple of Pompey geezers did run out of the escort at the time, and they were hitting them, and getting nicked. We were all shepherded into the ground. All penned in the large away end, which was filled up easy.

All the firm back together again. Froggie's firm was the main firm who had the rucks, 'cause they actually went in the shed, about 50 of them got in there before the game. This was like half-one, and they had a massive ruck. When all the Chelsea supporters realised what was going on, that's when it went off rotten. It was like 50/50, they never got their way. About 15 of them got nicked. My relative got locked up and, I tell you, Pompey never had a care in the world that day. One time we all got over the fence. It was in the corner and their mob came up to it, then we charged it and were jumping over. You could see them all backing off and as we got over to the pitch bit the Old Bill came. If they'd wanted they could have got on there with us, but they could see how many there was of us. Hundreds of Pompey – all up for it. The Old Bill were out in force: horses, dogs, the lot. So not a lot really happened during the game. It was a 2–2 draw on some sandy desert of a pitch.

The final whistle went. They decided to keep Pompey in the ground. On the side there was a fence *about six foot tall but it was mesh. They were all pulling on that, then over we went, over the fence, hundreds and hundreds of us, but then the Old Bill came and only about 300 to 400 got through. It was like the side of the North Stand, and there weren't seats there then. All that North Stand was already gone, all the terracing was gone. We ran along there and then the bottom bit of the shed, in the middle of it, through the top bit, and they were all just running everywhere, some even ran across the pitch. We all came out the back end of the shed, down the steps and out in the streets. Chelsea were there. There were hot dog vans there, and they got in our way, so they were turned over, anything we could get was picked up and we just run Chelsea down towards Fulham Broadway. Mind you, I don't think that was their firm, though, that we actually encountered there, it was more their scarfers. But when everyone realised what we were doing, the Old Bill come on to the pitch with horses and got all the escaping Pompey back. Our advance party came back around the other side and joined back up with the Pompey lot.*

There was one big ruck down the side street as we were walking back to the tube station. They came out of the street and broke through the Old Bill. Pompey just run Chelsea the whole length, right down to the tube station. Some Chelsea were stopping, trying to have a go, then running. We were just backing and backing them down. I don't think there was any serious injuries, no one really violently hurt. What it was that day that spoiled it a bit was that there was too many Pompey there that day, too many.

So now it's the usual story – some want to go straight back to Waterloo, some want to go here,

*others are going in the West End – all split up again.
I was in a group that had got back to Waterloo before
any of the others and there was Millwall waiting for
us. There were only about 30 of us there. For some
reason, out of a group of 800, it seem mad, but I
ended up with all the Havelock boys: Froggie, Mc,
Yatesy, Jimbo, Micky F and that. A few other names
were there but it was mostly Landport boys. And I've
gone off with them. We came unstuck. They had us,
and Froggie and that actually locked themselves in
the toilets, you know, just to keep indoors. We
actually got chased down the platform. There was
me, Stevie M, Yatesy and Charlie B. There was about
30 of them chasing us. Well, when we turned round
and looked again, some had given up the chase and
there was now about eight or nine of them. Yatesy
turned round and took a stand. We all turned round
and stood. Yatesy's ran across and, believe it or not,
he's actually done three Millwall geezers. They were
backing off, then they realised their mob weren't
behind them and it was 10 Millwall on a platform.
With that, we've heard the most almighty roar you've
ever heard in your life. It was like the cavalry coming.
It was the rest of the boys coming up from the
Underground. Millwall stood for a little while before
it was time for them to go.*

CHELSEA HOME '83–'84

Towards the end of the season Chelsea came down in that night
game. We got run by Chelsea. They had a bad bunch of lads there
and there was loads of trouble. A couple got stabbed before the
game, and a couple of Chelsea-following skates were put in a
serious way by a Pompey crew. They came prepared, there were
people squirted up in that same ruck in the road outside

Portsmouth and Southsea station. Nothing big, but there were little firms having it within their own little groups. They'd come down mob-handed because it was their promotion party – they only needed to win to be going up that particular season. The game was drawn 2–2 so they still needed a point elsewhere, and that result spoiled the party, so they did the notorious Chelsea thing and rioted inside the ground, ripping out and hurling seats; they got at the fences, smashing up advertising hoardings as the Old Bill tried to keep them behind after the final whistle. Chelsea were acting crazy that day but they weren't so crazy when they attempted to get into the Fratton by pulling the fence down before the game. They actually pulled the fence down but when it fell they sort of bottled it, a few came through but Pompey weren't having none of that from them.

I was on the Fratton End that day and some Chelsea loon came up behind us, completely on his own, giving it the 'Come on, let's have it' sort of thing. He was frothing at the mouth. But I looked at him and he scared the life out of me. I thought, He's like a monster. Lucky for me, Charlie P, the old Gosport boy, he sort of put him away, but I remember looking at him right to his face, Oh, they had a few evil ones with them in that night game, did Chelsea.

After the game we came out and everyone went down by the Milton End. The Old Bill kept Chelsea in for a bit and then it went off. Chelsea had come out. We run them at first, got them back past Milton Park and then more and more of their mob came. I remember a few of them pulled blades out, one even had like a machete blade and there was a bit of panic set in. Then, from Priory Crescent, they had us backing and they just run us back round past the front of the Milton. I mean, it was just one of them nights, no excuses, you know, we had numbers, they had numbers, there must've been a couple of hundred and we had about the same. Then you had all the little bits of offs like there always was before the game.

I remember up the Fawcett Road afterwards, Chelsea seemed to be everywhere. I was with Stocky, Leggy and Tony T and that. These Chelsea crossed over the road, but one didn't know who we were and was sitting on a wall eating his chips. One of ours went up to him. 'Fucking good result tonight, mate, weren't it?' 'Yeah, brilliant, blinder.' Then – bosh – they emptied his chip bag over his head.

QUICK DASH ACROSS LONDON

We were playing Charlton away so we drove up in a couple of motors to Waterloo station to meet up with everyone who had gone up on the earlier train. There would have been a good 400–500 travelling up on the train that day.

We parked up at Waterloo station and saw everybody just hanging about Casey Jones – 6.57, Somers Town, Paulsgrove lot, pretty much everyone and an entire firm of dressers, all standing about, you know, in the split Lois jeans, Nike trainers, Pringles, Ellesse jackets and that. In '83–'84 Pompey had a full-on big casual crew, big numbers all over the country.

So we're at Waterloo and it's about three hours before kick-off at Charlton and someone decides they want to go Chelsea v Leicester. Immediately everyone charges down the tube and we are on our way to Earls Court. We get off at Earls Court, and the Old Bill come over. 'What's going on? What's going on?' Everyone starts talking in ridiculous accents saying they're from Leicester and we end up being escorted towards Stamford Bridge. We turned up at Fulham Broadway and we started to see a few Chelsea over the road, and some started to walk alongside to let 'em know who we were. When we got to the King's Head, one of their main boozers, and the pub opposite, they were all in there and, as they all come out, we all bounced up and that was it. The Old Bill rumbled we were Pompey and pushed us all back on to the train. It was all a little too early, not enough crowd on the streets. We could only make a showing before the Old Bill had it sussed. But we'd got enough of Chelsea's boys all wound up. They said, 'You fucking cheeky cunts,' and all that.

We had a thing going with Chelsea for a couple of years and, to be honest, I think we embarrassed 'em. I wouldn't think it was the normal thing for anybody to turn up at Chelsea, for they had a reputation as a firm, home and away. Ken Bates made a thing that he considered there was a problem at Chelsea. 'Why was a team that was not connected with Chelsea or Leicester and had their team playing on the other side of London, why did they turn up at Chelsea? We don't need other fans coming to Chelsea who had nothing to do with that game that day causing trouble.'

He was attempting to sort of stick up for Chelsea, making a point of why the fuck would these supporters turn up to a Chelsea game that had nothing to do with them – I don't think we were even in the same division, were we?

THE JOKERS WERE WEARING
NORMAL CLOTHES

Wimbledon away on Boxing Day in the'78–'79 season, the old Fourth Division at the famous Plough Lane. I still remember that dump of a ground. We had a coach that day going up from Stamshaw and just to get into the Christmas spirit we thought we'd all go in fancy dress. It was a coach full of mushes on there and we were all dressed up just having a good laugh. We were on the piss early morning as usual. We used to stop at the Wooden Bridge in Guildford, an old Pompey haunt going to London games. We'd get all pissed up in the old Wooden Bridge and the coach driver took us to the ground, dropped us all off, and for some reason he had to shoot off and had arranged to pick us up at Waterloo station at closing time.

So we went to the game. Boring game. Wimbledon, they've got no geezers or nothing. I think we won 4–2, but believe me it was boring over there. Game over and there's 45 geezers all in fancy dress and we've got to get back across from Wimbledon to south London to get back to Waterloo to pick the coach up. So we went to a few local pubs first, then we got the train back to Waterloo. At Waterloo we went for a drink in the Wellington. We were all in there having a good old shout and that, and unbeknown to us we were being weighed up by a load of Chelsea geezers. We're all in fancy dress and someone said, 'Look, it's definitely Chelsea over there. But nothing happened in the Wellington. It all came when we left and they followed us. We went to a pub near the station – I think it used to be called the Drum, just above Waterloo station. We all walked in and then in came this 20-odd firm of Chelsea. It all started to get a bit tense. They didn't know who we were. One of them walked over and said, 'Who are you lot?' Now, while you're reading this, you've got to picture the scene here, with us in fancy dress. We just said, 'We're Pompey. We've just been to fucking Wimbledon,' and the Chelsea said, 'We don't want any trouble. We just wondered who you were and that.' I said, 'Who are you then?' He said, 'Oh we're Chelsea.' We said, 'We're Pompey, do you fucking want some?'. The Chelsea main man said, 'Well, you've got one choice, you'd better turn round and fuck off or we're going to put you through the windows.' We outnumbered them and just steamed them and they legged it out the pub.

CHELSEA GIVE IT

I've always wondered to this day what they thought, you know, fucking 20 Chelsea geezers getting steamed by fucking Spiderman, Elvis and the Three Musketeers and we're all fighting dressed in fancy dress and chasing them across Waterloo station. And I expect the Chelsea geezers probably brought it back to the Shed that following fucking Saturday saying they'd just been done by Andy Pandy, Spiderman and fucking Donald Duck. I expect they'll remember that one.

Newcastle,
The Warriors

One of the favourite football stories involving the 6.57 was Newcastle away at the height of the football casual. So much happened that it wasn't unlike a scene straight out of *The Warriors*, a classic gang-story film. And for a 90-minute game, it was one hell of a long weekend that just didn't stop kicking. If you weren't there, you could never comprehend fully what that day felt like, but if you were, and weren't really into the football violence scene, you would have been after that day, 'cause you would have been addicted to it. If we had all the 6.57 giving accounts of that day going to Newcastle away, there still would have been a little row somewhere they'd forgotten to mention. But I think those who were there will have completed their jigsaw having heard this account taken from the recollections of Eddie, Bill W, Steve W, and Trev. Just read on and tell me a madder day than this.

Most probably one of the biggest days for actual total
violence all day was on 1 October 1983, the vintage

*year of the football casual dressers and the 6.57 crew.
We'd been promoted to a division two that had every
bloody firm in it: Chelsea, Man City, Leeds, Cardiff,
Boro, Newcastle and ourselves, 6.57.*

*The 6.57 name came about because someone wrote
a letter to* The Face *magazine – the first men's lifestyle
magazine that took a big interest in the football
fashion up and down the terraces. Someone wrote a
letter saying, 'You northerners are shit, the clothes you
wear', and this and that. And then Zee wrote a letter
in saying something and he signed it '6.57 crew'. That
letter signed 6.57 crew was printed and the name
stuck from then on.*

Everyone knows the story of Zee's letter to The Face
*magazine. He was a Pompey lad, one of two brothers
from Milton. Their old man, Jack – he's brilliant, Jack
– he's late seventies now, but he still goes. He always
says to me, 'I was at Newcastle, one of the two
Pompey fans at Newcastle when we won 5–0 on a
Wednesday afternoon game.' Because he had a
haulage firm then, he went in his lorry. He was in
Newcastle that afternoon so he went to the game. He
said there were two of us in the ground and we won
5–0. The championship years of the fifties, ah.*

*Anyway, it's '83 – that's the one that sticks in my
mind 'cause quite a lot went on that day. I was up all
night with five or six of my little firm. We were in a
place called Foster's Snooker Hall in Fratton Road. It
was an all-night snooker club and if I actually went
home and went to sleep I most probably wouldn't
have got up and made the 6.57 train. A last-minute
rob on the club fruit machine got us the money to go
and meet the rest, coming out of the nightclubs 3 or 4
o'clock in the morning. We all went down and had a*

sleep on the train station. That way we didn't miss the game. We used to go in the clothes we'd been out in the night before, so we didn't miss the game.

With a bit of luck we used to bunk on the train to Waterloo and a lot of times a few of the boys had their Persil tickets, student railcards or one of the family deals where three kids go free, for a pound. A lot of them used to bunk on there, never used to pay at all.

So it's Portsmouth and Southsea station, half-past six in the morning, usual faces there, good old crew. There's the Air Balloon again, plus the rest from all the surrounding areas in Pompey. We were bang up for it, all excited and that, big old game, Newcastle away, all of us really up for it. We all got on the 6.57 up to Waterloo and by the time we got to Waterloo we had a good 150 to 200 geezers just mad for it.

At Waterloo, there was about 50 Millwall having a float about, like they do. Then they were gone when they realised the amount there was of us – few little scuffles and off, they were gone. Then we went off to King's Cross. On the way we heard rumours that there was going to be Chelsea waiting for us at King's Cross. I think they had a game that day but they knew that we were travelling north. That's what used to happen, you'd look at what other teams were doing that day and you would take a little detour. They knew 'cause we were on the south coast we obviously had to go into London and face a possible meet up with the London firms. It was almost guaranteed you'd have it, and that was all part of the excitement knowing that you were not only having it with the team you were playing, but also with any of the London clubs' firms, which made it more exciting.

When we got to King's Cross it was fucking crazy.

Somehow the firm had got split up. The train was already in and a load had already got on the train, about half the mob. The other half went running into Chelsea 'cause a big old mob of Chelsea turned up outside as there was still 100 of us milling about the station. We sussed they were Chelsea straight away, 'cause someone mentioned they'd seen one of their boys and thought it was Hickey's mob. So we just run straight into them and battered them all over King's Cross, running 'em all outside, and while we're doing this we missed the fucking train.

So half of them were already on their way up there, and we had to get the next one, the slow one running about a half-hour behind. But we still give it to Chelsea, so it was well worth it.

What happened was, we were on the next train behind them and they were all waiting for us at Newcastle. There was probably about 70 of them waiting at Newcastle Station when we got off. So we all firmed back up at Newcastle and told them what we'd done – 'Where were you?' and all that. 'We just fucking had it with Chelsea but we didn't need you anyway 'cause there was enough of us.' We give them a good old hiding and that. Then our mate said, when they'd left King's Cross, this Chelsea main man Hickey had got on the same train as them. Chelsea were playing at Huddersfield but they were going to Doncaster, so Hickey got on with a half-dozen cronies in his trademark flight jacket and a fighter pilot's hat on, the type with the floppy ears and everything. So they're all talking to him and he's quite a tall fella, this Hickey, but everyone was all right, just having a drink, talking and that. They got off at Doncaster. We all went on up to Newcastle, but we took note of that stop for the way back 'cause we knew when Hickey met up with his boys they'd want revenge, wouldn't they? So we were all bang up for it on the way back and all, but we had Newcastle to deal with first.

As we got outside the station there were a few Old Bill there asking us to wait up, so they can organise an escort for our own safety. They said Newcastle had a few boys out and that. And I'll never forget the policeman when he said, 'You go that way, you get to the ground; you go that way, you don't reach the ground.' We all looked at each other and said, 'Where do we go for a drink?' He said, 'You gotta go that way.' Obviously we didn't want none of that escort shit so we just, like, legged it up the road. We got up the main road, looked across and we saw their boys starting to come out of a pub, which apparently was their main pub.

There were 150–170 of us, and everyone was really up for it. We had two Leeds geezers with us. One was called Griff, but I can't remember the other geezer's name – they used to come with us. Also with us, he was well known at the time 'cause he was a one-off, you know, a skate who went by the name of Addo. Now a skate is what we called a sailor in the Navy. The Leeds fellas had already been up with Leeds that season or the season before and they said they'd take us to these two Geordie pubs. 'But there ain't enough of you here, you know, you're going to get done,' he said. 'They're mental these Newcastle. Powerful geezers.' With that, us being Pompey and being a bit mad, we said, 'Take us, come on, we want to go there.' So we had to go past these two pubs, and they spilled out into the road from both pubs. I think the Adelaide was one and the Bull was the other. It's up on the right-hand side if you walk down out of the station.

All of us legged it across the main road. The Old Bill following caught up but couldn't contain it, there was too large a number there. From where I was I could just see this Addo, mad geezer from Grimsby, go in on his own with a couple of other Pompey geezers behind him into these Newcastle geezers. And with that, half of Pompey split to one pub and half split to the other. I remember Addo was struggling through the door with this Kev from Fratton behind him. We were just trying to get through the doors, windows were going through and that, and we just heard loads of screaming inside the pub. We were just fighting with them in the streets for about a full-on five minutes, but fucking hell, what a row. The Old Bill got control but it took their riot squad – usual stuff, pushing us on the streets, back on the pavement and that. A couple of the boys got nicked – I think Kev did. A few of us tried legging it but the Old Bill just rounded us up and marched us to the ground.

All the way to the ground they kept coming out of everywhere, chucking bottles, glasses, the odd housebrick. There was little mobs of Newcastle coming down side streets and we were just running up the roads trying to get away from the Old Bill, trying to get into them.

Then as we were going into the ground, there were a few Geordie geezers standing outside with kilts on, wearing great big fucking Dr Martens, and quite a few had these black and white, curly-haired wigs on. I thought, Fucking hell, they're strange up here. And these Leeds geezers couldn't believe it. One of them

said, 'Well, Pompey, that was unbelievable.' He said
they'd run Leeds all over the place when they were
up there. He said there'd been 200–300 of them
against the same mob of Geordies. Addo obviously
got a big name for himself that day. He was well
talked about and became well known after –
although he did get nicked for his claim to fame,
along with our Kev from Fratton.

Inside the ground we were all put in an end.
Obviously the Old Bill had us all under control and
a police cordon around us in this away supporters'
end, which was pretty standard for the day then. I
think Pompey quickly went 4–0 down, and Pompey
didn't care. We didn't care in them days whether we
won or lost. And we'd even take the piss out of
ourselves. Every time Newcastle had the ball we
were all cheering, sitting down, jumping up. We
went mad. We'd just play silly games and everyone
around us thought we were mad. Then Pompey
popped one in and they scored another one, brought
it back to 4–2. We all started getting serious again,
thinking, Oi, oi, we've got a chance here, and we
started supporting our team again. And that ended
up the final score.

We got kept in after the game for about 10–15
minutes while they cleared all the Newcastle. When
we came out of the ground, unfortunately for us
there was an escort back to the station with no
trouble. But there was more to come on the way
back. Our train stopped at Doncaster on the way
back and, lo and behold, someone shouted out,
'There's Chelsea.' Two platforms across was another
train that had just pulled in before ours. A King's
Cross-bound train coming back from Huddersfield

*full of Chelsea supporters, mob-handed. They must
have known and been waiting for our train. Well,
Pompey fellas were climbing out of windows, not
even trying to open the doors, that's how mad we
were, getting out, running across the platform and
steaming into these Chelsea geezers.*

*The whole train just emptied out and run them
straight off the platform. They had a little show but
they got back on their train. The Old Bill were there
as well and managed to separate us, a few little
things got thrown and we all remember Hickey was
just stood there saying, 'You're out of order,
Pompey.' He was just stood there – what's that
stupid hat he use to wear? Like a flying officer –
'You're out of order, Pompey, out of order.' He
thought, 'cause of that morning, it was all right. I
always remember that. After we'd done all that,
there used to be 20 or 30 Doncaster supporters come
and watch Portsmouth. The Donnies realised what a
firm we had. They used to come and watch when we
were up north, regular.*

*With the Doncaster ruck over, it was back on the
train and back to London, knowing they're going to
be waiting for us, or if we get there first, we're going
to be waiting for them. And by then we'd found out
that a Chelsea fan had been killed that day. I think he
had his head severely kicked in by Huddersfield. I
think he was just a normal supporter who was in the
wrong place at the wrong time, which is sad, and it's
one of them things that happened. We got back to
London, and they were there – they'd got there before
us. We got off the train, straight through the gates, no
hesitation whatsoever, jumped the barriers and, as we
got out of the station, they just ran at us. We just*

stopped, turned round and straight into Chelsea and it's fair to say that Pompey fucking blitzed them, chased them all up the road. Hickey was about the last one to run and I remember him shouting, 'Chelsea, stay and stand' and all that, and Pompey were all over them. In the end he turned and ran as well. We kicked a few of them, gave them a bit of a dig and that, but they didn't want to know.

So if you count that, from a day out, we've had the firm behind us and had it with them, done them on the way up there, we've done Newcastle, their two pubs on the way up there, that was both our firms together, 150 of us. On the way back we were all together again, and we've done Chelsea at Doncaster and at again King's Cross. And that's obviously five or six big fracas. That day was one of the main days out for me with Pompey.

If you survived not getting nicked or stabbed, whatever, you done well. After that it was back to Waterloo and Casey Jones, absolutely shattered, knackered, filthy, still with the clothes on from Friday night. But everyone stayed together 'cause you know there could be a little bit more. I mean, nine times out of ten it was a burger in Casey Jones, get on the train and home. We thought there might be a few of the other London mobs moving around, but they didn't show that night. We also thought Chelsea might come back, but obviously they'd had enough of 6.57 that day. So we stayed there till the last train, like we do. We went to a couple of strip clubs, got well shantied up, went to the Queen Anne, the Scotsman and that, just abusing everyone, smashing things up, like we normally do, having it with anyone who was there. There used to be 30 or 40 of us would stay together and then we used to get the mail train home about half-past three, pissed out of our heads. We'd catch the mail train and get home early hours Sunday morning singing, 'Play up Pompey'. Hey, we still talk about that Newcastle game.

Leeds

LEEDS AWAY '83–'84

There was a good mob, a good 350. This was the first time I ever went to Leeds. We caught the 6.57, got to Waterloo like normal and went over to King's Cross. We got the train up there, but, as we came into Leeds, what we actually did was we pulled the cord and everyone got off the train before it pulled in. The ground's on the right in an industrial estate, and as we got off the train we were going down all these embankments, but the Old Bill were waiting at the train station for us, you could see, it was about half a mile, three-quarters of a mile away. When they realised where we were going they all got in their vans, and came round to the industrial estate after us. We've got off the train, and we've got about half a mile away, 300 of us, all down the embankment. As we came across a field we saw the dogs, and the Old Bill let the bloody dogs go, so everyone had to run to get back on to the train. Have you ever tried getting off the train without a platform there? Honestly, it's as tall as me, that's how big the train is. I'm struggling to get back up and, like, all the fat ones couldn't get back up on to the train. But somehow we all managed and then we went on to Leeds.

When we got to Leeds they never turned out. We actually walked from the train station to the ground and we never encountered anything. We had broken free from the Old Bill, and went straight back into the town centre, all split up, all met again. So there were 300–350 Pompey went right through that town centre, right up to the football ground, no Old Bill with us, never encountered one bit of trouble. They were nowhere, and this was like 1 o'clock in the afternoon. We never saw a Leeds supporter until we were by the ground. The Old Bill got round us then – there was a little tunnel with police with dogs and they were on the bridges and round us. When the Old Bill were round us, that's when the Leeds supporters started giving it: 'Ah, we'll have you after the game, we'll have you after the game.' It was absolutely freezing – everyone was up there in Ellesse T-shirts, all the gear on. We got up there and it was like snowing. It wasn't cold, it was absolutely freezing.

* * *

Me and my mate Williams bought the wrong tickets outside the ground and ended up in their bit of the ground, and they beat us from one end to the other and chucked us on to the pitch. Me and Williams were bruised all over. As soon as we got on to the pitch we ran into the Pompey bit.

There was no trouble before the game, nothing, they never even turned out. So the main thing that happened that day was after the game. We'd all come down these really steep steps and we could see there was about 400–500 of them outside, and now they're ready for it. There's this stupid old man on the gate, and it's these roller shutter gates. Someone just went over, pulled the gates open and walked through. Next thing, we've all just run straight into them and run them all down the road and it was their firm outside. It went on for about 10 minutes, and we run them into a great big car-park – they were just running everywhere. We had a good ruck with them. Then they regrouped, and we had another ruck. Off they went again and that was it – they didn't turn out any more. I was very disappointed with Leeds. What I'd heard before I went there was that we were going to encounter a lot of trouble so I was very disappointed. Even when we went back to the train station, we were mobbed up, like 300 of us, we never had any encounters there. We were waiting at the train station and about 50 Pompey broke away, done the business with them, and they were gone.

That's when they tried to put us on a train, and I swear it was a cattle train, 'cause we weren't going to leave. We had to make a connection, 'cause when you go to Leeds you've got to get a connection on to another train. But they've tried to put us on this cattle truck – ah, all the old wooden slats, you know, you see a cow with its head through them, that's what it was like. Then they actually had a fire on the platform with about 400 Pompey there. We were still there in

*Leeds about 8 o'clock at night. We couldn't get home,
'cause we refused to get on the train. Plenty of hustle
and bustle but they wouldn't let us on the train, so we
wouldn't get on the cattle train. Eventually when we
all got back to Waterloo, everyone caught the mail
train home. I used to catch the mail train home quite
often, half-past three, but that night everyone had to
because we'd missed our last connection by the time
we got back to London.*

LEEDS HOME '84–'88

Running battles were the order of the day when the Leeds mob
came down in '84. Despite a heavy police presence to escort the
Leeds fans that got off at Fratton station, the Leeds lads were
trying to have it with pockets of Pompey all along Goldsmith
Avenue. They found it big time when a decent firm of 70–100
of them slipped past the Old Bill guarding the entrance to
Frogmore Road to reach Pompey fans queuing to get in the
turnstiles. This has never been known. The Old Bill have always
been able to control the away fans' entry into the ground, but
they'd taken their eye off the ball this time. As the Leeds casuals
charged into a street packed with Pompey they had that element
of surprise – normal Pompey fans didn't know which way to
turn as a few of the boys waded in trading punches briefly
before vanloads of Old Bill arrived quickly on the scene making
plenty of arrests.

*Leeds would pay for their audacity after the game
when word got about there was about 300 of us and
we backed them up everywhere. I'll tell you where
they ended up, in the glass factory with the Old Bill
all round them. Yeah, the Milton glass place behind
the Shepherd's Crook. The Old Bill tried to move
them off and get them to the railway station but the*

*same firm got waylaid when we got them further up
the road by the paint factory with a little car-park.
What happened was we were running into them
down there as Pompey were coming back up from
that end of town. Word got about, and all them
boys from the Milton came down that way, as all the
lot from Fratton Road was coming the other way.
They had nowhere to go, and they ended up
cordoned off, totally cornered. Portsmouth
magistrates took a dim view of all the trouble that
day, refusing people bail and anyone pleading guilty
was getting 28–60 days' detention for things like
using threatening words or behaviour.*

Another time Leeds made the headlines down here was the game
when Pompey beat Leeds 4–0 in 1988, third game of the new
season down in division two. It only involved a small band of
Leeds and the odds against were a bit of a liberty really. One of
their main faces was known to Pompey. They even had a few
come along when we travelled north, Newcastle was one game
that comes to mind and the link was the connections made on
past England trips. The mistake this crew of Leeds faces made
was deciding to stray from the path and pass the Milton Arms
and they were recognised straight away by a full-on mob of
Pompey. They got chased all down Meon Road and were forced
to take refuge in a corner shop. Cans of beans and lagers came
flying out from the Leeds crew as bricks, bottles and even a
shopping trolley went back in, demolishing the entire front of
the shop. It was out of order, but football is like that sometimes
and this was an incident the police Optica spotter plane, which
was drafted in to watch for any fans roaming the back streets,
failed to pick up. Leeds to their credit do bring the numbers
down for a northern club, and there must have been 3,000 Leeds
there that day.

LEEDS REVISITED: FA CUP 5TH ROUND 1997

This is more of an account of the thrill and the buzz you experience in the build-up to a big game. The fans wind themselves up for what they refer to as the big ones. Leeds away this particular season was a big, big game, particularly in the minds of the Fareham loyal Pompey crew travelling up in their hired minibus.

At the time we were shit. We weren't doing a great deal but, when it came up on the telly, Leeds away, we all cheered. We were shit in the League, bottom of the First Division, and we still sold 5,000 tickets within a couple of days. Everybody I knew was going to Leeds, and was getting the tickets. It was our big day out of the year, and everybody was up for a row with Leeds – everyone fucking hates Leeds, mouthy Yorkshire bastards, everyone from Cardiff to Man U hates them. We were meeting in the Red Lion in Fareham to get it all organised about who was going up and how we were going up there and shit. There was a few of us sat in there, having a chat, early days, how we were getting up there, what the score was. Everybody was up for it. It was going to be a fucking good day out because everybody knew that, at the end of the day, you don't travel 250 miles north and 250 miles back without it kicking off sometime – it's gonna happen, you know that straight away.

This guy organised a good coach. He organised a minibus and the good thing about minibuses is you don't have to worry about who's fucking driving. The build-up before the game was almost as good as the day because everybody knew that anyone who was anyone was going and it wasn't anything to do with us thinking about the team's chances. Nah,

nah, we didn't give a fuck about winning. If we won, we won, that was going to be a bonus, but the situation was we were going to Leeds and we were going firm-handed.

At that time, that great people's favourite, yeah, Terry fucking Venables, was our manager, and he was just a twat – he still is. He got put in charge of Portsmouth Football Club who weren't doing particularly well. But back to the actual Leeds game and it was definitely one of the biggest games for me because it was the build-up around it, knowing that everyone was up for kicking some northern arse, there was no doubt about it. Not only that, it's a long journey, and everybody wants to go so you get all your favourite mates, friends and everything and you get them on a bus or whatever and you travel up and you know there's going to be loads of sniff. Every firm in Pompey – it didn't matter where they came from, whether it had been Fareham, Gosport, Leigh Park, Portsmouth, whatever, Salisbury – had all organised their own little way of getting up there but everybody knew where we were going and where we were meeting come whatever. That's typically Pompey, that is, where everyone's got their own little minibus doing their thing.

We've turned up in Leeds town centre and gone straight in the pub, just us, Fareham Loyal. 15 or 20 of us on the coach. Middle of Leeds, straight in a pub, drinking with them, talking with them, straight away admitting we're from Pompey, no hiding it, giving it to them, just talking. We felt comfortable with the 15 or so that we had, we were happy. No hiding in any way. Had a drink, loads of Leeds people everywhere. It was one of them days, and I was out of my nut from 9 o'clock in the morning till 9 o'clock at night. Mark had a broken arm and all his stash was down his cast, everything like that, it was fantastic. Everyone volunteered, I sussed really early and I volunteered to sit next to Mark. Like the Ulster volunteers I was straight in alongside. I went straight in there. I was gone, really out of it, one of the others will remember more...

* * *

The biggest game for me, certainly around them couple of years, was Leeds 'cause we'd done nothing else, we'd done nothing – the club was going nowhere, and we weren't going to get the chance to go again. We chatted to the lads, and they were all up for it, everybody wanted to be involved. There was a big hype a week, two weeks before the game. As soon the draw came up, everybody knew we were going up to a Premiership club. We wanted to win, but it wasn't that important. The important thing was that we were going up to Yorkshire, we were going to Leeds United, who were doing well at the time as well, and we wanted to get involved in some serious fucking grief and we did it. I definitely wanted to make sure it was sorted. I spoke to the old woman to make sure the minibus was sorted out, made sure the money was sorted and the right people were on the coach. We made sure we were tooled up on the minibus, there was no doubt about it whatsoever. But nobody took the sort of tools which, if we'd been pulled by the Old Bill, the Old Bill could say, 'You've got a knife or gun.' The tools were there but they were things like a car-jack – you could get your hands on them quick. If it's in a minibus nobody would think much about a spanner or a screwdriver. There was loads of gear on the minibus on the way up there and it was definitely all sorted out just in case that did happen. The thing is, with all football, it always happens, you know. On the way there the main thing is to get pissed up and make sure you've got the right gear to keep you going for the day, the beers there, your bags there. Everybody was well up for it.

The build-up, when we got on that coach, a 15-seater minibus, straight away we were all tinnied up. There was plenty of booze on there and we all knew we had a long journey ahead of us. We were going to start drinking at half-past seven in the morning, and the only way to keep going is to make sure you've got a bit of company, which we all did. It was a fucking brilliant trip up, everybody was on a high.

Aggro-wise it was fairly quiet on the way up, we saw some other teams on the motorway up, as you do. We had a great sing-song. Fareham are the best singers, no doubt whatsoever, we sing our own songs whether it be loyalist songs, whether it be Pompey songs. We sing some great football chants, we've even got some of our own songs we made up ourselves which are good piss-take songs. And if I was to pick the best 10 out of all our firm, they were on that minibus that day and, getting into Leeds, you didn't give a fuck who you came across, how many were there, we were going to have it with them.

We got to Leeds, and there wasn't a great deal of Leeds there. I was a bit disappointed at first, finding out that they didn't have a great firm that were going to come and have a go. There were rumours going round, people were speaking to each other, telling each other where we were going, what we were going to do – Fareham were speaking to Leigh Park, Leigh Park were speaking to Pompey, you know, everybody knew where every firm was and, if it kicked off at all, everybody would have gone to somebody's rescue or gone to where it was going to happen.

We'd been to Leeds before but, as I say, it didn't really kick off beforehand. The Old Bill were fairly heavy, and there was a lot of Pompey there, as we'd sold a massive amount of tickets. We parked just outside the ground in the big car-park close to the dustbowl, right next to the exit. Now, what I do remember is walking down the road, and their main boozer was like opposite the ground, and they were stood outside. By that time Pompey, Fareham and Leigh Park and everybody's little firm were there and we were fucking awesome – we looked like one hell of a mob. We got in the ground and even though it didn't really kick off, the result was absolutely fantastic. To see Pompey win, the goals go in, pissed up, at a Premiership club, it was fantastic. But, when we got out of that ground, they'd got it together, Leeds had got a firm together, they were at that same boozer and they were what, 100-handed? Easy. Up till then it was subdued but what turned the tide with the Leeds was that Pompey had been taking the piss everywhere, and Leeds started giving it back to us was when we beat them 3–2. All of a sudden they were game as fuck and we were ready for them.

They held us in for 15 minutes, I remember that, and when we all came out of our end we burst out of the doors to come into the street. We were with Mark J and I was with Mark D and his brother and a few others, and Leeds came straight across the road to get us, but the Old Bill were there and there were coaches stopping us from getting across the road. Leeds stopped short of the coaches 'cause they couldn't get between the coaches to get at us, but there was a gap of about 4 or 5 feet and Leeds started crushing their way through there and the Old Bill couldn't get in there, fucking twats. Northern coppers are the worst coppers you're ever going to get – they are just so anti-southerners, it's unreal. So, anyway, bang into the fucking large gap, they came through, and Mark J, who was on my right-hand side, top fucking geezer as well, was straight across. He'd gone into them while they were coming through. About four or five of them burst through between the coaches. I was with his brother and a few others and we had it there in a 4-foot gap between the coaches and the side of the wall. It was crushed to fuck, it was like biting fighting, 'cause you couldn't throw punches it was that fucking tight against the wall. We had it all up along there and as we got to the end the Old Bill shut off the road and there was missiles coming over, fucking traffic cones, bricks, bottles.

By that time, Pompey were firm-handed and we were trying to push back to get into them but there was no going. The Old Bill were all over the place. We moved back up to the car park, and I met Mark D again and he had a fucking steamer of a black eye on him. He'd been fucking hammered, but he just ran straight into them, he was like that. He was always going off on his own, steaming firms all on his own. Anyway we got back to the minibus, and Mark's in the minibus, with a right old eye on him, and in a right raving hump, giving it the large one – 'What's going on, let's get back' and all that. We couldn't go back 'cause there was no going back, the Old Bill were like three and four thick and, of course, they turned over Pompey. Northern coppers are all right with northerners but with southerners, they're not interested, they want to beat the fuck out of you all the time.

So the plan was to get back in the minibus, get back into the town centre, firm up with all the other bods, yeah, and have it in the town centre. It was Saturday night, so we'd see what they had in there. Anyway, we managed to get back into the minibus, and we looked up the road and saw about 30 geezers running down the road towards the minibus in the direction we've just come. Well, somebody pointed out they were Pompey, so we didn't know what was happening at first, why they were running down towards us. What had happened was they'd come out the ground, this firm of Pompey, walked away from the ground and been run back down towards the ground again by Leeds. Of course, we jumped off the minibus. A couple of them knew that we were Pompey, and they were saying to us, 'Come on, there's a firm out here and they want it.' Douggie was pissed off because Mark had taken a hiding and he said to me, 'Open the fucking door, open it.' The situation was the Leeds came down, we jumped out the minibus and we stood. Most of this lot of Pompey were running past us 'cause they didn't know who we were. The Leeds ran into us getting out of the minibus 'cause Doug had fucking sussed out what the score was and, as they came down, we started fucking launching into them, as we do, 15 on the minibus went straight into them. The Pompey that ran past us had stopped, so therefore you had the 30–40 that had run past us and the 15 that had got off the minibus with their mob just running into us – it was just fucking toe to toe straight in the middle of the street. I'm fucking having it with some geezer right next to the minibus, and I remember dragging him down by the back of his really heavy duffle coat. And as he fell down he hit his head on the stairwell of the minibus and he half-knocked himself out by that. And as I went to give him some fucking punches someone else who was coming out of the minibus gave him a couple of digs too, and stamped on his head a couple of bits.

I went down the road and I remember there was a fucking great billboard and there was missiles coming over the top of the billboard, which were being chucked by the Leeds nippers, all the youngsters were throwing shit over the top. So one of their geezers came running out this road, with a bottle in his hand, and he fronted me up with the bottle. When he launched at me with the bottle I stood thinking, I'm going to get a bottle in the head if I steam him, and, before I had a chance to steam him, Douggie came over. He went on his arse, he fell down, and he was fucking choking. Then Dave M ran past us. Leeds started running back into their own ground, but they made another stand. By that time we were 30- or 40-handed and started walking back down the road towards them. Now, fair play to them, they had the front to fucking stand their ground, but the nippers who were behind the billboards came running round, about a dozen of them, all 15- and 16-year-olds, came running down and carried on throwing missiles. Of course, they got caught by the other Pompey who were coming from behind, and they got fucking toed to bits.

Eventually the Old Bill turned up and the funny thing I remember about it is, when they gathered us up and got us back to the minibus, they said, 'If you've got any booze in this minibus whatsoever it's got to go.' Right at the back was an empty crate. I picked it up as if it was full of beer and I said to this copper, 'There's a lot of fucking cans.' Of course, he drew his truncheon out in the minibus but I moved out of the way. We were just having a laugh with him. Just having a bit of crack with the northern cunt. There were loads of people coming out of the car park who were Pompey people, not hooligans, nothing like that, just normal family people, but there was only one way out of the car park and, as you left, this firm was out there picking off cars. And people were actually getting out saying to the Old Bill that we were only defending ourselves. They were all sticking up for us and everything. They were saying, 'They've done nothing wrong.'

Team Called Scum

Throughout this chapter you will find comments along with various accounts that typify how a Portsmouth–Southampton affair is no 'love thy neighbour'.

Whenever Southampton and Portsmouth get to play each other it is not just another game. There's a real loathing and a real animosity felt that's on a par with any of the other much-hyped and talked-up football derbies, like your Liverpool–Everton, Tottenham–Arsenal, Sunderland-Newcastle, the all-Manchester derby and, of course, the Old Firm encounters. That's if you can still class that as a true derby, considering how many times those two manage to play each other in one full season, in what is effectively a two-club league. Whatever your view about that classic north of the border, the south-coast encounter is pure old-fashioned rivalry in the truest sense of a local derby match. You certainly won't find a mix of day-tripper corporates flown in for the big game, along with all the other non-regional voyeurs that have tried to attach themselves to all the big-match derbies.

Portsmouth–Southampton is a derby in the truest football tradition. It can sell out at least three times over and, given the size of the police operations put in place to control the crowds, it is no less passionate or vociferous than any of the others.

Maybe it is fortunate that in the last 30–40 years they have hardly ever met in competing match encounters.

THE PLAYERS

When the clubs met in the FA Cup for the first time, Pompey's blonde striker Alan Biley, a former Everton player, brought first-hand experience of the famous Merseyside derbies, which he described as a walk in the park because there is friendly banter between the fans, and he commented on how unlike here it was. 'Here the supporters' future way of life depends on the result,' he said. 'For the winners it means complete one-upmanship until the next time. There's been a war of words between the fans for so long. I've heard some say we should try to forget about that side of the game, but it can't be swept under the carpet. The support for Pompey is fanatical. You've got to be Portsmouth or Southampton – you can't just go there to enjoy the match. That's what has hit me most since I came here. The rivalry is not merely down to the youngsters, it's the older generation as well.'

Rod Stewart-lookalike Biley lived in an area that was half-Pompey and half-Saints and, as a player, he could feel the tensions.

Another player regarded with affection and associated with the old Portsmouth team is Steve Clarridge, whom the lads hold in high regard.

Clarridge, yeah, we've had some brilliant players come down here and play. Clarridge is local, he's only from Titchfield, a little village just outside Fareham, where they have a big carnival every year and there's like 30,000 people turn up and every year they burn an effigy of the Lord of Southampton. It's a story that

*goes back to the old days. He blocked off the river
that goes through there, so the people of Titchfield –
Pikies and all sorts up there, good people, the last
stronghold of Portsmouth before you go into
Southampton – every year at this carnival they burn
an effigy of the Earl of Southampton or whoever it
was 'cause he blocked the river off and stopped the
trade coming into Titchfield. And they have a special
committee there called the Titchfield Bonfire Boys. It's
an open society whose primary purpose is to preserve
one of the biggest and best carnivals in the south of
England. They raise a lot of money for charity and
Clarridge is one of them, if he's not doing his bollocks
in the bookies.*

The bad-tempered FA Cup tie of 1984 season that saw
Portsmouth lose 1–0 was lost in the time added on for the coin-
throwing Pompey louts who felled Saints defender Mark
Dennis. These were the disgraceful scenes that provoked uproar
from within the Football Association, a complete contrast to the
cool-headed player himself. When asked for his comments on
the incident, he said, 'I don't blame them for what has
happened.' He went on to say he could understand their
frustrations because he used to live in Bermondsey and stand on
the terraces watching Millwall.

And as young England striker Steve Moran found the target in
the time added on in that game, to score what was the winner, he
rammed the Pompey taunts back down their throats. A feat that
didn't go down too well with Pompey fans and you can imagine
the smugness they felt when reading of this particular incident.
Steve Moran was punched after a row in a Portsmouth disco, and
having read the exploits of many of the Pompey lads you might
not be surprised, but the assailant who walloped him had played
for one of Portsmouth's teams and, whatever the disagreement

was about, it goes to show that the bad feeling doesn't always just remain with the fans.

Even on a lower level, the Hampshire FA once received a terrifying report of a local football team from Gosport being forced to run the gauntlet of angry Portsmouth supporters, armed with iron bars and bricks, after a match played in Portchester. A harassed team manager stated that, 'Even though we won 9-0, there wasn't a problem until the yobs saw one of our players leaving the changing rooms wearing a Southampton shirt. They began shouting "Scummers" at us and the whole situation turned ugly.'

The decline of a once great Pompey football team that was very successful in the fifties, finding itself tumbling down to the depths of the Fourth Division, while its much reviled neighbour, a comparatively small club has kept itself in the top flight may be to blame. Nevertheless, the emotion-charged atmosphere whenever the two clubs meet stirs local passions beyond those of a football match. There's real hatred together with a real need to show a loyalty, whether just healthy fan rivalry or some that want to, and will, take it further than that.

Living amongst the community you find it surfaces in everyday life, beyond just the graffiti written on the walls. The depth of feeling is such that nobody that was prepared to be interviewed in the book could bring themselves to even mention the words Southampton Football Club.

When I was living in my old house I had a lodger. He'd been a taxi driver and he said he went in the Festing one morning to have a beer because he'd been working all night. He said he'd walked in the pub half-ten in the morning, and there's an old boy sat in the corner reading his paper. He said he was at the bar, there's no one else in the pub, and another bloke walks in and goes, 'All right, Albie?' 'All right, Bert.' He said, 'Yeah,

see the Scum got beat last night then.' Just two old
boys in a pub, having a passing conversation.

Looking at the history of this deep-seated rivalry between
Portsmouth and Southampton supporters, the actual root causes
are far from clear-cut. Looking through Pompey eyes, is it a
geography thing? Even though Southampton is 20 motorway
miles away, they are still the closest neighbours. Are we looking at
the story of two cities? With Portsmouth claiming they have the
heritage after being designated a city by Royal Charter since 1194,
whilst Southampton only achieved city status in 1964. If you take
a look at the cities then, you are comparing its communities and
the traditional rivalry there, being as both are docks, one
merchant and the other Royal Navy; one community has more
sort of town folk and the other more rural sort of people.

But a far bigger gauge of this rivalry and where it really raises
its ugly head is in the city's two football teams. Pompey have
always thought they are the bigger football club of the two, with
its footballing history of three FA Cup Final appearances in 1929,
1939, 1950; winning the '39 Cup; they can add two successive
League Championships of '49 and '50 to that. Unrivalled by any
on the south coast, it was a history that said Pompey would
always be the 'big' club, until the World Cup years, and ever since,
when they were rattled by the scourge of their much-scorned
neighbours, Southampton, which rose to become the south's
leading club by establishing consistent top-flight football in the
highest league. While Portsmouth Football Club in the same
period went into a decline.

While the two cities' football clubs remain entrenched in strong
communities it could have only served as a blessing that the two
football teams have met only rarely in the past 30-odd years. The
worst match remembered for trouble was where the result of the
match had an influence. The game played at Fratton Park on 6
April 1976 was a real sickener and it's still remembered, for if it

wasn't bad enough that Southampton had made the FA Cup Final that year (which they won for their only trophy to show for however many years of top-flight football), they also went and won the game at Portsmouth with a Mick Channon goal in the last minute to relegate Pompey down and out of Division Two.

A very young Rob Silvester remembers the game vividly. 'I was very young, but I still remember that day. We're talking about '76, big flared jeans and the old crepe soles with wedges but bigger, the long hair gives that period of time away, anyway. It was scarves round the neck. It makes me laugh when you see the old clips on telly and you see the old three-star jumpers and scarves around each wrist, and big fucking brown bovver boots. But that was the first time that I actually saw football violence.

'Anyway the Scum came down here, and Channon made it 1–0 in the last minute. The ground just emptied, we were straight out of there, Frogmore Road, straight down Carisbrooke Road, heading towards the Milton End where all the Southampton fans were. I mean I was only 12 at the time. I just went straight up there, did a right and went home. Now a mile up the road and this was the first time I got to notice what was football aggro, it was the thud and thundering of feet running. I turned round and three Pompey blokes had hold of this Southampton, who we call Scummers, and they kicked fuck out of him.

'In a way I wasn't frightened 'cause I knew the hatred goes back with Southampton to a dock strike where they, well, we were on strike down there, and they brought their own people in. That's why we call them Scummers, scabs and every other vile word you can think of. But it made me laugh seeing all, like, the big flares and the crepe soles, you know the thudding, the kicking. I was with a couple of school friends, like I say, I was only 12, and I couldn't wait to get to school the next day and make out we were involved. You know, telling all the girls, "We got hold of this Scummer last night, kicked fuck out of him." Being 12 and being part of it, seeing it.

'The first competitive meeting of the sides since that awful day at Fratton Park in '76 was to be a fourth-round FA Cup on 28 January 1984 back at Portsmouth's ground. For eight years the loyal Pompey support had waited for his game, and all the old rivalry began to resurface along with the dreams of revenge. The tensions were obvious and the Hampshire Police became involved in the biggest crowd control operation the city had ever seen. The police were on red alert to keep the supporters segregated and get 9,000 Saints fans in and out of Fratton Park safely at what would be an all-ticket sell-out crowd of 36,000. Police no-go zones were in place all around Fratton Park. Several roads were totally closed, and part of Goldsmith Avenue, Frogmore Road, Carisbrook Road, Ruskin, Apsley and Claydon Roads. Pedestrians and car parking were all banned along these zones, and there were pub closures.

'But, in spite of this massive police operation and particularly after the game in which a Pompey loss was blamed on coin-throwing Pompey louts, 60 fans were arrested and 18 put in hospital, surrounding shops had been smashed and damaged, as well as several police vehicles. Relations between police and fans remained a hotbed of tension. In the aftermath the Football Association conducted its usual enquiry and the outraged late Bert Millichip said, "I don't think I have to tell anyone that it is a social problem – it's total lawlessness, minor terrorism."

'This was a desperate call from Millichip, who'd felt like Moses crying in the wilderness, to get some help for a tougher stance from the government who up to now had felt the responsibility was for football to sort its own affairs. There were big problems, but that was not how the fans saw it – the Pompey lads were on a different buzz.'

Roy, a Pompey-born lad living in Reading, bears testament to how far the Portsmouth catchment area goes:

We used to love coming down on Saturdays, we'd meet up at our station, usually a dozen of us, bunking on with your platform ticket. The train from Reading would go straight through to Pompey. As soon as you got to Fareham and Portchester, it was packed. The trains were absolutely packed, any game, great support and it was the best way to travel then. There would always be a great atmosphere, fantastic. And you would get out at Fratton station and it was brilliant, all the way along Goldsmith Avenue, I mean it's all change now. These all-seating stadiums. We used to like all the swaying and the surging and today, the youngsters have only got the shirts, we used to have the scarves and sing and chant, you know the Liverpool-style walk-ons. It was great – a great atmosphere. If you got 20,000-plus in that old ground or 30,000-plus, the Pompey chants were always brilliant 'cause it is an echo after all.

And I think the biggest mob of Pompey I ever saw was that fourth-round FA Cup match with Southampton. They reckon they could've sold up to 70,000 tickets for that game if the ground was big enough. That was always going to be the game. They were first, we were second – First Division, Second Division. And it was the old Fratton Park then. They nearly had 40,000 in there, and I mean even Southampton filled the away end, which helped – about 9,000. But I'll never forget it. I was down there a couple of hours before the game. We went down Fratton Road for a bite to eat 'cause of travelling and there was three of us sitting in the café in Fratton Road. And I'm not kidding you, from the time we ordered our grub to the time we finished, there was a mob from one side of Fratton Road to the other which must have been about 40-deep just going past all the time, not 'cause it was en route to Fratton Park, this was Pompey lads.

TEAM CALLED SCUM

*They must have emptied out from Buckland,
Landport, everywhere, North End – it was the
biggest mob I'd ever seen. Although it was en route to
Fratton Park, the main road, it was, you know, it was
the biggest mob I ever saw. They must have all gone
together. It was absolutely fantastic – a real top
Pompey firm, proper mob. I mean Southampton,
they had, you know, like 9,000 in the away end. But
as a mob – not really. I mean, you got scuffles
everywhere. You know, wherever they could get hold
of 'em, they was rucking, but not a mob really. I
mean, you got a lot of families coming down with
them, it was a family club.*

*Inside the ground that day, there was no serious
aggro, just the usual abuse at each other, you know,
giving it all the Scummers and all that. Even before
my dad was born, they'd called Southampton that.
I think it goes right back. There still wasn't any real
trouble inside the ground that day, although there
was a lot of coin throwing. Then they scored in the
last minutes. We couldn't believe it, that was it
then. Don't forget a lot of people had been in the
ground since 11 or 12 o'clock. It was like the old
days, you know, big, big, mass crowds. But, you
know, even being pretty pissed off, it was good to
see Fratton Park full again.*

I imagine I'm only touching the surface where the football
rivalry brings it all out, but I'm confused as to whether it is
rivalry or hatred. Roy, the Pompey-born fan who moved out to
Reading when his father took a job out there, can still recall
many a Pompey fan that couldn't afford to travel when Pompey
were playing far away, in those early years before there was the
cheap travel on the specials, and they would go over to

Southampton by the trainload on home-match days and support the other team.

But back to the rivalry about who is the bigger club:

> *We had massive support and we were in Division Four. Scummers, now they say,' Oh, we get 30,000 every week,' and you've just got to turn round and say, 'We got a 32,000 crowd for a Fourth Division game,' and they can't ever beat that. We used to take thousands everywhere in the Fourth Division games.*

The one-upmanship doesn't end there. Southampton found a new ground after years of Pompey talking about doing the same, but before their neighbours could crow, this circular was put out.

SCUMMER'S NEW GROUND

I'd like to tell a story
All Scummers need to know
The truth about their brand new ground
And why they shouldn't go
We know they're both excited
But they should fear the worst
For when they finally crawl inside
They'll find we've been there first
Beneath those new foundations
Preserved from rain and dirt
You'll find a pair of Pompey shorts
And matching Pompey shirt
Deep beneath the Scummer End
Amongst the leaves and roots
We've laid to rest a Pompey scarf
And Andy Awford's boots
Compressed inside the brickwork
And plain as it can be

TEAM CALLED SCUM

That moon and star from up above
The badge of PFC
We've raised the turf and sown the seeds
Which prove my story true
By early spring that Scummer pitch
Will turn a shade of blue
Close by a capsule keeping time
With tales of steel and zest
In years to come all Scum will know
The lads in blue were best
At night when eerie sounds are heard
Don't fret or wonder why
No doubt it's Westwood's bugle playing
'Portsmouth Till I Die'.

So we're getting a football mix and a social mix as to why nobody interviewed can bring themselves to mention that other team's name. It's all pointing to a long history of a community rivalry that becomes worse whenever there is a football connection. I mean, judge for yourself as I leave the final say to the one-time travel organiser of the Pompey fans' away trips – Old Fooksie.

As young as I was, we never played them, of course, 'cause they were always in the third, or the second – even in the old third division, Southampton never did anything. We were the top team in the area and then, of course, they came on some, had some good players, started whacking us at the match, the football match, that is, and it was just an inborn thing. I think the first time I heard the word Scummer used was by a lad called Barry H who used to run coaches. Barry H, that grey-haired old git, you know, who stands by the tunnel now – the Pompey sailor. He and I wouldn't be far wrong in thinking that he even thought of the word Scummer himself. He was the first one I ever heard, and from that day, you just tell your kids, Scummer. And, as soon as they're old enough, you tell your kids, 'Scum, you don't run from Scum – you don't run from them, you run at them. Don't run, run at them.' You just do – silly, but you just do. It's just a thing. It's a funny town Portsmouth. I've often thought, Why are we so different? We're only 20 miles up the road, we're both in Hampshire, right on the coast. It's a really funny mixed-up congregation Portsmouth, 'cause it's a naval port, and all different people from all over the country have met Pompey girls and settled here. You see, like, a sailor from Newcastle, Wales, London, Liverpool, in the Navy, comes here, meets a Pompey bird and settles down, but he settles down here, he doesn't go back home to Liverpool, Wales or London. They meet a Pompey bird, settle down here, have kids and I think this is why we've got a very mixed-up sort of creed of people. Whereas you go just 20 miles up the coast and it's all farmers. So it's a funny city.

Cardiff, You've Got To Respect

Cardiff – we've always had it at Cardiff, haven't we? And they've always turned out for Pompey, haven't they? The old Cardiff firm or that Soul Crew Cardiff lot. We've got a lot of respect for them.

Cardiff is the capital and largest city in Wales, with arguably the most attractive football club in that part of the world. Any thug within a huge catchment area follows Cardiff, giving the Soul Crew a fierce reputation.

Pompey have a fair bit of history with Cardiff, and in the mid-seventies we had a major battle in their side, known as the Grange, by all accounts going pretty well. Indeed, both sets of supporters still talk about that one today – one of the classics of hooligan folklore. Fareham Jack was of the generation which turned over Cardiff in the Deacon years of the '73–'74 season, the old division two and Pompey's first away game of that season.

It was a funny old season. People had longer hair and the skinhead phase was well finished. You still had the staunch one who'd stick through it, but you had your more fashion-conscious people changing as the fashion went more into flares and stuff. Work-wise it was quite good in those days. Saying that, there were power cuts later on in the year which affected a lot of games involving Pompey. There were elections, and an oil crisis, and Pompey bought a generator so they could have their games at normal times and all the rest of it. There were a few workers strikes going on around the country and the miners were definitely out. So with them kind of problems around, I don't think Cardiff even could realise what the turnout from Pompey would be that day.

Cardiff away had a big turn out. I wouldn't like to put a figure on it, but the actual number of boys wanting to have a go was very good. We're talking 600-plus, all wanted to have a go, plus all the others that were there. Everyone was getting a little more independent and they had their own little crews going, doing their own thing rather than one person organising everything. People were starting to drive now. You still had coaches, and the trains, but once you got there it was the same result – you were installed together and it didn't matter where you came from.

Cardiff's Grange End was good. We were congratulated by the Cardiff Police, believe it or not, for being the first crew ever to turn Cardiff over. In fact, the police were quite lenient, so I don't know what the press picked up at the time. There were a few stabbings going on, both ways. Yeah, there was some serious stuff going on. The police basically tried to stop it all, but they realised that Cardiff supporters were getting a bit of a pasting and basically eased back because they said they had it coming to them, it's about time they got a taste of their own medicine. So, yes, everyone was quite happy about that. You had some right characters there, everyone that's a character at Pompey was there and it looked like everyone wanted to have a go as well.

You know, you're probably talking about 800–900. We were there first and when Cardiff came in it was quite frightening – they all came hammering at us and, give people credit, they just stood their ground, they thought, We're not running, and that was it. I think people were looking around nervously, thinking, Well, they're not going to move, we're not going to move, and that's what happened. So they slowed up as they got close to you, as always happens, and then we were on the offensive. And I can tell you, it was the most satisfying day, the reason being that they think they're quite a little crowd up there. Big, big reputation, so I think they get a lot of benefits – a lot of people don't go there, so they've always got a bigger mob. And I would say that usually the police protect them quite well, but that particular day the police didn't want to know, just let it go for a bit, a bit of their own medicine.

CARDIFF AWAY '82

Since that epic encounter with Cardiff in the early seventies we never met again until the autumn of 1982 but we knew what to expect of an encounter with their mob. It had kicked off when they turned up at Newport County in '81 too. Newport always bought a good little crew of skins themselves to Fratton Park, led by a nutty bird, so when we next played them in the early eighties we knew we would have some fun.

The first time up at their place in '82 was largely uneventful, but we took a strong mob and were put into the ground early. We had travelled there in transits, engaging in inter-van egg fights on the way, drawing attention to ourselves, and we'd been tumbled by plod. As we waited in the ground, Cardiff were walking behind the stand shouting up at us. It was unbelievable but the wall to the terrace we were on was crumbling away, so we took lumps of it and dropped it down on to them. They went fucking mad. We simply couldn't work out why, as surely we weren't the first to think that up.

It was just after the Falklands war and, as Cardiff were mobbing up, we were horrified to hear them chanting, 'Ar-gen-tina, Ar-gen-tina'. Everybody immediately rushed the fence, a rag-tag mass of mesh, to get over to the side where they were mobbed up. The fence was rapidly disintegrating as the police baton charged us back. Two wrongs don't make a right, I know, but as we were pushed back Pompey were chanting, 'Fifty Welsh guards, fifty Welsh guards, allo, allo,' which was out of order and a reference to the direct hit the *Sir Galahad* suffered from an Argentinian exocet in the same conflict, the incident when war hero Simon Weston suffered horrific burns, so looking back it was not one of our finest moments. Those sort of chants are a far cry from the campfire-like 'Shall we sing a song for you' that echoes round Fratton Park nowadays, making any thug, active or not, cringe with embarrassment. We jumped on an old army bus to get home afterwards that one of the older lot had filled. We then stopped in Bath and fought with anyone who was remotely interested in a ruck as the pubs chucked out.

CARDIFF HOME '83

We were now getting to know all the same faces and all getting the same trains, and the same sort of things were happening, but one of the incidents which really helped to bond us all together was when we met Cardiff – Cardiff being one of our main rivals for promotion that year in the old Third Division.

Everyone had been to Cardiff early on in the season and there was just loads of trouble. So everyone for the home game was expecting a couple of thousand Cardiff to turn up with maybe a couple hundred of their boys. But when they came they must have had 3,000 away fans and 1,000 of them were geezers – big, fat, horrible old Welsh geezers in donkey jackets, the 25- and 30-year-olds from the pits and the valleys. The only dressers in evidence among them were their young lot: the 16- and 17-year-olds who had the casual look.

When they came that day it was late, about five to three. We'd had scouts and lookouts everywhere, some on pushbikes, while everyone waited and gathered around the barn and the back of Fratton Park. It was the same geezers, and the same firm swelling in ever-increasing numbers with every game. Someone saw their mob come off the train and it was on. We went for ambushing them up every side street we knew and, by the time they got in the ground, I thought they were the gamest firms ever to come to Pompey. Inside the ground the banter was both wicked and nasty but both supporters were kept apart. The Cardiff fans rampaged among themselves, ripping up our famous old clock that was always sited in the Milton End – something they still haven't stopped crowing about. Every time we used to see them after that, if they were on a coach or whatever, they always used to do these little clock signs to you.

I remember still being outside the ground when the Cardiff fans were first waiting to go in and a few of us went up and started talking to some of them. We were having a close study of them, couldn't help noticing how a lot of them had Armani on, Armani jumpers and cords, the new-style trainers, stuff like that. They still had too many of them scruffy ones in jean jackets and with long hair, and a few of them still had baggy trousers. This was terrible, ever our normals, the geezers down town would at least be into that awful Spandau Ballet look.

At the end of the game they kept Cardiff in, holding them inside for what seemed like hours but in reality was probably only 20 minutes after the game. We all mobbed up at the back of the ground round by the barn, knowing full well that they would be escorted down to Fratton Park station. It was some firm we had on show, absolutely hundreds of Pompey, the only other times I've seen a firm at home like that was when we played Scum in the Cup and Chelsea on a bank holiday in the following season. But as both Cardiff and us had a real show and turnout, so did the Old Bill in what was a massive police operation on a par with what they'd put out for Millwall, Chelsea and Scum at home. We did everything we could just to get at them, we attacked at every single street and all the side streets in attempts to get at them and they had some game geezers, who were up for putting right the embarrassment we gave them at theirs earlier that season. But they didn't have what I call desperate groups of people that all seem to know each other. There wasn't that organisation about them. We were running down one street attacking 'em, and then going all the way back to launch another attack around the back of them from another street. All the time we were attacking up every street we could see the police didn't appear to be arresting anyone, anyone they grabbed hold of they seemed content to just give them a clip round the ear and chuck them *away. This would be a different time to when the Pompey Police were given all their powers to crack down on what was going on, which happened to the 6.57 later. It must be said that Cardiff were well up for it too, missiles rained backwards and forwards but there was no major contact made. Maybe Cardiff with the firm they had could have made more of it, but they didn't really try to break out of their escort, or do anything outrageous or extraordinary – we had to take it to them and we did. There must have been a combined total of 2,000 thugs trying to get it on with them. But they gained our respect for that grand show of strength and certainly they did well outside the station when some of us managed to get to them.*

The Old Bill were really dishing it out to our lot that day. They were baton-charging our lot and never the other firm, which is the usual story at Pompey matches. They must be unique in this, as it's never seen at any other grounds and it certainly doesn't help when you're trying to have a fight. Eventually Cardiff were escorted away and out of Portsmouth, and the Old Bill's attacks on us along Fratton Road went on long after Cardiff had left.

CARDIFF AWAY '83

September '83, we went away to Cardiff and there was a really big turnout because we hadn't played them for years and years. What's more, Cardiff had always acknowledged Pompey were the only team to have taken their side. I think that was the first time we went there as the 6.57 crew and there was a lot of violence that day. A lot of fighting and it would be the cause of an ongoing thing with Cardiff, which went on for two or three years.

Again, we took good numbers – I mean, travelling on the train together, by the time you get there you could be talking up to 600–700, you know, actual thugs who wanted a fight. But I think in our mob there was about half that, maybe more. I mean, obviously you get people who are with you who don't want trouble and they drift off and make their own way. I think actual numbers of those who were really bowling about looking for it was 250–350 again. For some reason, I don't know what it was, but you never ever felt that anyone could touch you. If you were with these certain groups of boys, certain groups of people, you just felt invincible. I don't know how to describe that feeling. We knew we had a good mob but it wasn't just that, there was just something extra there. And you just felt that the lads of Pompey had gone through all the leagues and had it with everyone, and I suppose we did have it our own way with most teams. But Cardiff boys stick out because, you know, to be fair to them they've always put up a good show and always had a good mob there themselves.

We got off at Cardiff and we managed to get out of the station in one piece without too much trouble from the police. Everyone was just like walking along talking, going down this road and suddenly we heard the roar go off. 'Here it is!' went up the call, and as Cardiff came piling out of their Philharmonic pub, it went off. Both mobs filled up the road and went straight into each other. It went off, sort of hand to hand for a couple of minutes. I remember Paul L doing well. Cardiff were now bouncing around on the other side of the road, backing off out of it. They didn't reckon on the firm that came running straight at them. Once that familiar roar went up, everybody charged and a blur of casuals poured out of the station, a full blitz of Tacchini-, Ellesse- and Pringle-clad warriors marched on through Cardiff and we were invincible that day.

The momentum we built up as we left the station simply didn't stop. They were demoralised, as any of them who stood just got battered. It got even worse for the Soul Crew as a few minibuses of nasty Paulsgrove had joined in the fun, as we got closer to the ground. We never gave an inch all day as the fighting and chasing continued all the way, and there was sporadic trouble all the time. We gave it the big one right outside the Ninian Arms and, although Cardiff are a really game crew, it was our day, we really had them that day. There was no such thing as respect given to anyone that year and the end result was a succession of these types of victories, which has given Portsmouth's 6.57 crew the reputation it has to this day.

It also went off in the ground, but to be fair to Cardiff they stood their ground and it was pretty even as 150 rival fans went for it in the grandstand. The Old Bill didn't have a clue – Cardiff had their casuals, we had ours and the Old Bill never realised what was going to go down. When they did see what was happening, they escorted Pompey fans back over to the visiting section. They got it together a bit better after the game when we were getting escorted back, but you could get out the escort pretty easy. The Old Bill just weren't sure who was who. So a few of us broke away and a little mob of Cardiff came down the road. We were having it down one road and there were isolated scuffles down others. The main damage was done, however, and we went home happy that night. We had turned them right over and the papers were full of it on Sunday and Monday morning, and the 50–60 arrests, which were split between us. But the headlines read: POMPEY FANS ON THE RAMPAGE AS PUB WRECKED. *This resulted in the return fixture being played at 12 o'clock.*

CARDIFF AWAY '84

Cardiff away again and still early in the season, but we'd been thinking of a way to outmanoeuvre their Old Bill because of what had happened last season and we knew the police were going to be on top of us. Everyone was getting dressed up then, so someone says, 'Well, why don't we all put blazers and shirts and tie and everything on, and we'll make out we're going to a wedding.' We had the wedding invitations printed and everyone put on a blazer with a pair of Farrahs and what have you, and we went up and we had a reasonable firm all on one train.

At the time, football was all about clothes – it was a different lifestyle from those who weren't into football. The clothes that people that weren't into going football used to wear were dire, absolutely disgusting – they would wear what Spandau Ballet would be wearing while we would be wearing Burberry, Aquascutum, whatever, and that's how you could tell the difference. Average Pompey football fans had Levis jeans, Fiorucci jeans, Armani jumpers and T-shirts, all different types of ski coats, Tacchini. In those days the general clothes you used to get in your high-street shops were pretty cheap and shoddy, not like today. I'd like to think that through people going to football, all over the country, we helped shops move away from the cheap crap they were selling at the time

CARDIFF, YOU'VE GOT TO RESPECT

For Cardiff we were all up for it. We knew they had a decent mob up there and it would just be a question of how the Old Bill were going to react. Sometimes they had buses waiting for you, and sometimes they were quite relaxed. We got to Cardiff by 12 o'clock, got off the train and the British Transport Police came up to us. They said, 'Football?' We said, 'No, we're here for so-and-so's wedding.' And about 30 of us got out of the waiting police escort on the strength of the wedding ruse. The rest had had it – the Cardiff Police were pretty heavy straight away. And some of the lads got picked out and sussed by two Portsmouth CID officers. This was something new by the police for that season – the use of trained spotters whose job was to get to know the 6.57 crew and identify its ringleaders. The result here was that Pompey was surrounded by their Old Bill and marched to the football ground, with the Old Bill keeping an eye on us.

There wasn't a lot doing at Cardiff in the ground. It was an uneventful day in south Wales, really, much to everyone's disappointment after the last time there. Although there was the amusing sight of one of our lot in their side on his own, getting sussed and throwing caution to the wind as he windmilled into them on his own. It was not deemed a sensible move, and he was rescued by the police while he was being kicked all round the floor.

Nothing after the game. The Old Bill thought they had it sussed. The Cardiff geezers wanted to know, and we wanted to know. We had a good mob. Cardiff had a good mob. It surprised us really how they were now all clued up with their clothes. Wales, you'd think they were all sheep-shaggers really, but they had some good, big boys. You know, we were really quite young, all early twenties. They walked on one side of the road and we were on the other side going to the station. There were a few little incidents at Cardiff station, but nothing to speak of really.

A stop-off in Southampton on the way back home livened things up a bit, though. The Painted Wagon, their main pub at the time, emptied after a couple of our lot poked their heads in and the 20 waiting outside had to reluctantly retreat to the station as 100 tanked-up fools came running out. The next train was full of thugs who had heard about the Painted Wagon incident and went mad when the Old Bill kept the train doors shut and moved it on. Later on that night, six of our well-known faces infiltrated the Wagon and were bombarded with glasses and other missiles by this pub full of idiots, but not a punch was thrown. Why they didn't simply kick the granny out of them is a total mystery to all of us in Portsmouth and is talked about to this day. One of our finest suffered a nasty injury that night. The odds were ridiculous and even the most fervent die-hard Scummer knows that it was piss-poor and cannot be explained.

Cardiff have since travelled to Fratton in the nineties and by all accounts have been just as impressive. They have maintained this standard right up to the present day and are considered over the years to be just about anyone's equals on their day. Pompey, as well as everyone else, rate them highly. Off the pitch we have never come second to them, and there can't be many firms who can say that.

We Went Through the Divisions

ARSENAL

The mighty Arsenal. Alas, Pompey on the pitch were never in the same league during the period we're talking about, but nevertheless there was always the magic of a Cup draw and, of course, any friendly games that could be had. The pull of the Arsenal and that famous side that won the double with the likes of Armstrong, Radford, Kennedy and the gifted Charlie George was never more evident than when you look at the gate Pompey had at home in the third round – 20,000 against promotion winners Sheffield United, compared with the Arsenal in the next round and a massive 40,000 attendance. 23 January 1971 was a day many of the older prominent 6.57 lads, mere impressionable young boys at the time, would remember for the impression the London side's fans would leave on Pompey, more than for any result on the field of play – the fashion, suede Budgie jackets and all that, and the London thing of infiltrating an end.

What I remember most about Arsenal was being up the Fratton End. In those days the Fratton End would be like split in two. We had the hot-dog side and they had the other side. Pompey were 1–0 down at half-time. Then, late in the game, really late, something like the last minute, we scored to make it 1–1, and they went off on one and, basically, they done a runner. I remember the Old Bill trying to hold 'em and everyone left. They just came through and they left me – they run straight through me. It's one of them things, Do you run or do you stay? I didn't stay for a punch-up, I just looked. I couldn't get away, basically. Don't forget these were the days when we could go in any part of the ground and, you know, with big crowds like that you would get away supporters in any part of the ground. I was about 11 or 12 at the time.

Arsenal in a friendly in the early or mid-eighties always reminds me of a real character over Pompey – really well known was Fish. He's dead now but we still talk about him, he was a good laugh. He used to go around with the Stamshaw lot, game as anything, but he turned to drink in the end.

I remember it was the pre-season friendly when Charlie Nicholas made his debut for Arsenal and Fish was wearing a Spurs shirt that day. He didn't support Spurs, but I think they went shoplifting in the morning and he got a Spurs shirt. So he wore it to the game. Arsenal were going fucking mental.

After the game we went round to Lee's house, he used to live outside the Fratton End. We used to go in his house, wait about 10 minutes and then they'd bring the away fans out. So they were bringing Arsenal out and we started going down the road towards the Shepherd's Crook, and a few of the Arsenal, instead of coming up, broke off and they went into Winter Road. So we ran across into Haslemere Road, the first road as we came to it – we are now one end of it, they're at the other. We called out to them and they came charging down the road, and we sort of had a five-minute hand to hand from the corner of the road. We did all right and then all their top boys sort of turned up and there was getting to be too many of them in the end. There must have been only about 20 of us, but even so it took the Old Bill to stop the row.

Denton was there and a few others for Arsenal, but they come up, when it stopped, and they said, 'Oh yeah, good row, lads, well done. You done really well there.'

BARNSLEY AWAY '83–'84

I remember going to Barnsley in '84. We were all in the pub having a drink. There was about 30, 6.57 and a few Eastos, a few Air Balloon, a few Paulsgrove and that. We were all sniffing poppers, as you did in the early eighties and there was a bit of blow, I think, and a bit of billy, 'cause that was what it was all about then. We couldn't afford Charlie, and it wasn't really around much then anyway. We were all sitting in a pub and then someone said there's a mob of about 60 Barnsley coming up towards us in the pub. There was only 30 of us, so we ran out. I think I was the first, well, I thought I was the first one out of the pub being like on poppers and that. I ran straight out, grabbed hold of a geezer and started smacking him and that. And he's going, 'No, I'm Leigh Park, I'm Leigh Park.' Pompey, I thought, fuck it, I wasn't the first one out.

So, as I've legged it, there was a grass verge and this Barnsley geezer came running towards me, and done a karate kick thing. As he flew past me, I grabbed his foot and he fell on the floor. Everyone just toed him in. And there was only young Barnsley and they must have thought we was mad, 'cause they had about 60 and there was only, like, 30 of us. We steamed straight into them and just chased them all up the road and that and they didn't want to know. Within minutes, like, the young 'uns have gone to get the older lot and they all come back. There must have been, I'd say, twice as many of them as there were of us. And we still give it to them. And I remember this Barnsley geezer saying, 'You must be fucking mad' and that, 'We well outnumbered you.' And there was one Pompey lad getting a good old kicking and this Barnsley geezer picked him up and, like, pushed him out the way, but they didn't want to know. They just fucking legged it up the road and that was it. We done them.

Years later, I got to know this Barnsley fan, 'Old Barnsley', whose recollection of that day was that the 6.57 in Barnsley in the early eighties used, in his words, the old 'code of conduct'...

'I walked into the town with my mate and was fronted by 30 or so 6.57. There must have been 60 Barnsley youth, but we were part of the older firm. The young 'uns looked at me and my mate, being older, to take hold of the situation and lead them into battle. Well, we gave the 6.57 the come on and they obliged without batting an eyelid, which I found really brave or really stupid 'cause there was only 30 of them. And there was 60 of us. And they steamed

straight past me and my mate, and proceeded to run the young 'uns down the road leaving us be completely. Within minutes the young 'uns had returned with a load of older ones, a larger firm of Barnsley who laid into the 30 Pompey, giving them a good old-fashioned slapping. But some of the young 'uns, who had legged it earlier, had turned round and started kicking shit out of one Pompey fan. I turned, pulled the young 'uns off of him, picked up this Pompey kid and sent him on his way. I always respected Pompey before this happened and always will respect them, even more so after that. Respect and good luck in your quest for the Premiership.'

BIRMINGHAM

January '77, Pompey went to Birmingham for an FA Cup match, all up on coaches including a coach full of loons from the Fox. It was the same round of the Cup in which Pompey went to Birmingham the year before and the Pompey fans had got turned over.

We turned up in Birmingham and a lot of people were wary, as it was still the old-style ground where you had no segregation. I still think, even in those days, maybe at a certain age you're on nodding terms with people because you've seen them enough times, but when you're young you're not on that sort of level. You just turn up and tag along. I won't say you were scared 'cause there were 5,000–6,000 Pompey fans travelling up. Away games like that were a matter of getting there and getting in the away end – the Tilton Road End. In those days it was really great, not like today with seats, you had all the fans swaying and all that. At a massive ground like at Villa and

Birmingham and Sheffield Wednesday, you could have a mob of a couple of hundred and you wouldn't even see them – those ends were massive and I remember saying to my mate, 'There's definitely Birmingham in here with Pompey.' I could see it going off. But just at that point all the Fox lot came round the back of Pompey. Their coach had just got in late from Fratton Park. They'd obviously seen what was going on and just piled straight in on it. And I don't think we saw much of them until after the game in there.

It was all like bombsites outside Birmingham's ground at the time. After the game all I saw was Birmingham fans getting kicked to bits. I would say Pompey had the better of Birmingham really. You know its all talk of the Zulus, Birmingham's boys, today, but when you look back you don't recognise them as gangs – you didn't have these elite top boy firms, it was just supporters, mob versus mob all on the same level.

That season before, when Trevor Francis became the Wonder Kid of English football, it was the replay that took us up there. They had come down and fought equally with Pompey outside the Fratton End. So Pompey had always known about Birmingham's lot of lads, just as we had with Cardiff going back to the seventies era.

But in '84 we had them at their place and most of us went by road, arranging to meet up at New Street station. When we got there it immediately went off in the subway outside with a tasty gang of black lads who did well until they had to do one when our numbers swelled too high for them.

A few of our lot knew some of their firm and had arranged to meet them in the seats. But whatever had been said, the look of disbelief on their faces as they started to walk in to their stronghold with 100 of us parked up was truly memorable and it didn't look as though they had taken us seriously. A few of the chaps spoiled the moment by steaming into the first few as they were trying to get organised and get some numbers in. It spilled on to the pitch and we were moved out into our end. The Zulus were furious as they gathered and, although a result is not being claimed, they weren't expecting our front and they were not happy at all. We were all taking the piss out of them at the fence throughout the game. In addition to this we scattered a so-so mob of them after the game as we charged across bombsites – it wasn't their cream but they were still giving it and we duly obliged. They were given fair warning that we were coming and we felt they had taken it with a pinch of salt. Now they knew they had an additional fixture to look forward to later that season. They couldn't take Pompey for granted.

After the game one of our lot, who had become separated and lost, was actually chased up some building scaffold next to New Street station, as he had nowhere else to run. They were climbing up after him when the police arrived and he was really quite distressed about it as he swore blind he was 50 feet up as they advanced after him at an alarming speed.

Later that season on the return leg we waited in anticipation at the Robert Peel in Somers Town for the Zulus to show on match day. We had well and truly upset them up there and it was payback time. We knew they would come and we were not disappointed. It was 11 o'clock in the morning when the pub phone rang. They were off the train in town, 250-strong, having a drink and they wanted directions to get to us. The only other team to bring a mob of this size to our city centre this early had been Millwall in '81. They were almost polite as we sorted out a suitable meeting place. A couple of ours went up to tell them the score and equal numbers left the Peel marching towards the Guildhall Square. The Old Bill had by now sussed it and formed a line just before we met head on, so we all headed back towards

Somers Town. The Zulus, to their credit, then broke away and we met them head on in Winston Churchill Avenue where there was a good even battle. This was total anarchy as it was right outside the law courts and the Central Police Station. Two good mobs were bang at it right outside the very institutions that taxpayers were funding to stop and deal with such problems. It went off for a good minute until it was broken up. Everyone was well pissed off as the police, as usual, charged us not them. Obviously a tactic they used because they felt it worked for them. Also the severity of the nearby magistrates' courts was in the back of our minds, and once plod started their antics we moved away.

The Zulus were not aware of this and would have carried on fighting regardless. It was extremely hard for us to try and engage them as the boys in blue chased us into the nearby flats. At the time, Portsmouth magistrates had the powers to lock you up on the spot for threatening behaviour. People were getting three months. This was one of the first places to get all that. Any new powers, anything new, CS gas and the American-style batons, and Portsmouth Police always seemed to get them first. I don't know why, maybe it's a training place for them, 'cause we've had the hoolie van, and the cameras were always down here. But they used video evidence to their cost not ours, 'cause every trial they've had down here has collapsed.

As we were regrouping at the Peel a few Brummies almost got to the door before being moved away. We were happy that they were as keen as us, but for the rest of the day the police were the top firm.

The next time they came down, however, they had a ball at our expense and it has to be admitted they came out well on top. It was 1986 and although everyone was still going, football had just started to lose its edge in Portsmouth. It was becoming difficult to manoeuvre, as our beloved spotters, CID officers King and Hiscock, now knew all of us by name. Getting things sorted with other firms was becoming a nightmare. The police were starting to sew things up and dawn raids were becoming commonplace around the country.

The Zulus didn't seem to give a fuck about any of this and brought a good mob down who did the business in some style on Fratton Bridge after the game. Against the odds they broke up some fencing and went to work with pieces of wood, and to be fair we took a slapping. They battled really well that day and continued this all the way up to the Air Balloon, where again a small but bang-up-for-it crew of them really performed. They had jogged all the way from Fratton Bridge to the pub for a fight, a distance of about three miles. The Zulus were like men possessed that day and we were second best. Even the most biased of our boys will agree to this.

You have to say that Birmingham gave the best man-for-man display ever seen at Fratton that day. They were the business. In our defence, their timing was good as without a doubt by '86 football violence was past its peak in Portsmouth. They would not have enjoyed the same success a few years earlier, but credit where it's due. Within a year of this, in the wake of Heysel and the Derby away riot at Peartree Road, we were all but disbanded. But Birmingham are the only team to come to our two main boozers and for that alone they are well respected here. They are organised and a really game crew.

BORO

No football book past or present would be complete without a piece on Boro. The thing that everyone should remember is that this town is even smaller than ours so they remind us of ourselves to a degree. It's a very rough place. Middlesbrough has a population of 150,000 and is on its own. Boro should not have the mob they've got – they must put something in the babies' milk up there. As I said before there are a lot of similarities to us. They have Newcastle up the road irritating them on the pitch like we have Southampton, but the Geordies would not get near them off the pitch as we have encountered both and the Frontline are much more to talk about mob-wise.

We have had a few run-ins with them and, although we have never met their full mob head on, there are a few healthy moments to speak of and a definite two-way respect between the 6.57 and the Frontline. They came down in '77 for an evening Cup game, and you had to feel for them as there were about 100 of them stuck in the Milton End fighting for their lives as the Old Bill just left us to it. We didn't have any segregation in those days and Fratton Park was, in a word, vile if you were an away fan. We had a 33,000 crowd that night so you can imagine what they were up against, they didn't budge but then they couldn't really and it was a case of 'form a circle, shut your eyes and swing like mad' for them. Any Boro older boys will remember that night with a wry smile.

We then played them at Fratton on the first game of the season in '83–'84. An early morning attack was launched by our lot on a minibus full of Boro at the Ferryport and it resulted in some nasty charges and one of our good pals getting 12 months for leading the attack. He is still known as the General, but this is only in piss-take to him and the system that called him it. That day a mob of Pompey even got the train to Waterloo to wait for Boro but missed them – this was the only time we ever did this apart from when we took 200 up to hang about when we were banned from Millwall in '84. That resulted in a good tear-up as the Whackers always got it sorted.

During the game, about five or six cheeky bastards came on to the pitch when Boro scored. Without further notice the North Bank emptied and about 600 Pompey went over the pitch to the Milton End. They were keener than Sheffield United when this happened a couple of years later and the police dog-handlers battled to keep us apart. If anyone had seen the firm we had on the pitch the bets would have been on us as it's a long way to Boro and they didn't have the numbers or the initiative. It would be fair to say they were lucky the fences and Old Bill were there. The game was stopped for about 20 minutes.

One of our gamest boys who has performed to a consistent high for many years got through the wall of plod, scaled the fence and steamed into the lot of them on his own. It had to be seen to be believed and Boro will verify this, as there were enough of them there. He was dragged out and took a few digs but he got a rapturous ovation from us, and anyone who saw that will never forget it. It is some feat to jump into any end like that, let alone a top mob's end, but it has been done, as we can confirm. Millwall's infamous big black fella and main face took a hiding as he walked about in our end at the old Den on a night game in 82. He was also on his own, and he was, of course, easily sussed as we had no 6ft 6in black guys in the 6.57!

A few Boro were jumped as they got separated after the game. Boro didn't ever seem to come *en masse* to us as we always seemed to pick off small groups of them at our place. It wouldn't be talking out of turn to say they have been relieved on a few occasions to get to the ground and see the plod at our place as they were back-pedalling and fending us off. They certainly had a few in the ground but always seemed to travel in minibuses and cars. Fine by us if you wanted an uphill battle getting to and from the ground without an escort. It was either brave or stupid, as everyone else seemed to stick together when they came to Fratton Park.

Talking of sticking together, you certainly had to do that at the old Ayresome Park, on a freezing day later that season as 100 ski-coat-wearing thugs embarked on the 6.57 to Waterloo en route to Teeside. We took a quality firm that day and did well in some isolated battles around the ground, standing firm. A few of ours got separated and legged off the platform down the tracks by a load of horrible bastards at the station – it was a warning shot across the bows. In the ground, a few of ours took it to them as they mobbed up, this was only a scuffle and they were keen as well. After the game, about 20 of us got separated and we had to punch and kick our way back to the station. Their local Old Bill just didn't have a clue, and every time we thought that was it, they came out of another side street and, bang, it went again. It's a dark and intimidating route to the station and it went on for ever. The after-buzz was certainly more enjoyable than the actual trek. We had had enough by the time we got back to the station, but luckily we were never outnumbered too badly and were not overwhelmed. One of our boys took a truncheon from a horseback copper. This made both mobs angry at the filth and took the attention off us as Boro rightly kicked off with the Old Bill. The rest of our boys had had a few skirmishes on the way back too and had stood their ground every time, Boro just couldn't see them off, but this was only minor stuff and not full-on battling.

One last quality moment was on the station as we were put back on the train after an even ding-dong just outside. One of our boys was stuck on the platform with all of them and, as they set about him, we were all cheering him on. This sounds like we didn't care but, if you knew him like we do, you would know he would find it funny if it was one of us. He was a game fucker and could have a fight and he was putting on a good show as the Old Bill dragged him back and slung him back on our train. We were all slapping him on the back and laughing as he dusted himself off, coating the life out of us for taking the piss. We went home pretty pleased with the day's events – we had taken a good mob and had a good day out. But, as I said, the two mobs didn't really have a crunch meeting or even near it that day. It was just pockets of fighting here and there.

They came again in the early nineties when we were past our best and we had an even go with them by Milton Park and in Goldsmith Avenue. The numbers on both sides were again small but the fighting was quite prolonged and fierce, resulting in one of our boys getting a badly broken leg. They stood all the way as usual, and we did too, and it was a real slugging match. It's hard to see anyone really taking the piss with Boro, although it happens to every firm sometimes, but they are always up for it and well respected. They have remained a force over the country and they think as highly of us as we do of them. They took an awesome mob to Chelsea in the play-offs in '88 and walked around like they owned the place. Chelsea did get their act together but they were caught off-guard that day resulting in pitch invasions and other mayhem as Chelsea stayed down and Boro went up that year.

The facts are plain and simple with Boro: pound for pound they're very good and they will have a proper go. It must be said, though, that, if the question was asked who our best rucks have been with over the years, you couldn't include Boro in them because both mobs were always thwarted trying to get it on in any really decent numbers. We still think on our day we would have edged them, but then they would probably think that about us. One thing is for certain, they wouldn't slag us up there, even though there was no real mass action.

BRADFORD

The main turnout with Bradford was the old Fourth Division, 1979–80. It was a promotion clash, which saw a gate of nearly 10,000 as against the piss-poor turnout of 2,000-odd the season before, when Pompey and Bradford finished with exactly the same points with us nicking the last promotion place on goal difference.

The old Fourth Division was the roots of a growing fan base amongst the Pompey support who took to rucking in streets with little terraced houses and the most sort of silly places you end up going to if your team was ever unlucky enough to be in that division. Through '79–'80, we had Wigan away – trouble; Rochdale – trouble; Huddersfield – lots of trouble; Doncaster – fighting on the terraces; Newport – gangs outside; Walsall – now that used to be a nasty place.

There was a firm of Pompey lads coming together that, if you didn't know them personally, you were on nodding terms. It was probably the start of things getting more organised, particularly away travel. OK, you can say it wasn't hard going here or there, but it was the start of people going places en masse and having a ruck. Bradford, being our promotion rivals, was the main one. At the time they were like the northern version of Millwall. The first time we went to Bradford it was for a night game.

> We got up there, on Jonesy's coach – just the one coachload, no one else. Once again, we've gone straight in their end expecting trouble and there was no one there that night, and the reason was that the rugby team was playing the same night and everyone goes to rugby. We stood in their end and all the little kids were saying the boys will be along in a minute and they'll do you. We spent the whole 90 minutes expecting trouble and nothing happened. But the following year was when it really went off.
>
> The match sold out within two hours. We couldn't believe it. All sold out. Scum played Bradford the season before in a big Cup game. Scum were in the Cup and they returned 6,000 tickets. With Pompey everyone went for it. Terrific. We went by train and, when we got there, their Old Bill escorted us from the station to the ground and our own train stewards, all Jonesy's lot, Leigh Park, were all up the front. We went round the corner and there was a big piece of open ground with a pub, up a hill. The area all around it was derelict but you had this pub. And as the front of our train mob went round this corner, they all started coming out of this pub and coming down the hill. Well, that was it. The first 50 Pompey round the corner just started running up the hill, and the Bradford would have thought, Well, that's all they

got, we'll have some of this, and even more of them were coming out of the pub. And as more of them were coming out of the pub so there were more of us Pompey coming round this corner. This column of people is walking round the corner with the escort, and all of a sudden they've broken free and they're running. Everyone was running up this hill towards the pub. They did turn round, Bradford, but wallop, off they went back up the hill and Jonesy didn't stop and neither did about 200–300 Pompey.

When you got up to the ground you had to go through their bit to get in our bit, the away end. Everyone's queuing up at this away end with its two separate sections. Both sets of fans queuing up together, no trouble. Then, as soon as you get into the ground, everyone's throwing rocks at each other, and there were bricks flying. The terracing was all crumbling, literally falling to bits, and that's where we were getting the ammo from. The Old Bill were going, 'Don't throw no more' and we were going, 'All right then.'

CAMBRIDGE '84

At one game when everyone was 6.57, we all took pushbikes. That was funny as fuck actually. Someone had said that Arsenal went to Aston Villa or Birmingham and they took skateboards. So, as a laugh in the Milton, someone suggested, well, why don't we go to Cambridge and take bikes. So we turned up in the morning down the town and, I don't know, it must have been about 30 or so turned up on pushbikes. You used to be able to put your bike on the train in the guard's compartment. So we've all got these bikes piled up in this guard's compartment. We

*get to London and pulled across to sort our tickets,
then we rode across from Waterloo to Liverpool
Street, which wasn't all done up like it is now. They
didn't have all the upstairs shops done and everything.
We pulled up and we're all come on these pushbikes,
and I had an old Post Office bike with a basket on the
front and I had someone sat in the front of that. I
remember West Ham were playing at Norwich that
day and there were a few about. I remember the ICF's
Taffy, who everyone seemed to know, was on the
platform. He was lying down on a bench just
watching. And he went to me, 'This will never fucking
catch on.' I think he got there early because we
recognised Downes, a big bloke pushing 40, who used
to go to all the West Ham games. The ICF used to call
him Pompey.*

*So we turn up at Cambridge on these pushbikes and
what happened – Cambridge, obviously being a
university city, there's bikes everywhere, so everyone
just had half of them away. They weren't locked up so
people were just nicking bikes. It ended up with there
now being a firm of about 100 of us, all pedalling
down the road to the ground. And I remember we got
outside this pub and we all just chucked the bikes in a
pile. These Americans and Japanese went by and they
were all looking at these bikes. So we're all outside
this pub, you know, we've just got off the bikes,
chucked them on the pile, got a drink and come out.
All these Japanese and Americans were there,
scratching their heads. And I went up and said, 'This
is the new type of art,' so they all got out their
camcorders and their cameras and started flashing
away at these bikes all chucked in a pile. I said, 'We're
at the university and this is our art project we're*

doing.' So there's more taking photos and all that. Back in Japan, you'll probably see it on the internet one day – English art.

HEREFORD

We went to Hereford of all places towards the end of the season. Pompey were on the way down anyway and the stories were that Hereford used the SAS for security at the football ground. I just thought, There won't be any trouble there, then. We got to Hereford and I think the gate was only 3,000-odd but we end up actually being followed by a mob at Hereford's ground. This is no word of a lie – about 30 of them and about 10 of us. No word of a lie, I'm not saying that I was the bravest but we were all in front and we were walking quicker than those behind. At the top of my voice, I shouted, 'Don't run, it's all psychological,' and we've had a laugh over it ever since. And I always remember Mickey D. I don't know how he did it, but I've got this vision of it now – he's in mid-air, and he's reached someone's head in mid-air, so his whole body is like in a straight line. After that, they just legged it.

***

Hereford, I remember well one year, it was my 18th birthday, 31 August, but I had to go, it was one of the first rounds of the League Cup – I don't know what it was then, Milk Cup or whatever. We went up by coach, which we called the Boogie Bus, Eddie organised it. It was just mad on the way up there. On the way back, we ransacked a service station and the police stopped us on the motorway to try to get us to

173

pay up. We had a whip round and managed to get £4.40 or something from 52 geezers.

As for the game, on the day, there was nothing. We all got there and got off the coach. And all I can remember is one Hereford skinhead on a racing bike abusing Pompey, and Pompey just chased him up the road. What he didn't realise was that there was another mob of Pompey up the road. They got hold of him, but then they let him go and just jumped up and down on his bike. There were so many Pompey up that day, we were running into each other, just running past and the Old Bill didn't know what was going on, thinking there was two big mobs there. But it was just a nothing day, nothing happened at the ground, and I think we lost the game 3–2. But on the coach journey, we made a stop and went into some bar and thieved a statue being used as some ornament. One of the boys put this big brass statue next to the coach, then they put it in the driver's seat while the coach driver had gone for a piss somewhere. The driver came back, saw it, picked it up and went to walk off with it. As he's done it, the Old Bill have turned up thinking he's thieving this statue 'cause the people from the pub have phoned the police about it.

We kept singing Rolf Harris songs all the way home and he threatened to fucking just pack up and walk home and leave us all there. 'Tie me kangaroo down sport.'

Next stop was a service station. Everyone took liberties and had the works: three-course meals, as much as they could have and no one paid a penny. The Old Bill stopped us about 20 miles down the road. They said, 'This is very serious, lads. We'd appreciate it if you all had a whip round and paid for

the food at the service station.' That's when they got
about £4-odd out of 52 people. And, as everyone else
was nicking Mars bars and cans of Coke, that Ray
went up and put a handful of beans and fried eggs in
the pocket of his full-length leather. He got back on
the coach and got fried eggs, beans and sausages out
of his coat pocket and started eating it. He called it a
late breakfast.

Seeing the driver had put up with so much, we all
decided to have a whip round for him. So everyone
unscrewed the knobs on the reclining seats and put
them in the bucket. His job for the next day was going
around screwing on 52 knobs. He'd been screwed
twice by 52 knobs.

HUDDERSFIELD AWAY

At Huddersfield we always used to have a tear-up
every year and every year we run their side out. They
had a massive side and an end called the Cowshed but
they all used to go on the sides. So Pompey were in the
Cowshed End – about 40 of us, all in the end, so they
turned round and then there was about a 15-minute
running battle that went on. We run them out on to
the pitch at one point. A couple of Pompey got nicked,
but it went on for about 15 minutes and the players
were warming up on the pitch at the time. Terry
Brisley used to play for Pompey then, and I remember
seeing him at a game a couple of weeks after and he
said, 'Fucking hell. You lot was at it for ages. We were
warming up, we were all watching on the side.' But,
yeah, eventually we got moved out and put in the
Pompey end. But the row did go on for what was ages
in football terms. They would run and then they'd
regroup and come back, and we just sort of held this

area with some crash barriers round us so they couldn't get in too much.

***

Flares, scarves round your wrist, longer hair, and they used to wear those big zip-up cardigans with the collars. We used to play Huddersfield a lot. We played them every season for years 'cause, like our club, they fell through all the divisions. We always used to have a little go up there. I remember one year it was Christmas time, and we went up in a couple of cars. We were coming out of the ground in two carloads and we bumped straight into their mob and there was a bit of a scuffle in the car park, but we were outnumbered so we got backed off and we all ended up in one car because we couldn't get to the other car. We had to drive out of the car-park, with them all chasing us, and we were hanging out of the windows chucking stuff at them.

***

The most memorable year at Huddersfield was the season '79-'80, when the crowd was 16,500. That was big for those days. They had that great big bank of terracing. We had gone up on that minibus from the Portland pub in Southsea, a place we used to go. There was probably about three or four minibuses, and a few went on the train. We had parked up, and you didn't really bother with the pub. We saw some Pompey queuing up to get in their side and we just sort of thought we'd follow them, and we accidentally went in the Huddersfield side.

WE WENT THROUGH THE DIVISIONS

Like I say it wasn't on purpose, just everyone queuing up, but it just snowballed from there. As we got in there, there's a mob of us, a mob of them, and just went into them. We literally ran the whole ground, right the way from our end, all ran to the Cowshed, which was their end, and from the Cowshed into the other seats. And what made me laugh, you had to get over about a 7-foot fence to get out and they all climbed that. Northerners with hobnailed boots and fucking flared trousers and donkey jackets. And they were climbing out of the ground and that.

LEICESTER

Leicester hate us at Pompey with a passion. It must be said that we don't hate them like they hate us. They have a grudge with Chelsea too. I'm not saying that we don't hate them, though, and we do have a bit of needle with Leicester's firm who are known as the Baby Squad.

Our history with them started in London when we bumped into their main mob at the Cockney Pride in Covent Garden. It was 1984 and it was right when WPC Yvonne Fletcher had been shot and killed and the Iranian Embassy siege was under way. We were about 80-strong or so as we learned they were drinking in the Cockney and we proceeded to head towards the pub. It was a very good 80 that day and we were bang up for it, as we had been told through the grapevine they were one of the better Midland firms.

We took the Baby Squad by surprise as one of our main boys, who is sadly no longer with us, gassed the pub and they all came out coughing and spluttering. We steamed into them and it was a huge advantage as quite a few of them were kicked around the floor. The fighting intensified as they got their act together to a certain extent and it was without a doubt their main mob. We had them on the back foot most of the time, as the gas had definitely softened them up and the fighting continued all round Covent Garden. The running battles (with us doing the chasing) even spread to where the cordon was up around the stand-off at the Iranian Embassy. Then it was time to go as armed police were not an option and we had done Leicester anyway, so it kind of fizzled out. They did have a few game fuckers, though, and if you wanted to be generous the gas had made it difficult for them. However, if they want a rematch, no gloves and referees would be provided by us, although it must be stressed we were never a tool-happy firm like Millwall at home have become and the Scousers. We went home on a high and Leicester didn't that day.

The next time anything of note happened with Leicester was in '93, we had just blown promotion and drew them in the play-offs. The first game was at Trent Bridge. We lost 1–0 and it went off on the Bridge, but no one really had the upper hand and it was only 40 or so in total having a ruck anyway.

We also lost at Fratton Park and feelings were running high as the ground emptied – we were not going up. The police let everyone out together and the Leicester fans were really winding us up. It has to be said, as lairy as they were, some of them were not the mob but they still got knocked out as everyone was going mad. Looking back on it now, it was a bit naughty. One of our really popular boys was fighting for his life in Whitley Bay after being bashed by some Midlands tossers from Coventry after it had all gone wrong coming back from Sunderland away. Feelings ran high and were taken out on Leicester. It was sorted out as people were held back and, as the normal fans were allowed to walk back to their cars, the winding up was abruptly stopped. You can't walk down Goldsmith Avenue singing, 'We're going up, we're going up. You're not, you're not,' as we line the side of the roads, having been dumped out of the play-offs.

To set the record straight with Leicester and anyone else who is reading, women and kids have never been attacked at Fratton Park, it only happens at Molineux. Stories get blown up out of proportion and that is crap.

They came down spitting blood two years later when we played them and attacked the bookies opposite the Milton Arms just after kick-off as no one was in the pub. A handful of our boys held them off at the doors and were pretty shaken up. You have to give Leicester credit for this as they were coming to have a go at the pub – they just arrived too late.

We drew them in the Cup the next season and again they brought a good mob, this time a good 200 boys, and although no one really met head on, they certainly meant business. We were not our best in these times and, as it has been stressed time and time again in this book, we were a force earlier than these incidents, barring the Cockney Pride. That's not taking anything away from the players who were involved through the nineties but as everyone knows the likes of Leicester wouldn't have even walked down Milton Road in the early eighties. That's not being disrespectful to them because they always seem fair game, it's just that we were better on our day. The hooligan grapevine will agree to this, they haven't got our pedigree or track record. But our day is not that often nowadays while they remain active as do a lot of Midland firms. Leicester and us have got a bit of a thing about each other but when we did properly clash in '84 we came out on top.

LINCOLN

We had a little rumble with Lincoln. They had a nice little mob – only about 40 or 50 lads I think. They were all right, game. We went to Lincoln when we went up that year. Again, we went up in a minibus and their town centre wasn't pedestrianised then so they had a main road going through it. So we're driving through Lincoln, and we saw a geezer outside

*a pub, black hair and black jumper and someone's
given him the wanker sign. The traffic lights changed
to red. Suddenly the whole boozer's turned out and
they were like 50-strong and Malcolm's driving. He
said, 'Get out the van, they'll smash the van to fuck.
Don't let 'em mess the van up. It's gonna cost us
hundreds.' So we had to get out of the van. It went
off there and then, in the middle of the street, and
then the lights changed on the van so he's driving up
the road, and we're running like the clappers fighting
them off and trying to get back into the van at the
same time. At the time when it was all going off Lee
was in an escort van behind and he was trying to run
them over. Sheer madness.*

*And then we had it up by the ground with them
afterwards. When we parked up, went up by the
ground again. I remember that bloke they had, quite a
big fella, he had a black Fred Perry jumper on –
someone said after that he was one of Man United's
top boys. They were really quite game. Malc G who
used to drive us, he was a bank manager then and he
was about 21, we were about 17, 18. Once the vehicle
was parked up safe, he said, 'I ain't having that,' so we
stormed off, back down the town and we walked
smack into the middle of them again. Down by the
canal by the ground. It went off really well.*

*Also, we'd stopped at a place called Grantham on
the way up and there was a bingo hall, and they were
taking all this food in, 'cause it must have been a
bingo afternoon or something. So we watched a
woman take a tray of sandwiches in and we went up
and we nicked the other tray out the back, and we
had it in the back of the van. Someone took our
minibus number so, when we got back to the*

minibus after the game, the van was surrounded by police. We got banged up for about six hours. But the best thing was they came in and we're all laughing about it and they said, 'This isn't funny, it is a serious matter.' We said, 'All right then,' and they said, 'Who had the cheese and onion and who had the cheese?' and it was because there was about a 20p difference in the tray of sandwiches. Spraggsy had put some away, and he still had some of the sandwiches. When the Old Bill were outside he started eating them and he said to this copper, 'Do you want a sandwich, mate?' and the copper was eating a sandwich before he found out what was going on. Yeah, he was thoroughly enjoying his stolen goods and if they were cheese and onion he should be doing bird.

Then we had them in a night game a couple of years after and they all turned up with hammers and everything. There was a lot of Pompey up there. There was quite a bit of trouble but they always stood their ground, Lincoln. We had it a couple of times before the game and then after as well. We'd all come up together that time, and Fooksie would organise the train. There's a river from the station, and somehow you walk along this river and there was a bridge over the river. They had a couple of Old Bill there on the way to football. After the game, everyone came out, and there was no Old Bill there at all.

MAN CITY AWAY '84

There was a good firm of Pompey boys going to Man City. I'll tell you who we had an encounter with that day, Leeds United, who was coming on the train to London with the big blond fella when one of our

Pompey lads was going to have a fight with him. He ended coming to Pompey a few games. Gavva he was, he said he was from Doncaster but he was really from Leeds. But as we got to King's Cross Leeds were getting off the other train. The Old Bill were all there, there was a bit of a scuffle, but there was only like 30–40 of us and they didn't want to know. We had a little ruck with them, there was a little tussle, but when they realised how many there was of us they carried on going. That's when we got on the train, but half the people on the train never had tickets. There was about, I don't know, 200 of us, and when we were on the train, we're all playing cards for a gram of Charlie. Someone's put a gram in and they were playing shoot pontoon and three card brag.

There was a pot, but there was like 10 games going on, and the others were drinking whiskey. When we got to Manchester Piccadilly they had a row of police on the platform. When we'd bunked on the train, they'd thieved everything that was on the train, they cleared the buffet completely, everything. So when we got to Piccadilly, they pulled the train in and had us cornered. There was like 150–200 of us. They had buses waiting for us to take us straight to the ground, so as we got off, there was about 60 of us got through and got out, 'cause we never had tickets.

We were walking up the road, and I can remember it to this day, walking along and all of a sudden about 50 Mancs come around the corner. Oi, oi, here we go. By then, this was about half-past twelve, 12 o'clock, just before the rush hour. They came running down the road, and we just walked like we used to. As we stayed walking, they got nearer and nearer and they were running back, back and off they went. We carried on walking, and asked someone the way to Man City's football ground. There was this cleaner, with a big bucket, and he was cleaning all the steps, He said, 'You go that way, you go that way, mate.' Someone said, 'He's telling lies, I never went that way.' So they beat him up. They got his broom and beat the poor fella up. And then as we've walked down the road for about 10 minutes, a mob of about 120 come and there was only about 60 of us. Then 100 came, and we had a ruck with them for about 10 minutes, but when they could see how game we were, they went. Then we walked about another 10 minutes, quarter of an hour, and 150 came back. It was like the Alamo in the end, first of all there was, like, 60 of us and about 80–100 of them. Done them, they've gone – there wasn't even a punch thrown. They came towards us, then off they've gone. After about a quarter of an hour 80–100 of them came back, we had a ruck with them for about five minutes in the middle of the road, and now they can see that we're game as fuck. Off they go.

Now we're walking, now we're right into where it's Manchester town centre. We're in the precinct and it looks like about there's 150 coming. Someone said better get a bit of tool together, so we picked up bricks and all that, and someone, I don't remember who, said, 'Wait until it gets within 50 yards of them, hit them with everything we've got and just pile into them.' So we've hit them with everything we've got, bricks, bottles, whoof, straight into them – and then we've gone into them. They had us on our feet, and they never had the bottle to do us. There was about 150 of them and there was only about 60 of us, and they've legged it. We've walked through this town centre, thinking we've got away with this, heading towards the ground, which is only about a mile away.

Then they come round the corner, like ants and they kept on coming and they kept on coming, by which time there must have been, I don't know, 400. The word's getting round Manchester that there's a firm from Pompey. But it wasn't the whole firm, if the whole firm had got off we'd have done the business on them. There was only about 60 of us. We had a few casualties, a few slipped off, so we were down to about 50. We walked through the town centre and out in this open space and they came around this corner and there must have been about a good 400 and everyone was looking at each other thinking, What are we going to do?' Well, I said it's silly running, 'cause they're going to catch us.' We had to stand our ground. We just picked up anything we could and we were there toe to toe for about 15 or 20 minutes. There was just too many of them. You couldn't believe it, you were having a ruck with one and there was me, another one and another, and we were all like feeling we're together but then we're just going further and further down the road. We're not running, but they're just beating us back. Two Pompey fell on the floor over there, and there was 10 of them kicking them. There was me, Richie, Derek, Rob, Andy, Charlie, I think there was about six of us, and we ended up inside the doorway of Woolworths. But the people in Woolworths wouldn't undo the actual door, 'cause we were only in the doorway. By then, they had us everywhere, there was hundreds of them, and there was only 50–60 of us. But that was the time when you wanted to hear sirens. When we heard the sirens coming, that was, like, well, I could see what Dunkirk *was about. After all the rucks had finished my eye was up, I had an eye up there, a bruise on my back, where one of them hit me with a pole – I don't know if it was an iron pole or a bit of wood.*

When we actually got to the ground, and we got together, there was only about 40 of us left, a few got split up, a few went. We walked up to the ground and we had the Old Bill escorting us and, when we got to the ground, these Man City supporters were coming up to us saying, 'We've never seen a firm like you lot, you just wouldn't give in.' But after the game, when we come out the ground and we'd got the whole firm there together, like, 250–300 of us, they just didn't want to know. They just didn't want to know at all. I was really disappointed after the game 'cause I thought they'd be up for it. But they weren't. It was an easy walk back to Piccadilly, a couple of scuffles going back to the train station, but there was nothing. Nothing happened.

Funnily enough when we actually got back on to the train they were all up for it. With the northerners they all talk a good fight – we'll meet you here, we'll meet you there – but you'll turn up, and they'll never be there. And we used to get pissed off, 'cause we'd turn up everywhere we used to go. After the game, they had the opportunity – we had to walk about two and a half miles to the train station. First of all they had the same amount of us, and they didn't even want to know, then, even when there was 100 of them, they didn't really want to know. But when there was a lot of them, it was different, there was just fighting going on everywhere. You'd see old women, all the shop doors were all closed – it was like a proper battle. But it was better for us when we got out in the middle of

this road, as they were just kicking us everywhere, so
we got into a bit of cover. The road was smaller and
we could all stand toe to toe then, but they did do us.
There was just too many of them. You were frightened
to go on the floor, 'cause I saw Williams go on the
floor and they were all kicking him round the floor.
You couldn't get to him, 'cause you had to stay on
your feet yourself. As I was a big fella, I thought if I
go over I'm not going to get back up. But that went
on from when we got off the train at, like, a quarter
to twelve till we actually got to the stadium at two,
quarter-past two. So we were rucking from the time
we got off the train to the time we got there.

SHEFFIELD UNITED

I think I've been to Sheffield United about 15 times – it's like we
play Sheffield every year. The Yorkshire club has taken an
identical path to ours. It should be a big club, its support is loyal
enough yet somehow it tumbled all the way down the divisions
and ended up in the Fourth Division in '81–'82. Clubwise, our
supporters will have a lot in common over the years as our clubs
have both gone full circle.

We had a real good row at Sheffield one year, the row
Cowens describes in his book Blades Business Crew.
Pompey 6.57 crew remember it well. We turned up at
Sheffield and we all came off the train. They had a
couple of spotters out so they knew we were about.
We started walking in the direction of their ground
and we saw a pub on the way. From what I remember
it's called the Rutland and when you've been there
that many times you know all the pubs. When we got
there, there was already a big mob of Pompey
drinking, Johnny D and all that lot. So everyone feels

fucking brilliant, and there's a firm of 250–300 Pompey in this pub that's sort of halfway down. There a hill at the top called London Road that comes right down into it.

So we got in the boozer and we're all having a drink and the roar went up: 'They're here.' So we all empty out of the pub and see about 100 of them at the top of the road. A few of their front boys are coming down the road throwing bottles and bricks. Pompey went straight into them and we run 'em. All Sheffield did was come down the hill, chucked everything they had and then ran back up the hill.

So, everyone's gone back into the pub, and we're all sitting there having a drink. About a quarter of an hour, 20 minutes later, a load more Sheffield came, they'd rounded up a load more. Pompey come out of the pub, went straight into them again, run them everywhere, and we went back into the pub again. And they kept sending a geezer down, well, a kid really. He says, 'I'm not Sheffield Utd mate, I'm Rotherham.' We say, 'Oh yeah.' He says, 'I know where their lads are drinking. Do you want me to take you to them?' I say, 'No, you're all right, they know where we are. We're here. If they want it, let them come.'

Twenty minutes later, they came, even more Sheffield this time. They came down and it was like the air just filled up with bricks and everything. But I only remember John P being hit bad by anything. He got a brick on the head, and it was literally pouring with blood. But as soon as they ran out of ammo we steamed into them. Quite a few of them stayed, but most of them got on their toes. We all sort of joined in the chase, with someone running up the hill with his ghetto-blaster with him, it was quite funny to see. And

ROLLING WITH THE 6.57 CREW

I can remember being with Pete C and he had a brick in his hand and he smacked this big bloke, who must have been about 40 years old, blonde hair and a sheepskin, he put him straight down and everyone was on him like a pack of dogs. He got a kicking and then someone picked him up and let him go.

Pompey's firm did really well seeing that the northerners had the top of the hill and we were halfway down it. Eventually the Old Bill arrived to escort us down to the ground. We then went and all sat in their seats. We got chucked out. Everyone was throwing things at us and then the Old Bill came and turfed us out, put us on the sides. All their boys were on the side, and they tried to get at Pompey and Pompey were just laughing at them.

We used to have the Fareham Rockabillies that used to come with us. I remember one used to have long blond hair and always wore a jean jacket. Two of them got nicked when it kicked off before the game. They all got let out after the game, though, and they got the train back with us. There was nothing afterwards, the Old Bill had it sussed. They just walked us back to the train station.

We were just about to get on the train and we saw all the younger lot. They had a minibus so they went back out of the station to get their minibus and they had a row, it was about a 15-a-side row with Sheffield. While the Old Bill were getting us on the train, we could see this row from the station. It was going toe to toe like. So that must have been the row Cowens talks about in his book. Like I said, we played Sheffield many times and they always had lads up for it, but that was the best time in Sheffield that '82–'83 season in that pub the Rutland.

WE WENT THROUGH THE DIVISIONS

We were playing their neighbours Wednesday one season and we left Portsmouth in the early hours. The idea was to get to Sheffield and meet at the station in the morning or meet at the nearest services first then go into Sheffield to the station. About three Luton van loads of us and Sheffield were going somewhere, the United. We all started piling out of the van, they didn't even know we were there. Sheffield United came piling into the station, and they had a good mob of about 100–150 of them. Everyone just got back into the vans and beat a hasty retreat.

When Sheffield United came down to us in '82 it was the first game of the season. They'd just come back up from the Fourth Division. They brought down a massive mob, 4,000 or so. There were battles all day long, little firms all over the place. That was the game when this geezer went through the window in the Milton Arms. It just always goes off with them, you always know they've got a mob.

Now, this was the early eighties and we'd started getting a really good mob up together and it's the first game of the season – Sheffield United, they'd just won promotion and they'd bought a few players in the summer – so, you know, it's a big old game, and there was a big old buzz around the place. And Sheffield United turned out with a good mob down here. And a few of them went into the Milton Arms. I think they thought that was a bit of a mistake afterwards. I remember they got a drink and everyone was milling about saying, 'What are they fucking doing in here?' and that. Someone went up and had a word with them, and said, 'Look, have a drink and get out,' but one of them got a bit mouthy, so he got smacked and the next thing they were just getting smashed all over the place. I remember one went through the window and another one of their lads ran out of the pub – it was like he didn't know what to do – and he ran on to the crossing outside the pub and a car just went straight into him and he flew up in the air. So he came back down to earth with a bump there.

Pompey always look forward to playing Sheffield, particular if it's United. They've got their lads and their show for you.

SHEFFIELD WEDNESDAY

Let's be frank here, we don't exactly rate Sheffield Wednesday, particularly when you take into account the size of their city and the fact they do have a mob. This is because of their showing at Fratton Park or rather the lack of it, and we're talking about their boys here. We've played them a few times and whatever our number we've gone there and made a show, and it would be us taking it to them. The accounts we give don't have us having it all our own way. As we said, Wednesday have a mob like most teams do, but you need to play them at theirs to find out.

Sheffield Wednesday, away '78, and we drew 0–0 and Figgins saved a penalty. I think it was '78 and we were in their Spion Kop End, about 20 of us. I had a sheepskin on and I was fucking shivering. Couldn't have been no more than 20 of us, in a little huddle. Twenty, maybe 25 of us, stick together, with 5,000 fucking Sheffield Wednesday around us. They had a mush called Sammy, who was the leader, and they walked around going, 'Sammy, Sammy'. Sheffield Wednesday's whole ground was going, 'Sammy, Sammy', when this mush came in.

***

Wednesday Away '83. 'Cause we were used to playing smaller city clubs we were looking forward to this one. This was one of our top-of-the-list-type things. We caught the usual three minutes to seven train, the 6.57 train to Waterloo, although quite a few of ours caught the earlier train, 'cause there were never any guards so you could get up to London for nothing and just pay for your ticket from there. But then we were on the student railcard so we were getting everything for half price. There was no trouble at Waterloo but we were aware it could happen. But we were always so early and we met up with the other firms from Pompey and the ones from Devizes, Chippenham, Reading, so the crew almost doubled once it got to Waterloo.

There was 70–80 on the train, maybe more, but a few were making their way up on minibuses that day. We were all in Armani, Head ski-coats – typical casual firm of the time. A lot of the Old Bill had sussed us out over the previous couple of years, and we were aware that they had radioed through and there would probably be an escort for us once we arrived in Sheffield. So, as we came into Sheffield, someone pulled the communication cord about half a mile from the station and everyone just leaped off the train and was running down the track leaving the rozzers on an empty train.

We kept on running down the track until we found a hole in the fence into some scrap metal place, we went through and just found the nearest pub where we could re-gather and keep a low profile for an hour. There was a good 60–70 of us got off the train, so there may have been a few more than I thought on that train. Anyway we decided to head towards the

*town centre. As we got to the top of the town's centre
precinct, this mob just ran at us, Sheffield Wednesday.
We had it toe to toe in the town centre and they
backed off – same sort of numbers as us but they were
retreating to a pub on the left, set back, and they were
all holed up in there. We were stood outside, throwing
punches at them in the doorway, and they were
cowering in the pub doorway when someone let off a
flare at them.*

*Just a bit of fun really, you know 6.57, we thought
nothing of it really until I then heard someone whisper,
'Ginger, Ginge.' I said, 'What's up?' 'Hundreds, look
we've got hundreds of the cunts.' I look round and, shit,
there's about five of us left. For some reason this geezer
– and I won't name him – felt the need to take everyone
back up the road away from the pub, probably 'cause of
that flare going off. Big mistake 'cause by then it's made
all the Sheffield Weds geezers come out of the pub. By
then, they were coming in all directions, and we had to
join up with the others fast – they were coming from
everywhere, running. We were having it but we got
done, we got chased through the town centre and it got
really wild then. It pissed me off that, people were
running, even though we were outnumbered we should
have made a stand and a few of us did want to. It can
really grate on you. We never used to get done and we
wouldn't have got done if it weren't for a certain person
who didn't want to be there. The really annoying thing
was, just as we got away all the Somers Town boys came
up. They'd spotted us and got out of their van, but not
soon enough. Because all the Old Bill came up too –
game over. I just felt if only they had been there a few
minutes earlier.*

When we got to the ground, we couldn't get away

*from the Old Bill, so we split up into small groups.
Then a few of us got away and met a small mob of
theirs, just had it here and there, a few skirmishes
around the ground. We did have a good Pompey mob
up there, but the only aggro in the ground was with
the Old Bill. We had this feeling that they thought we
were soft southerners, so we'd wind the Old Bill up
and take piss out of 'em.*

*After the game, most of us got herded on the train.
Normally we went back to London for a beer. Some
of us used to go to Covent Garden, Soho, maybe nick
a few bottles of nitro, run riot a little bit, three, four
of you having a bit of fun. A couple of times we ran
into Marilyn, the pop singer, in his car and we were
rocking his car. We nicked that Mark Almond's hat
once. Then we'd hang around at Waterloo East, have
a few beers and wait for Millwall.*

STOCKPORT

*In 1980 we went to Stockport away on a Monday
night. There was about 20–30 of us all went up by
train. When you go to Stockport, there's a pub literally
at the top of the station. We were in this pub when it
filled up from outside with gangs of men. The pub just
turned into a big ruck, as they'd come through the other
bar and just came up in between the two bars. But the
funny story from that night was, Storm said to me years
later, 'Ray, you caught me over one, at Stockport.
You've made me stand in front of you.' I had to place
him so I've got him dead right, and then I swung a
punch at the bloke in front of him, knocked him down
and Storm's got nicked for it, which you can laugh
about now. I'll always remember that Monday night.
We went up by train and it took all night to get back as*

well, as you can imagine. We got back to Euston at about one-ish and there was a gang of us walking through London to get the half-five train home.

* * *

The other time in Stockport, the Friday night one, once again it was probably at the peak of people going by vans from different areas. Afterwards, people were calling it the battle of Coronation Street, 'cause all around Stockport is like in Coronation Street. *It hasn't even changed now. It was rows of terraced houses with alleyways, a bit like it is round Man City's ground. Everyone was just fighting afterwards. The funny thing was I had a mate called Lee, a little bloke, and he'd gone the next day to watch the Manchester United and West Brom match, classic game sort of thing back then, and he's going to that, planning to stay overnight. On the train up he could hear people in the seats behind him going, 'We went to Stockport last night, they're fucking mental. Pompey load of skinheads, they're all fucking mental, all they want to do is fight.' And he's trying to keep quiet in the seat in front of them, you know. But that was just a weird night, Friday night, Stockport, everybody went and everybody seemed up for it.*

* * *

Stockport, it was hilarious when we made a more recent trip. There was only about 15 of us who'd gone up on the train. We came out of the ground with my young boy. He said, 'Dad, there's a couple of blokes over there with Burberry caps on and that.' So we clocked them and carried on walking, and then we walked past a pub and there were about 10 of them outside, all dressed up and everything. So, we caught up with the others and I said, 'They've got a bit of a firm back there, I reckon they're looking for it.' Everyone's like laughing at Stockport. Suddenly we've heard, 'Come on then, Pompey.' We turned round and they're running up the road. There was about 15 of us, about equal sides. So we just, like, spread out across the road and we went, 'Well, come on then,' and they went, 'Come on then.' It was like that, you know, and we were all like laughing at them and then they said, 'Get rid of the kid,' and he went, 'What did you say? Fuck off you northern mug', and they all sort of stepped back. Giss was stood in the middle of them laughing and they're going, 'What's up with your mate?' and then they went, 'Ah it's all camered up.' [there were closed circuit TV cameras everywhere]. But we've got a geezer that goes with us now – Aidie F who was married into a gypsy family and everything like that. Now Aidie is a big old lump but a really nice bloke, bit of a gypsy like. Suddenly there's him and Stockport's biggest geezer and they're squaring up to each other but they're going, 'C'mon' to each other and taking turns to give a little push at each other. I was holding the wall, laughing in hysterics. I said, 'Are you two going to hit each other in a minute or what?' Still nothing actually happened until we went to get on the minibus and then one of their geezers ran forward and Dave just went smack. Straight on his arse.

Later we met with some Stockport at the England game. They said, 'Who are you?' and I said, 'Pompey.' They said, 'Oh, we had it with you the other week',

and we said, 'Who's the boy who went on the floor?'
They said, 'Oh he always charges in and ends up on
the floor.'

SUNDERLAND

At the end of the '92–'93 season Pompey put a tremendous run of results together and were chasing automatic promotion. Our last away game was Sunderland. Paul Walsh was God at that time and on a warm afternoon we took 8,000 fans to a packed Roker Park. A lot of the lads had decided to go to Whitley Bay for the weekend and had checked into various B&Bs for a beer-filled weekend. A win virtually guaranteed promotion. A defeat was unthinkable.

Although things were a bit different off the pitch all over the country – the aggro had undoubtedly subsided – the big games tend to bring all the old faces out. The police must be praying that Pompey are never involved in a play-off final in Cardiff as even today we would all turn out for it.

On 1 May 1993 disaster struck on the pitch. We got hammered 4–1, Walsh and Guy Butters were sent off and the other results left us a mountain to climb. We never made the summit, with Leicester beating us in the play-offs. On top of that, Sunderland were safe from relegation. The mood turned ugly the minute the gates opened as the first 50 Pompey steamed straight into the waiting Mackems, backing a larger mob of them away. Everyone got together and ran down a hill to a roundabout where Sunderland were regrouping and it went off again. We came out on top, with the Salisbury lot doing their usual good business and one of Paulsgrove's main boys going ballistic into a pack of them on his own. There were a couple of Sunderland spark out on the floor as it ended. No one went to town on them though, which was surprising considering the circumstances and the scoreline. It obviously hadn't gone down well, though, as the season after, when we didn't turn out, eight of our lot were nearly killed by 200 revenge-seeking Mackems, and had to get taxis to Newcastle to vacate the area. They were understandably shaken up and relieved to escape.

Some of our top players were staying with friends in a little village called Shildon that weekend, which is half Newcastle and half Sunderland. They brought their hosts along for the day to watch the game and one of the Shildon lads copped a punch in the mouth during the mêlée. Our mates couldn't apologise enough. Everyone went back to Whitley Bay that night and it was going off all over the place. Our good Zulu friends from Birmingham even came for the piss-up. But the night turned nasty as one of our very good friends and one of the most popular lads on the football scene was severely beaten up by some bottleless cowards from Coventry. A few of our firm had been drinking late in a small hotel and a bit of piss-taking had got out of hand and the rest is history. We were all just so relieved that he pulled through. Some gas had been let off and he had wandered outside where they'd done him.

It was quite a bad weekend all round really and everybody was glad to get home. Rumours have circled since that Pompey went to Coventry last season and caused absolute mayhem. It has been said that the trouble was organised because of Whitley Bay. The hooligan grapevine and the internet have been rife with accusations about it, blaming a revenge attack. It was the first time we have played at Coventry since this incident, but it is also known that the blokes who did it were not part of their football mob. There is no specific reason why it happened, it's just that once a season everybody seems to pick a game to go to. Coventry was that game. And it was just coincidence.

TOTTENHAM

We first came across the Yids in a pre-season friendly at our place in 1980. We knew they would come so we had a good 150 waiting on the Milton End for them. As expected roughly 60–70 of them filed in, all boys. The tension mounted as we were all around. A big black lad of theirs shouted, 'Come on, Tottenham. We'll smash this shit into the ground.' Just after this they scored and without hesitation everyone steamed into them from everywhere. We battered them and chased them down on to the pitch, where they were put into the lower South Stand for their own protection. They were a sorry sight as they were shepherded away.

We all took the piss as we had well spanked them, and they had a hard time after the game too. In fairness to them, I don't think they were aware of the reception they would get at Fratton and obliged us with much better numbers next time. Any Spurs who were present will remember this drubbing.

Next time up we drew them in the Milk Cup away in '85–'86 and we took an absolute army of 10,000 for a night game. As always happened when we took too many everyone was disorganised and the wrong type of people were there. So-called hard nuts from the town, who weren't really clued up on the strategy of football rucking, were present and given a caning by the Yids.

Disaster struck in the murky ethnic shithole that is the Seven Sisters Road. We were all over the place as Tottenham set about us after the game. They seemed well organised and well up for it and we got well and truly legged. We kept trying to regroup but they had their foot hard down and we ended up as a shambles. It was so dark everyone got separated and there just seemed to be hordes of them. They saw us off that night and we hold our hands up there. The Yids had given us payback. You can't win them all.

That match was a draw, however, so we all swore to get them back and mobbed up all over the town, waiting on the night of the replay. News spread that two coachloads of Yids were drinking in the Traveller's Rest in Somers Town a couple of hours before kick-off, so about 60 of us set off from the Peel.

Everyone was collecting bricks and bits of wood as we trotted towards Somers Road. It was a top buzz as we made it right up to the doors and proceeded to destroy all the plate-glass windows in the pub with them inside. A couple who came out got a dig and as the missiles rained in they looked completely shocked. We had taken them by surprise.

As the sirens wailed nearby, we all did one back into the flats as the police pulled up, but what the Yids didn't bank on as they came flying out of the boozer well tooled up was the strictness of Pompey Old Bill. They only made the bingo hall at the top of Bradford Junction before they were rounded up. Ninety-five of them all got nicked and not one of us. They couldn't believe it as they were all loaded into the meat wagons. They hadn't really done anything as we had instigated it and all they were doing was arming up to retaliate. They must have been well upset, but we laughed like fuck, and they got bound over in court the next morning. Sorry about that!

We played them in the old First Division in '87–'88 and there were some skirmishes on the tube, but nothing to speak of and the next time it went off with them was in the FA Cup in '91 at ours. They brought 6,000 that day. It was the year Gazza was unplayable, but he was brilliant at our place that day as he scored the equaliser in their 2–1 win. About 30 of our lot went over on to the pitch and straight into the Yids behind the Milton End goal. The Old Bill moved them out but it went off for a bit before they did. It looked really funny, such a game little crew having that much front. Mind you, it was just as well they got moved out, as it was coming on top for them.

That's about it with Tottenham – we have done them and they have done us. We hear they are just about the top firm around at the moment along with Man Utd maybe. We also know quite a few of their chaps and they are decent blokes. You could always guarantee a ruck with Spurs and that will never change, certainly in a different league to Arsenal off the pitch. We have good memories and a lot of time for the Yid Army.

VILLA

In front of a good old crowd at Fratton Park, I can remember Pompey were cruising, they were 2–0 up with 10 minutes to go. It was a League Cup game with Aston Villa – called the Milk Cup at the time. We thought, Oh, here we go. Then Villa scored and then they scored again. It was 2–2. All of a sudden we'd got a replay at Villa in a mid-week night game. Everyone was quite excited about the game and the ground, because we hadn't been there before. We went in two Luton vans, hired from Southern Self Drive. We'd decided to change our routine of getting the trains to avoid the escort waiting for us every time we got off the train.

So it was all organised, bunk off work and leave from outside the Air Balloon. We used to call these vans Space Vans. They had roll-up backs where you could pull the shutter up and down. We just used to pull the shutter three-quarters down to get a bit of air in. The Milton Arms had one with about 30–40 in the back. Leigh Park crammed in the other, and we had back-up. They were a few old transits that could only do about 40–50 miles an hour, and we always used to have to go slow to let them keep up with us. It was a good old firm of everyone, you know, Stampshaw, Eastney, a few from the Havelock, everybody messing about and having a laugh travelling up in convoy.

We arrived there a good hour before kick-off, after

stopping for a drink 20 miles outside Villa. Somehow we managed to park on some car park right outside their end and we all steamed off the bus. But to my knowledge not a lot happened before the game. It was all to come afterwards. We were all put in a side with seats that was to the left of the main core of Pompey fans. We all started taking an interest in the football, and it was a great game of football, a really good thriller that included an unforgettable Kevin Dillon-chipped goal, and I think it went into extra time. We got done 3–2 in extra time. That's when things were just starting to boil over.

We came out the ground and the police just let everyone mingle in with everyone and it was the first time it'd really happened to us, 'cause we were escorted everywhere in them days. So you try to stay together the best you can, try and stay with the main boys. There must have been a good 300–400 of us, and we were 10- or 20-deep. We never used to run, we used to walk. They heard us coming down the road, chucking bricks, bottles and all that and we just kept on walking. Then we just charged straight up, and the fighting erupted immediately. I would say at least 300 Pompey ran towards the Holt End as the Holt End came out. Then, without hesitation, everyone went in. Police pushed the Pompey fans back. I remember a fan driving across and immediately the windscreen was put through with a concrete block. We were near a row of terraced houses outside the ground when mounted police came in and people were trying to pull one of the coppers off his horse. There was sporadic fighting outside the Holt End with the Villa fans – not really their firm but mainly people coming out the ground and mouthing off. Fighting was short-lived and nothing too major, except the police vans, and everyone dispersed back to the Lutons.

Back in the Luton vans we made our way back to the motorway – people were sitting on the back of the van and dangling their legs, others used to stand on the sides – it looked like the minibus of the Baldies against the Warriors – hanging out the van.

We must have been two or three miles away from the ground and from out of nowhere came Derek and Eddie being chased by a load of Villa and they looked quite panicked and flustered. 'Come on, there's a load of Villa, there's a load of Villa.' Both vans emptied immediately so you are talking 60–70 Pompey and we were confronted by at least 100 Villa. They were older than us with a few in their mid-thirties at the front. The average age of our crew would have been between 20 and 22, a few 24–25 but predominantly 20–22. We got organised and went straight in. It went off straight away. We were going downwards and, although there were more of them, they had a massive disadvantage 'cause the hill was quite steep. The battle raged and we backed them away. And when they could see we weren't going to stop, they just turned, they were on their toes and then we could run them. It was going off through the streets, there was a great big wasteland with buildings, like a bombsite, where they kept stopping and chucking bricks. But what actually happened, one of the Lutons got smashed up and it never came home, the actual Luton actually never come home. Another thing I'll never forget, we had these flares. Walking down the road and as they were coming towards us, we were letting the flares go and they just didn't know what hit them. It was just mayhem, and we had them all running down the road.

About 50–100 yards to the crossroads, they decided to make a stand and it was pretty evenly matched – no one really gave an inch. Again there was 100 of them and 50–60 possibly 70 of us. Anyway, there was more of them than us. When we backed them to the crossroads a car screeched up and there was a bloke and his bird in it, fighting. They just jumped out, left the lights on, music blaring – I swear it was Yazoo or Alison Moyet or something like that – and left the car doors open and the keys in it. Villa were now in full retreat because a couple of them had got quite cut up – which ended in all of us getting nicked – and they were 20–30 yards down the road. So we got into the motor and turned it towards the Villa who were legging it to a pub at the bottom of the hill to get away from us.

Just as the last Villa fan's got into the pub, one of us – I won't say who – decided to drive the car straight into the pub. There was this mental crashing, clanging noise as the car went into the double doors. I swear if he had hit it a couple of seconds earlier he would have crushed a couple of people to death. He never was a very careful driver even at the best of times. Everyone looked at each other with an 'Oh my God, what has he done?' expression on their faces. We all burst out laughing and ran back to the Lutons as fast as we could. It was an absolute classic. We lasted all of five minutes before we were rounded up. Don't forget there was two people stabbed that night, two Villa supporters. On the way back they confiscated one of the Lutons 'cause the other was smashed up. We were arrested en masse. The game was finished for us well and truly. The Old Bill rounded us up, tapes, fingerprints, names, everything. Two days of fruitless questioning, and ID parades when everyone kept

*making faces. We were all released without charge
and arrived back in town on the Thursday, tired and
in need of a good kip. It was a cracking day out.*

Football violence was in vogue. Everyone wanted to do
something, everyone wanted to be part of it. Portsmouth and the
surrounding area had a particularly strong pull. I think if you get
1,000 people in a tense situation like a football match, the
inevitable will happen but particularly in Portsmouth. They made
their mark in the eighties. It was a youth cult thing that seems to
have gone away now – a sort of fashion that came along with all
the clothes. Apart from a few hardcore people it seems to be a lot
more politically motivated nowadays than it was then. Nowadays
with CCTV and the powers the police have, with attitudes being
a bit different, and possibly drugs, it seems to have calmed down.
But in certain areas, maybe south London, Cardiff, there's a lot of
people with nothing to do and a lot of angry people. Local kids
want to come out and throw bricks at the police.

Going back to the football casual days, each town's police
force did its own thing. You never had that national pooling of
resources, like you get today with all the NCIS [National
Criminal Intelligence Service] stats intelligence. I mean they had
their trusty old hoolie van out everywhere (you can see a photo
of this in that excellent pictorial book titled *A Casual Look*).
They used the odd helicopter up in the skies and got wise to us
with the use of police spotters. Even so it was never as
sophisticated as some of the methods tried and used today. For a
start that old hoolie van was as subtle as a Trojan horse and, for
all the work out in the field, it was back at the house of justice
that it was decided whether the stuff that shamed the streets of
Britain could ever be contained.

So we, the authors, thought we couldn't complete the story of
the Pompey outrage at Villa without giving this account, looking
at it through the eyes of a 6.57 member who wasn't involved in

the main rows, yet still had a bird's-eye view whilst handcuffed up out of it. It's just another account that shows when having you're having a mad, mad day at football there's never ever just one story – it all depends how you see it from where you're standing. This is Steve's account:

I got back to the car park, and made my way back to the van. Everyone would be there and we'd do what we're gonna do from there. So, I've got back there, and none of them's there. There was me and a couple of others, and obviously the Villa had seen us waiting by the van and it's ended up going off. I've ended up having a fight in the car-park, me and a mate I'm with. We were both chased and arrested by the police. But, unbeknown to us when we were arrested, the rest of our boys from the two vans and the transit were out on the street in Aston Villa's area. They were having it, you know, fighting with what was a lot of black lads there. I think it was like an estate – and they came out. Well, anyway, me and my friend was chained to the floor in a meat wagon, you know, an Old Bill van. We were chained to the floor in handcuffs, and we couldn't see out the windows, but we knew we were chasing our boys in the meat wagon.

I don't know if they were short of police out that way or what, but they were chasing them with us in the van. And we heard them say, 'There's the one with the sleeves, there's the one with the tattoo,' and it was night, so he must have had a T-shirt on. You obviously knew what was going on out there, there'd been fighting, there'd been chasing, and now we were chasing them. With that, more people were getting nicked. They decided to take us back to the police station.

ROLLING WITH THE 6.57 CREW

I've gone in the police station, one of the first ones to be brought in – I didn't know that everyone else was going to get arrested later on. I'm standing in the doorway waiting to be booked in at the police station. This Villa geezer's come up and asked me the time. I told him to fuck off, and, as I've said that, he's chinned me. So I've started, like, rucking with him in the police station. They pulled us apart and all that, then they slung me in the cell and that was the last I heard for about three hours. Then they pulled me out and booked me in. While they were booking me in I could see the names up on the board and I'm looking down the list. I've seen name after name after name after name – all the boys that I know. Then they put me in another cell with some Pompey boys who I knew. They told me all what'd been going on, the stories and all that. There was stabbings, there was bricks thrown at people, and they even went on to say that one bloke got stabbed three times, but he got up, and he was saying to all the Pompey, 'Is that the best you can do to me?' and all that. And as he's said that, he's turned round and a wall brick's hit him straight in the head – KO'd him. Well, maybe no now, but thought that was pretty amusing at the time. With that, we were locked up all night.

We were taken to Birmingham New Street, locked up. It was like being in prison. The courthouse was like a mini-prison: it had three landings. It was really old-fashioned. Their court building joined to a police station and going in there, it was a frightening place. I mean, it didn't really daunt me, 'cause I'd been in DC and youth custody and prison and that, but to other people who hadn't tasted that before it would be a daunting place.

Rob Silvester, author of the *6.57 Crew*.

Inset: We got the club crest in this book somehow! Thank you Harry's Gang.

Above: The original Pompey skins, Blackpool 1968.

Below: Blackpool 1969. Portsmouth supporters returned with close-cropped hair and adopted this peculiar style of dress. As the *Daily Mirror* investigation told the world, the new skinhead fashion was sweeping the nation.

On the way to Leeds in the early '80s, when someone pulled the emergency cord at Wakefield.

Inset: Stoke away. All visiting supporters pass the graveyard on their way to the ground.

Above: The Eastney boys in 1981.

Below: When the station clock strikes 6.57, we're rolling, picking up more lads on the way until the 6.57 Crew is out in full force.

Above: The Nutty Air Balloon lot, inside Fratton Park at the end of the 1980 season.

Below: A day trip to Bournemouth, '82–'83 season.

Scenes from 1980. *Above left*: Bradford away. A decade on and the Pompey skins were at the height of music and fashion.

Above right: Barnsley away.

Below: Halifax away.

Above: As we were: a young casual firm that stayed together as we went through the divisions.

Below: We're on your manor. 6.57 Crew daring any Sheffield Wednesday to front up, '83–'84 season.

May 1983, Pompey clinch Division Three at Plymouth. *Above*: A police helmet goes flying through the air behind the goal at one end, while fans invade the pitch at the other. *Middle*: Police rush on to the pitch to try to stop more fans joining in. *Below*: Too late, all on.

I was locked up with a couple of boys who were Pompey boys but they weren't what you'd call our group, the hardcore, or whatever – they weren't 6.57, but I did know them. We were talking, obviously they were banged up and that. Anyway, one chap's gone up in front of me, never been in trouble in his life. They took him up first, and he's come down and he was a bit upset. I said, 'What happened?' and he said, 'I got 28 days,' like that. I went, 'Fucking hell.'

That was the first time he'd ever been in trouble. So, in my infinite wisdom, I was thinking, What do I do here, 'cause I'm going to get more than his 28 days. I decided to plead 'not guilty'. So I went up, and they put me in this court and it was like the judge was looking down at me. They were up above me and I was like in a cage. It was all old wood and everything – really antique court building. Anyway, I pleaded 'not guilty' and they decide to adjourn it and give me bail. So obviously I was released and bunked the train home – I actually got caught bunking the train home and was prosecuted for that.

I'd been bailed to appear back in court for a further date. But in between I'd been arrested for something else in Portsmouth and was put on remand. I was told to write a letter to the clerk of the justice to Birmingham magistrates' court telling them my predicament. I did this from Winchester Prison – the Doll's House it was called at the time, because of all the young offenders it housed. Well, I never heard any more but about 15 years later I had a knock on the door early one Tuesday morning. It was Portsmouth Police arresting me for non-appearance in court for that offence 15 years before. I was taken to Birmingham, the charges were read out to me and because of the length of time that had passed, they gave me a conditional discharge. No fine, nothing. I just had to think of that fella in front of me, never been in trouble, 28 days. I would probably have got three months back then. So I was quite pleased with that and had a little chuckle.

WEST HAM

There's no disputing the credentials of West Ham but we have seen very little combat with them amongst other Premiership teams. It is very close between them and Millwall who we would consider to be the top firm in the country and that is the opinion of everyone in Portsmouth. West Ham are not really that active any more and it is hard to draw comparisons with teams now when they'd all but fucked it off by the mid- to late eighties. It's the same for Pompey to a degree – there can be no argument that our main years as the 6.57 crew were '81–'86.

In the early eighties, it was meant to be just about impossible to get a result off the pitch at Upton Park, but we were never given the opportunity to go. The long walk from the tube to the South Bank turnstiles would have been an interesting one. One thing is for certain, we would have gone in big numbers just like we did to Millwall on every occasion. We raised our game to the best and West Ham would have been no exception.

The only real time we had any incident to speak of with the ICF and Shakes and his Under 5s was a home pre-season fixture in the early eighties.

Everyone was waiting in the Milton Arms when they turned up, steel flashing and bouncing across the road. Some of our cream were present and it went off outside the boozer with roughly 30-a-side on the Pelican crossing. One of our boys launched his pushbike into them, doing serious damage to one of their faces, who for years would show his scars to any Pompey who would listen, swearing vengeance.

In the ensuing battle, the Under 5s went to work with Stanley knives and, as our firm backed away to avoid the blades, one of our lads was badly cut, mainly on the arms as he tried to fend off the blows.

We were not happy with the way things had panned out, but the Old Bill turned up and dispersed everybody. We regrouped and our numbers swelled. Everyone was furious at the tactics employed. There are no rules in gang fighting but some of this firm of Pompey, known as the Eastney boys, would fancy winning a straightener with anyone. They had flown the flag for our city in some style on many occasions, notably once seeing off a good mob of Millwall on and around Waterloo station in May '82 and another classic moment was when 15 of them ploughed into three coaches of Denton's finest, along Goldsmith Avenue causing temporary disorder to the Arsenal ranks until they got their act together to stand and fight. ICF face Andy Swallow and a couple of Under 5s came walking back over without a care in the world after the rucking had stopped. They were very cocksure and wanted to know how to arrange some more action. Swallow had been well game in the previous fracas.

One particular Eastney lad and their top boy of this era took real offence at this and sized Swallow up as he argued with our firm. Swallow was flippant as he shrugged his shoulders and asked what the fuck we expected. It didn't cut any ice as the Eastney lot were tight-knit and still are to this day. He had made a mistake as the rulebook was out the window. The punch that hit him was an absolute cracker. SS, the

Eastney boy, had caught him with a gem of a right hook. Well, what the fuck did HE expect? That punch is legendary in these parts. Even though he had Old Bill all around him at the time and therefore wasn't perhaps expecting it, he's still a main face for the ICF and that will do for us. We were still not happy about the blades and spent the rest of the night trying to get it on, to no avail.

WOLVES

There was that time at Wolves, which is one I would personally rather forget but receiving nine months says I won't. It was the year Wolves got relegated and we just missed out on promotion to division one on goal difference. We all went up to Wolves in the cars, and their Tubeway Army or whatever they call themselves was supposed to be waiting for us, so we got there really early in the morning.

The crowd for that game was less than 8,000. We had about 1,500 Pompey there. It was still the old Wolves, the old Molineux then. They had one new stand and we were sat in the back of there. There was a bit of trouble in the morning, we had been into the town and had a few little scraps by some pubs and stuff. But when we were in the ground, sat in these seats, a couple of Wolves fans got a message to us. They said if you want it after the game by the subway, like. So we were there listening to these Wolves, and they was all cocky and everything.

So after the game we said, 'Oh, we'll walk round to the subway, then. Some of us went along the top way into the subway and some went along the bottom, which meant one group got too far ahead. Wolves went to steam this lot and the rest of us came round the back, did like a pincer movement on them. We got them trapped in the middle and it was going off. Surprisingly there weren't really a lot of them, but I always remember, me, Derek, Richard and someone else, we got miles ahead of everyone else. We were chasing them and I remember we chased some Wolves further on down the road and Richard had a flare gun, one of those light, hand-held ones – you pull the trigger and it shoots out a distress flare. It was a bit of a 6.57 trademark because the lads working in the dockyards could get them off the ships and everything. So we've got these Wolves running and we're firing this fucking flare gun at them and these flares are going off everywhere.

We were getting further out so we just turned round and, like, Pompey were starting to go back. We got back up to the top of the subway, and everything had calmed down, you know, the police were there nicking everyone. And as we got back to our car, the Old Bill just swooped. What had happened was one of the Wolves geezers had got separated from the others. They got hold of him and dropped him over the top of the subway on to the bottom. When we got nicked, there must have been about 80 in the cells. And then gradually it was getting less and less until there was just me and Philsy left. They kept us in till Monday. Well, I got charged with wounding with intent first. I went to court a couple of times, and I got committed to Crown Court. The day I went to Crown they dropped the charge to affray and my barrister said to just go with affray, you know, plead guilty to it. So, I got nine months for that – something that started out as something of an invitation.

ROLLING WITH THE 6.57 CREW

SUMMARY

It must be stressed when reading this book that the stories remembered will always have a slant towards Pompey and the 6.57 crew. Everyone has been done or chased at football and different firms will have a different account of a particular incident they have encountered with a rival mob. You can only recount a story as you saw it. Cardiff may think they had a result at Fratton station when they were running up behind 100 baton-wielding riot police. We don't think they did. But, if the boot was on the other foot, you can see why they would see it like that. There have been many instances of this all over the country for the past 30 years or more. It can be mightily frustrating when this sort of thing happens. If you are a top boy or run with a top 10 crew – or have done in the past – you can probably count on the fingers of one hand the times you have been well and truly turned over. We at Portsmouth fit into this bracket as we are in the upper echelons of football gangs in the country and this is recognised by all.

We are not the best but we have fought the best and had results against the best. Not bad for an isolated port on the south coast. Every thug who followed any team with a top crew would always relish the thought of Pompey home and away in the season. The aggro was always guaranteed.

There have been times when Pompey mobs have been chased all over the place. Not the cream Pompey mobs though – the times then rapidly decline, just like it does for all the other top firms from certain clubs. If you're running with the top 30–50 lads you are usually on safe ground and will nearly always get the victory if the right people are there. If you respect your opposition you've already lost, that's why we never respected anyone in those days – we just got off the train to have a fight. That is why we earned our good name – 6.57.

Turning Up When Not Playing

OTHER PEOPLE'S GAMES

There have been a number of occasions when Pompey games have either been called off or everyone has decided to get together and go to a different fixture for a punch-up. This was evident in the seventies and eighties before the police intelligence put a stop to it by being able to identify known troublemakers from different clubs. For example, in the seventies, 100 of us would all filter through in dribs and drabs into the enemy's end and, if the clueless local police said anything to us, a pathetic put-on accent would more often than not be enough to get by. You can imagine how easy it was to turn up to a different match with no scarves or colours, also in those days you could guarantee a fight just about anywhere. Everyone was at it.

In 1978 we arrived at Swindon on three coaches to find our game had been called off due to a waterlogged pitch. We were pissed off because we always went up the Town End and into their pub at the back of it – they always had a go and it was a good day out. Southampton were at home to Millwall so without hesitation we were off to the Dell – 150 Pompey boot boys en route for what promised to be very spicy entertainment and the talk was of Harry the Dog, F-Troop, Treatment and the Halfway Line Mob. It was a year after the first Panorama *in '77.*

We arrived and went straight into the Archers Road End where it was half Southampton and half Millwall. The sky-blue surgical masks really did exist and the line of Old Bill between them fell apart as we were sussed, and pandemonium broke out as everyone just started hitting everyone – it was seventies terrace fighting at its best. We gathered and took a slice of the terracing and, to be honest, they both wanted a piece of us. We were at the top as we were last in, and this was a huge advantage for us as the Archers was quite steep in some parts like the Milton Road. It could have been a different story if we had been stuck at the bottom. To be fair to Scum, for once they were having a good go at us too – this was in the days of Dougal and the Warrens boys and they had a few who could have a ruck. The fighting was sporadic and went on during the game, mainly in the second half. To make matters worse for Scum, Millwall won and dumped them out of the FA Cup. We were eventually moved out towards the end and put back on the coaches. A great day out was had by all and the 150 were a credit to Pompey.

***

Brighton vs Chester is an unusual fixture and God only knows what a coach full of Pompey were doing there after another postponement. This was also in '78. They had it on top with a mixture of Brighton and some Londoners on a beano after the game as the coach was badly attacked. There was a classic moment as Portsea Henry charged off the coach with big platform shoes on scattering a load of young Brighton fans in the bus station where the coach was parked – this was a few minutes before the big boys turned up.

***

Most Pompey boys would at one time or another go on the train to London to watch a game, a few would go to West Ham, Spurs or Chelsea. We went to West Ham twice and, even if you had a claret and blue scarf around your wrist, you would get asked the time about five times between the tube and the ground.

We went to the Forest game where they got massacred from all sides and it's true they did get sent packing. Everywhere the Old Bill tried to put them they got battered. It was in the days of the South Bank chant 'The West Ham United will never be defeated', and it was a horrible place to be an away fan. The other game was Watford in the FA Cup quarter-final. You had to feel sorry for them as loads of half-arsed boot boys came past the market singing, 'We're the Barmy Watford Army', and it was lights out as they were destroyed with frightening ease.

The train back from Waterloo was always funny as all the out-of-town London football fans would group up against each other, and it was amusing to see them all change sides as their allies got off at different stations.

***

Another good punch-up was at Coventry vs Aston Villa in '81, the year Villa won the League. They had 12,000 there, and they had also taken Cov's end. We had decided to go there after our game got called off at Burnley, and we had a coach full with the legend Ginger on the back seat with a handful of game older Cosham. As soon as we parked in this underground car park, no less than 100 Coventry came swarming around the coach and only a few of us were off as the Cov boys went to town. We were taking a proper slap at first and our mate Richie was getting kicked to fuck. A few had run back on to the coach and everyone was shouting at each other to get back off. Enter Ginger. The glasses and hat came off – the myth was true – the back door exit opened as his face reddened with rage, with spit flying out of his mouth as he screamed at them. This was just what the doctor ordered, and they started to back off as Ginger led the coach into battle. They ended up as a rabble as we piled into them. One of their boys at the front, a big lump with a sheepskin, was asking who the hell we were as he was decked with a flying side-fister and Ginger took his coat. We murdered them and they didn't even regroup. We marched to the ground victorious. Villa's end was not that dodgy, to be honest, and nothing really happened as all their boys were up the other end. Our coach was relocated to a massive coach park where all the coaches were lined up in file, and we were all writing back to front on the steamed-up windows: 'Villa wankers' and 'PFC' and stuff, and they were going mad. We went home, and stopped off in Banbury to get slaughtered.

***

TURNING UP AND NOT PLAYING

*The England under-21 at Southampton in about '85
was a farce. A meet with Scum had been arranged but
the inevitable happened when there were a good mob
of us – we ran them all the way through the city
centre, as the resistance was non-existent. That
internet warrior Flynn, a typical Scummer idiot, got
his teeth knocked out with a crow bar that night and
we were delighted.*

***

*Swansea vs Bognor was good, our mate was playing
for Bognor and we hired a coach with 30 good boys on
it. We were almost all nicked for hoisting on the way
and had to put all the gear back. Luckily we knew the
driver – he had arranged the double-decker to Forest –
he found it funny and we carried on. It was obvious we
were not welcome as we stood at the bottom of 1,500
Bognor fans during the game, but it was still
unexpected when a couple of black lads came down
and whacked our mate. Fierce fighting followed with
us penned in the corner. We were well out-numbered.
We were all over the shop to start with, but when you
all accept you can't go anywhere you dig in, and we
gave as good as we got. It went on for ever and the Old
Bill couldn't quell it. Outside we were whacking
everyone. We had a couple of real dangerous fuckers
on the coach – one copped a seven a few years later for
shooting a fella point blank in the head and blinding
him (quite rightly so, as the bastard had taken a real
liberty with his family). We were baying for blood and
the wankers who were giving it in the ground had
melted away. On the way out of the city our co-
operative driver slammed the anchors on as we flew*

out of the exits into some Taffs, and the Old Bill were glad to see the back of us in Wales that day.

Bognor had held the Swans, however, and it was back to Bognor for the replay. We took a convoy of motors to the replay, and there was about 70 of us walking round the sell-out crowd looking for the perpetrators who had kicked off with us at Swansea. We smacked a couple but they didn't want to know. We learned that some of them were Brighton fans from Littlehampton and Worthing, which explains why so many of them couldn't finish us the week before when we were stuck in that corner. We dispersed when we realised our undercover CID were present, and we were lined up and had our photos taken. That was the end of that for us, but it was nice to see Bognor win the replay and we were well chuffed for our mate Neil, their centre half.

Pompey also turned up at Scum vs Millwall in '85 and, although there was limited action, it has always been a thing to do. There are the other big ones, too, like 400 of us at Chelsea vs Leicester in '84, and going back to Wimbledon vs Millwall after a lunchtime KO at Stamford Bridge, again in '84.

Sometimes you have to go to extreme measures to have a fight and we are no different on the south coast. This would never happen nowadays and it wouldn't even be attempted. The only time anyone gets together now when Pompey are not playing is for England games, and that will probably be an offence soon.

Derby, No Race Riot

'I DID NOT SEE ANY BAD BEHAVIOUR OR ANY TROUBLE,
AND I WAS PROUD TO BE THERE WITH THE FANS.
LATER, I DID HEAR THERE HAD BEEN RASTAFARIAN
RIOTS – BUT I WAS TOLD THIS HAD NOTHING TO DO
WITH THE FOOTBALL.'
CHARLES MOS: CONSERVATIVE COUNCILLOR AND
LONG-TIME POMPEY FAN.

D erby away, Wednesday, 4 March 1987, looked to be an explosive night, a promotion clash that saw 2,500 Pompey fans swell the gate to a 21,000 attendance to give Derby County Football Club its biggest crowd of the season. A match played against the backdrop of an area where tensions were running high amongst the ethnic community neighbourhood surrounding the Midlands football club, something the locals would be all too aware of with all the talk of demonstrations planned following the death of Clinton McGurbin who had died after being arrested in nearby Wolverhampton. A riot was in the air – it only needed a spark.

But surely no one could predict a firm of lads, notoriously known as the 6.57 crew, would be the lighter fuel that sparked four hours of rioting following the attack on the Caribbean Centre in the predominantly black Pear Tree Road area of the city. Stolen cars were set ablaze, buildings and property were attacked, smashed and damaged, all within a couple of streets from the ground. You had bottles and bricks raining down on photographers and police as rioters took to the streets – and the game played on.

The aftermath left community relations in the district severely strained, long after the night of rioting and the investigation into it were over, and the chairmen for both football clubs were quick to disassociate their football clubs from any involvement in the trouble. Indeed, it was a stance taken by various leading police figures who supported the view that there was little known trouble at the match itself and that the travelling army of Portsmouth fans were as much a credit as the well-behaved home fans.

So you had a scene of something resembling a battle-zone just 400 yards from the ground, which many in attendance were oblivious to. Police reinforcements from all divisions of Derbyshire had to be called up to safely shepherd the large numbers of fans leaving after the match. This they did successfully, as the Pear Tree Road residents were left to remove the riot debris amid the distinct smell of burned-out vehicles.

But it didn't take long for the following day's newspaper headlines to pick up on the Derby riot bearing the hallmark of the 6.57. There were the odd mutterings of the usual link to a possible National Front involvement. Football, police and particularly the media, firmly laid the blame on to a group they believed were using football matches as a vehicle for inflicting violence. As 20 fans from Portsmouth remained under arrest and as the news of the public outrage reached the south coast, a Hampshire Police spokesman came out and stated, 'It is not the club's fault the 6.57 crew exists.' Pompey chairman John Deacon reiterated these 'are not genuine supporters of Portsmouth Football Club', while a Portsmouth councillor, claiming to have attended the match, said in a local press statement that they were 'Rastafarian riots'.

So what really went on here? There was obviously a terrifying night of disturbances and violence on the streets of Derby that turned ugly enough to trigger off race riots long into the night.

DERBY, NO RACE RIOT

What linked the notorious 6.57 to all this is best told by Steve T, who only went up to Derby on a last-minute fancy and ended up staying there longer than he'd planned.

We travelled up on the minibus that went from the Sir Robert Peel. Nowadays it's a local boozer, but back then it was a main meeting place. It used to be convenient due to its close proximity to the station and, with it being handily tucked away on a housing estate, we found it ideal for any visiting fans coming through.

With Derby being a midweek night game, I hadn't planned on going because of work next day, but during my lunch break I bumped into Shaun and Tony who had organised the minibus. They assured me there was a seat available, so I thought about it. I said, 'Give us an hour.' They were leaving at half-one, so I got my mum to phone up work, said I was going sick.

The journey up was pretty uneventful, it was a dry minibus although there was a bit of puff being smoked among certain people on there, but not a lot else happened. Derby was a ground I hadn't been to before, so that was my main interest in going, but all the talk on the minibus was about having it when we got up there. There were a few lads who had been there the previous season and had a row, and they allegedly had a mob called the DLF – the 'Derby Lunatic Fringe'. We were obviously going up hoping to engage this mob.

When we got to Derby, we parked up our minibus, 15-strong and went looking for the others. There must have been about 60 that met up by the Peel. Pompey fans. We were the only minibus, the rest had gone up in cars. We walked the streets, and bumped into the

rest of Pompey's firm. The total was 60. We had a
little discussion and said, 'Down this road', as it was
getting on towards kick-off time. So we turned into
this road that we now know as Pear Tree Road and
there was a black lad walking towards us – he looked
like a football geezer: trainers, jeans, puffa coat.
Someone approached him and said, 'Where's your
firm?' He just pointed straight ahead. Just down there,
he indicated. So 60 of us made our way. I was, like,
towards the back end of our firm and as we got
further down the road we could see a little firm
outside a building, which was called the Texas
Goldmine. At the time we didn't know it was an Afro-
Caribbean community centre. So we were walking
down there and people spotted this little firm, and for
the keener ones it was like the start of the 100 metres
in the Olympics, they shot off. We're still walking, the
others have gained some distance. They must have
been about 30-strong. They got down to the top of the
road, where this other mob were. Already there were
a few punches thrown, and they've run inside, into the
Texas Goldmine. As we got closer, you could
distinctly hear the sound of breaking glass, and what
had happened, someone had ripped a drainpipe off a
wall, and lobbed it through the window and someone
else had robbed a 'For Sale' sign from a house and that
had gone through as well.

It was over quite quickly, we were still making our
way down there and then 30-odd came charging back
towards us. I'm like, 'What's going on here?' With
that a mob had come out of the Texas Goldmine and
they were tooled up, they had every conceivable knife
you could imagine. They were up to about 40-strong
by this time. Everyone panicked 'cause Pompey were

not known for being a tooled-up firm. There was a park nearby, where there were these flower beds surrounded by wooden staked fencing, and everyone's trying to rip this fencing out of the ground, trying to defend ourselves. The only thing that saved us was the sound of the police. They'd got wind of it and they'd come up, all the Old Bill. That got the blacks off our backs for the time being.

With that, everyone thought, Let's get out of here, and we've all clambered over this fence into this other road, which was adjacent to Pear Tree Road. As soon as that happened the Old Bill pulled us up and another nightmare, in DS Hiscock, had appeared. DS Hiscock, along with King and Bird, they were Pompey's Police, and it was their job to follow the thugs around the country. Mr Hiscock's words will stay with me till my dying day. He said, 'OK, sweets, against the wall.' That was his words. We're all lined up against the wall trying to avoid eye contact with him as he's gone up and down the line. Everyone's staring blatantly at the floor, just trying to look innocent. With that we've been escorted to the ground. We thought it was only a bit of a fracas. As we've gone in, we've been videoed individually as we've gone into the ground.

The game was a bit of a non-event. It was a top of the table clash in the old division two, which finished 0–0. There was 21,000 there, with a good 3,000 travelling up from the south coast. No one really concentrated on the game because we were all talking about the night's events. Word had gone round that one of the lads, Chas, had been stabbed. This caused a great deal of concern.

We left the ground and got back on to the minibus

and pulled away. We were in the football traffic by now and Tony leaned out the window and in a big Pompey accent called out to one of the lads on the other side of the street. With that Mr Hiscock turned round, spotted the minibus and pointed at it. Derbyshire Old Bill have swarmed all over the minibus, they've pulled us over and three coppers have got on the bus. One of the officers warned us that we were being arrested for suspected criminal damage. So we're all sat there pretty glumly. We've got a meat wagon in front of us, one behind us, and we've got like police motorcycle outriders either side. They've whipped us through the traffic sharpish to take us back to the nearest police station and no one's really said a lot during this time.

Once we were in there, we were all lined up having our details taken by the desk sergeant, 15 of us formed like an orderly queue, and we've got the younger ones towards the back. Someone had taken a camera along for the trip and as we're all being serious, handing in our valuables, giving our details. Rich, Stevie, Jason, and a few others are posing for a team photograph with this camera without a care in the world. Bums up and all that. I thought, like, I don't need this. We were put away into cells, three or four to a cell. I was in there with one of my old mates Es, Ian and Kev. Also, in the meantime they've nicked another car load, so that had brought the numbers up to 20.

This was all over this Texas Goldmine incident. Now the Old Bill had half of us banged up. Pete B, he was lucky, he'd been nicked initially but Mr Hiscock had spotted him down the ground when the row had erupted, so he was in the clear. So they let Pete B go, and I thought that was quite decent of them, kicking him out into the street past midnight in a town he didn't know. Typical Old Bill, no transport home. In the meantime, Es assured me that it was only a matter of criminal damage, and we'd be out by 4 o'clock. Well, later on, there was a bit of a struggle outside the cell door and it was Louis. He was abusive and they bundled him into our cell. But he didn't stay for long 'cause he was another one who'd been spotted away from the trouble with Pete B. But then he was rearrested in the morning, as he was wanted for questioning regarding a stabbing at a party back home. On Thursday morning he was removed from our cell and driven back to Havant by Hampshire Constabulary.

On our first morning banged up, we had a breakfast which was totally inedible, consisting of beans, scrambled egg – well, the scrambled egg was a block – and bacon, all served on a paper plate with plastic knives and forks with a cup of sugary tea. Terrible, but you know we didn't have much of an appetite. We hadn't been charged yet, but we were still being held. Later on Es was moved out and we had someone else in with us. Still, Ian kept the spirits up. He played in a local band, and it's quite amusing hearing him sing the old Englebert Humperdink song 'Please Release Me'.

Later on that morning we were all given a sheet of paper with our rights details on them. These were torn up, rolled into little balls and we played a game rolling the paper balls across the floor to the opposite wall. It was just to pass the boredom really, kill a bit of time. Midday lunch was served – the usual crap: mash, mince, cabbage and sugary tea again. And I was thinking to myself, Cheers, Es, for that. Out by 4am!

In the afternoon, it was roughly 3pm, we were taken out for questioning. I was pretty confident with my story 'cause I'd gone over and over it, having had plenty of time being banged up all that time. And then the two CID who probed me were making accusations which I denied. I denied everything – I'd been on my own, I hadn't been on Pear Tree Road and I didn't know whoever. It was quite amusing, 'cause the CID looked exactly like Jeffrey Formiles, the posh, plummy neighbour in George and Mildred. *Someone made some remarks about Mick Quinn, our ace goal-getter. When I answered back, he retorted, 'He's a jailbird just like you.' Quinny had recently served a 21-day sentence for drink-driving. There was a hint that I was heading for a custodial sentence and I thought, I ain't getting banged up for that. I thought I'd done well anyway, but if anyone admitted to really being on Pear Tree Road they would have been under serious pressure and, as far as I was concerned, I was innocent. I wasn't with the first group and I didn't put the windows through.*

At this point we hadn't had any legal representation as such, we hadn't even been offered it. Later on, we had tea in the afternoon, really crap: a cheese sandwich, really salty crisps and sugary tea, and that was the basic three meals we had for the next three days. Then we had a solicitor assigned to us from a firm called Brealey Mann. The solicitor we had was called Mann and he was in his early thirties: thin, dark hair, pinstripe suit, but he was very sharp. And as the group of about 18 of us, gathered round and listened intently, we made our point. I was quite amused that everyone denied being in Pear Tree Road, everyone claimed they'd gone on their own and no one had basically been there. In that time he had informed us about the serious nature of the events, as it wasn't just a case of criminal damage.

The local black community had rioted that night in retaliation over the assault on the Texas Goldmine. They'd really gone to town, burning cars and attacking the Old Bill. The local black community had thought there'd been a racist attack by local Nazis. So now the Old Bill wanted blood and we were the scapegoats. Mr Mann then told us that we were to be faced with confrontation, which was similar to an ID parade but you sat there in a room on your own and then the five alleged witnesses would come in and they would say whether you were there or not. We were informed that if you scored more than three out of five you were in the shit. I only scored two. But it made me laugh when the so-called witnesses came in. Mr Mann had informed us that one of them was well known to the Old Bill anyway and he came into the room using his alias.

After the confrontation we had another meeting with Mr Mann, and he informed us that the police were running out of time now and if they didn't charge us soon they would have to let us go. But in the morning they were going to the magistrates to apply for an extension so they could detain us for a further 36 hours while they carried out their enquiries. It was coming up to 22 hours that we had been detained. Mr Mann also had paid us the backhanded compliment that he thought we were the most streetwise lads he had ever met. He said that on the Friday we would be interviewed for a second time and warned us that, no matter what they put to us, we were within our rights to just say 'no comment'. We were led back to our cells, yet everyone felt sorry for Paul and Steve, who was still a juvenile – he was still at school. Because he was a juvenile they had banged him up in a cell on his own. On his own, with no other company, at that age, a schoolboy and he never cracked, never told them anything – he was absolutely superb. As far as we were concerned he was a star.

The cells were roughly 12' by 12', deep mustard colour, with a tiny window that barely let in daylight. One bench-cum-bed and a toilet, yeah, a toilet in the cell. And it was the most degrading experience of my life when we had to go to the toilet, having a shit, in front of a room full of people – totally embarrassing. Still, we all had to go one time or another. And when one went, the rest would just hide their heads under their jumpers for 10 minutes. We were also given a foam mattress and a blanket. We could communicate with the lads in the other cells just by shouting. Apparently Tony had spent all the time banged up asleep – obviously not worried then, Tone. Shaun kept our spirits up by letting us know that anything less than three months was a bonus. Cheers, Shaun.

Friday afternoon and another interview. This was going to be the long one, as Mr Mann had warned us. He'd said to expect to be up there for two hours. The second interview got under way and it was quite farcical really. Mine must have lasted about 15 minutes due to the constant reply of 'No comment'. The two CID conducting the interview were going through the good cop, bad cop routine. 'Is this you photographed at the Sir Robert Peel pub in Portsmouth?' 'No comment.' 'I'll put it to you that you are the ringleader of the 6.57.' 'No comment.' The more you denied it with the 'No comment', the more wild the allegations became. And then one of them turned to me and said, 'Come on, Steve. We had your mate Jeff in here before you and he told us everything. He was sensible, why don't you do the same?' 'No comment.' With that the pen was slammed on the table. 'This interview is a waste of time. End of interview.' I was led back to the cell. We had now been joined by Jeff R – Jeff is that mate of mine. I said to Jeff, 'Yeah, they told me you told them everything,' and we just pissed ourselves laughing.

One aspect of being banged up that I couldn't come to terms with was the lack of hygiene. We were unable to clean our teeth. We were allowed a bath, but then we had to put our smelly old clothes back on. Everyone took a bath 'cause it got you out of the cell for 15 minutes. Can you imagine having a bath and then having to put back on the same socks and pants you've had on for the past two days? My mouth was like a sewer and my underwear was well crusty. I managed to get hold of a razor and I left a bit of growth on my top lip, as I thought if I looked like I was 'wielding', which is Pompey slang for a moustache, I might be mistaken for a local or for Old Bill. So as you can imagine, I was sat there, a scruffy moustachioed smelly twat – in other words, a real northerner.

With the Friday afternoon interview out of the way we were informed that we were going to be charged on the Saturday and, quite frankly, it couldn't have come quick enough. It was quite amusing though 'cause, by being charged, if we were granted bail we were being let out, and one of our lot turned round and said, 'That's good, we can go to West Brom', which was obviously the last thing on people's minds.

Saturday morning, and all 18 of us were charged

with affray. Everyone was excited about the possibility of getting let out, and we handed over our blankets and mattresses and were led out of the cells and into the magistrates' court, which was in the same building. The court sitting was rather amusing as well 'cause you had people like Alfie H who just sniggered loudly as the magistrates mispronounced names. We were all granted conditional bail, the conditions being that we were not allowed within a quarter of a mile of any football league ground and we'd all have to sign at the nearest police station on Saturday afternoons. The conditions of bail were a shame as we missed Pompey's promotion to the first division. As someone who loves Portsmouth Football Club, that hurt. Pompey lost the last game of that season to Sheffield United at Fratton Park, but that didn't matter 'cause we were already promoted, so the 18 of us had our own party outside the Central Police Station as we waited to sign on. One of the lads, who shall remain anonymous, broke the conditions of bail and attended the Sheffield United game. He got his girlfriend at the time to make his face up and he dressed up as a woman. He left early so she could drop him off at the Central Police Station to sign on. You can imagine our faces as he stood there with a woman's tracksuit, Alice band and make-up on.

Derby should never really have happened as it wasn't a racist attack as reported. Some press reports had really gone to town making such audacious claims that people travelled up several days before to stake the place out before collaborating with local Nazis to launch an attack. None of the 18 lads I know were racist as far as I'm aware, we were just scapegoats. OK, so a lot of the lads enjoyed a tear-up

*at the football but no one wanted what happened up
at Derby. You see Chas, the lad who got stabbed, he
also got charged but the Old Bill never went looking
for the people who stabbed him. No one got nicked
for that. But we all stuck together and the way we
stuck together was quite phenomenal. The mutual
respect amongst everyone was well high.*

In the June of that year 1987, Ian P, Tony P, Russell C, Kev D, Ian
E, Jason E, Jason H, Crispin H, Gary W, Martin A, Nigel B,
Andrew C, Jeff R, Richard S, Shaun S, Steve T, Darren V and Steve
N were all cleared due to lack of evidence, and all agreed to be
bound over on a sum of £250 to keep the peace for two years. At
that time affray carried a sentence of three years in jail.

Docker Hughes
6.57 Party

1987 was going to be different for us and it kicked off on New Year's Day with a prizefight between the Docker and his sidekick, nicknamed the 'Kalahari Kid'. People in the know had talked about nothing else for weeks and betting odds on the bout were updated regularly in spray paint around the walls of Fratton Park.

Marty Hughes, known as the 'Docker' after his job in the dockyard, was a small man in his mid-thirties and he was up against a much younger and fitter opponent. A hundred or so turned up at the all-weather football pitch in Somers Town to watch proceedings unfold. Not a policeman in sight, it was a real old-fashioned match all right, but it lasted little more than a minute, for the Docker had been decked twice in that time and the referee said that was enough. 'The Kid' had come out on top but the Docker had won over a new army of people on that cold winter's night.

For much of the eighties Pompey were crap and going nowhere.

Attendances at home were right down and not many normal, sane Pompey fans would bother to travel to watch them away. And so the club had an above-average hooligan following who would watch them wherever, but who weren't just interested in the game.

With us being right on the south coast, away games often meant having to leave early and so we had to be up for the 6:57am train from Portsmouth and Southsea. Train travel was flexible and not too expensive at the time, when you had railcards and so on to get discount tickets. The 6:57 would pick up at the town and Havant, and get the mob together nicely. Here plans for the day would be made but the routine was normally the same for wherever we were going. That meant going to the first pub outside the station and then a tour of the town to see what was about. There would be times when taking the train wasn't necessary and then it would be cars and minibuses instead. But it was always because of the 6.57, when there had been trouble at these games.

The 6.57 crew was a tag used by the press to explain any aggro and then by the police to incriminate us in the courts. We had a name all right and sometimes we blew it, but firms up and down the country knew there was a ruck guaranteed when Pompey were playing.

Docker had lost his job after 13 years working in Portsmouth naval base. Unemployed, he joined some of us in Southsea, living the life on every benefit going. During the day we were 'up to no good' and at nights we were at Fosters, the snooker hall up Fratton Road. We had time on our hands but never much money. Most of what we had went on football, with the rest being blown at the races. With Docker it was always the other way round though, and his gambling was never a source of amusement.

We dressed and lived differently from the rest of

the world as we saw it then. Clothes were always very important, as were our lifestyles – self-styled on non-conformity. Other football geezers may have gone about things in pretty much the same way, but for us it was Portsmouth that always came first. And this year we were going to go where no mob had gone before.

Football was big news on the telly whenever there was aggro but it was the forthcoming general election that was grabbing the headlines now. By May we were all sick of hearing about politics when two people came up with a 'wacky' idea. Why not have one of our own stand as a candidate and who better than the Docker for the constituency of Portsmouth South? The Docker, to be fair, was more aware of the going at Plumpton than he was of what was happening around him. And we could make up our own manifesto as well! The whole thing seemed just too brilliantly funny to ever happen and so we got down to work straight away.

The first thing was to get the £500 deposit that was needed for him to stand. The Docker just laughed at the idea and thought it would never happen. He signed the nomination form disbelievingly in the town centre Corals bookies, and we started the hunt for the money.

At first, none of our lot at football could believe it either but when we showed them the signed nomination papers the money began to flow. Nominations and candidate deposits had to be in at the election office by a certain time and so it was collection buckets round the pubs to make up the difference. One such boozer was packed full of sailors but in went the money even though they didn't know what for. We had a good laugh about that because *part of our manifesto was always going to be 'Skates out of Pompey'.*

Our HQ was a house not far from the King's Theatre and what went on in there was pure comedy. Our party was named, quite naturally, as 6.57 and the manifesto we produced included the following:

On law and order, all magistrates to have served time themselves, and dockers should have their own community policing 'owing to the inadequacies of the central boot boys (Central Police Station)'.

Economic proposals consist of getting Portsmouth out of Hampshire and a campaign for 'Duty Free' goods to be available on the Gosport Ferry. Further, the abolishment of 'Off Course' betting tax.
Social policy to help the aged especially war widows and war wounded, and to oust skates and sinbads out of Portsmouth.

'No Robsons or Waddles' (a reference to the mullet hairstyles around at the time) and moustaches will be banned in public.

On planning, we propose to create a race track on Southsea Common, to keep Portsdown Park, and to save the Tricorn, keeping Wimpy Homes out of Portsea.

Help Loyalist prisoners in Northern Ireland and have Apprentice Boys of Derry marches in the city.

Come 27 May and we had our paperwork in order and submitted at the Guildhall before the set deadline. What we had done was sensational because our official candidate photo, a head and shoulders shot of the Docker, in his Aquascutum, was now all over the front page of the afternoon paper. POMPEY FAN POLLS SHOCK, *read the headlines, and for once we were being taken seriously.*

The election was just two weeks away and so we had plenty to do. Most importantly we had to sustain the public interest in our campaign and so it was off to the printers to get leaflets and posters made up. One printer was worried about getting involved with us because of what he'd read in the paper. But when we came up with the money, he soon conceded. We printed thousands of flyers with messages such as 'Vote Docker – Your Vote for Portsmouth' and 'Portsea Homes for Portsea People'. Close to the docks, Portsea was always a traditional heartland of the city, but the developers were moving in and pricing its local people out.

And what of our candidate, 'the Docker', throughout this, you may wonder. Well, he gave the impression that nothing had happened – he still went racing and carried on around town as normal. Some may have cheered him and some perhaps shown pity, but he seemed oblivious to it all. He was so laid back about everything, except racing, and indeed on the night of the election itself he was found fast asleep on the stage!

Whilst the party was now up and running, Docker got hit with another hammer blow. His wife came out in public wanting a divorce. She hadn't known about Marty standing for Parliament until she picked up the papers. He had told her nothing about it. The Docker had no reservations about this news, and never raised an objection.

At some expense, A3-size posters were made up in the blue and white of Pompey. On them was a photo of the Docker, looking up from his Sporting Life, and a list of some of our policies. These came out really well and were sought after as collectables, so many disappeared from HQ. We told everyone we knew to put leaflets up in their windows 'cause we wanted to plaster the city with Docker.

They did start appearing all over the place but not in the numbers of the three main parties, it has to be confessed. Nonetheless, the Conservatives complained about our leaflets, saying that we had stolen the town's star and half-crescent emblem from the copyright of the City Council! They uttered not a word against our manifesto though, and so their complaint went no further.

We began door-to-door canvassing for the Docker – taking 6.57 out to the people. We worked in groups of two and concentrated on areas where we saw our leaflets. This meant going on the estates where people could see that we were only having fun. One team got a bit carried away and started banging on doors in Buckland, an area out of the constituency.

Some of our leaflets began appearing in Portsea, especially in the shop windows along Queen Street. But 'Portsea Homes for Portsea People' carried a bit of a backlash there from the local resident groups. They argued that theirs was a serious issue that shouldn't have been mixed in with our manifesto, which we felt was fair enough.

The most controversial of our policies was the Irish issue, the one about Apprentice Boys marches in the city. The 6.57 had to stand by this initially, although it was put into the manifesto by an individual and not by the group as a whole. Press interviews were coming *in from all directions on this subject and we couldn't be seen to be changing our minds. But the Orange Lodge in Portsmouth kicked up a stink about us in the same way as the residents of Portsea, and so we dropped the idea with an official apology to them. It was probably not too soon coming either, because the Docker was getting death threats from mad paddies over the phone!*

Meanwhile, the news and television interviews continued and the nationals were beginning to come in. The Daily Star *ran a page on us under the headline* PRIDE OF PRATS, *and we didn't like the way things were going. A* Sun *journalist turned up wanting a story but we sent him on his way empty-handed. We had to think of a way to turn things around.*

We knew we couldn't win Portsmouth South, but we still had to have voting targets. We went to the press to say that we would donate our deposit to a local body scanner appeal if we polled 5 per cent of the vote. In the end we got nowhere near that amount because we were fighting one of the tightest marginal seats in the country.

Next, it was decided to hold a public meeting in our quest to gain more votes. Again we had the same problems as with the printers, because no one was prepared to rent us a hall. We managed to get the hall at Somers Town First School only because someone knew the caretaker. The date for our meeting was set for the evening of 4 June, so we posted announcements in all the prominent places around town.

Come the day and the Docker was up for anything, for the previous day he had been to Epsom and had a very good Derby. The hall was just packed full of geezers – all his supporters, although there were one or two others who nobody knew, probably Old Bill.

Everything in our manifesto was already well documented so what did the Docker or his agent have left to say? It was decided to get theatrical so out went the lights before the Docker hit the stage. There was a wardrobe on the stage and he got into it. And as the lights went on, he walked out to a rapturous welcome – it worked perfectly! No one raised any questions, so in effect, the meeting was over. Off went the fire extinguishers, the Docker felt happy and so it was time to do the Old Bill.

More posters disappeared from the walls as the hall emptied quickly. A few chairs were thrown about and we got a bill for the damage later, which we paid. On towards Central Police Station to 'do the Old Bill', but as is often the case in these situations, there was practically no one left by the time that we got there!

A news journalist had been at the meeting and she'd produced a jovial report of it all. The pressure was off and we were free to lark about some more.

Docker Hughes, eyes are blue
Docker is the man for you!
Tralalala, lalala, la la

With only a week to go before the election day, we had to sustain local interest if we were to get any votes. Back at HQ, one of our 'committee' had come up with the idea of an open-top bus and he'd gone ahead and hired it. On Saturday morning, some 30 of us met at the Hard and got on our bus! We had banners hanging over the side and leaflets in every window.

Someone had brought along a loud hailer and we used this to get our message out to the public as we drove by. However, the public reaction to our 'battlebus' was indifferent at best. As they went about their daily business they weren't taking much notice of us. On one occasion, when we'd pulled up for a while, two shoppers hopped on, thinking it was a normal bus service!

But we were having fun and so was the driver by now, and he was going to do whatever we wanted. At one point we came across the Tory 'battlebus' so we asked our driver to pull up at the shop round the corner where we bought up all the eggs and flour we could get our hands on and let them have it!

When we came to Central Police Station, it was down to the business of abusing the 'Central Boot Boys', as we called them. There was a big roundabout and our driver went round it three times, whilst we hung over the side with our banners and slagged them all off rotten. The police hated everything to do with the 6.57 and they got their own back on us later.

Our campaigning was going better than expected but as 11 June neared, we were getting swamped by the 'Big Three'. The election office gave us 30 tickets to be present at the count, with 15 'checkers' to oversee things at the ballot box. We wondered how the Docker would do on the night and perhaps some were dreaming the impossible.

11 June arrived and the night of the count in the Guildhall. The Old Bill were very much in evidence around Guildhall Square and many of us had been in the Peel all afternoon, getting quite shantied. We lost half our party there thanks to the boot boys,

who nicked them for drunk and disorderly. The Docker had been drinking but he would be 'untouchable' tonight.

In the main hall there were rows of tables, each with council employees opening the ballot boxes. Beyond that, people sat facing the stage where dignitaries were wandering about looking important. Adjoining the hall was a large bar, which is where the candidates and their entourages were headed for – Conservatives, SDP, Labour and 6.57, all trying to settle down for the long night ahead.

We hogged the bar, it has to be said, but in the best tradition of British democracy, no way could it be described as a 'stand off'. The Labour candidate may have thought otherwise as he made to walk through the middle of our party. Whether he fell or was tripped is open to question, but the three somersaults he completed before hitting the floor were certainly quite impressive!

Periodically, one of our 'checkers' would wander over to the tables to check on the voting. The contents of the ballot boxes were stacking up in four piles – or three and the odd one here and there to be more exact! We could see that we would not be figuring prominently tonight and this was a bit disappointing, particularly for the Docker.

After one re-count, the result finally came through around 2am. Candidates and their agents took to the stage to learn that the Tories had taken the seat from SDP by a winning margin of 205. The Docker polled 455, which he later described as pathetic. But, in his speech, he remembered to thank all those who voted for him. In fact, his polled votes were far from pathetic, as they were thought by some to have swung the seat to the Tories, as the victory margin was under half of the total votes that Docker Hughes' party had polled.

Yeah, no Waddles and Robsons. It was like a real piss-take. But, what happened was the Liberal Democrat was Michael Hancock and on the big night of the election after the Tory candidate had won by 205 votes and Docker had 455 votes and all these pissed-off party election women were going, 'You stupid idiots. If you'd all voted for my candidate he'd have got in,' and all that.

And so this little episode in the story of the 6.57 was over. History will tell that the Docker polled more votes that 106 candidates around the country that year and had done it in one of the most marginal seats.

Docker Hughes's place in political history will always be there and his obituary appeared in the Daily Telegraph in August 1992. He is thought to have died of natural causes, and as an epileptic he was on medication, but he lived his life following the fortunes of his beloved football team and always, always had a copy of the Sporting Life in his hand. Amongst Pompey fans, and particularly the 6.57, the Docker was a harmless chap, at times a figure of fun who became something of a fans' mascot and a real character. Every Pompey fan seems to have a memory and fun story.

He was funny, Docker. He was a nice bloke and he was older than anyone – he looked like he'd been going to Pompey games for 80 years, and he used to talk like he had. 'Oh, I think they're bringing the firm down.' But he was good, he was a character. I remember we had him on our shoulders at one away game. 'There's only one Docker Hughes,' and all that. 'Who's that fucking Docker?' All these firms come down, 'Where's

Docker 6.57? Let's see him. Fucking hell ...' They expected to see a docker, not this geezer on our shoulders. He used to love it. He used to wear a Barbour jacket, all the time a Barbour coat, and he always had the Sporting Life and a carrier bag with him wherever he went.

I remember once we had Crystal Palace in the League Cup and we were having a drink after the game in the Milton, and he used to live on the road opposite the Milton. There's me and Steve in the pub and we saw Docker going by, and Steve says, 'Watch this.' So he opens the door and bawls out, 'Come here, you Pompey cunt,' like that, and Docker didn't stop. He was straight across the road and up the hill, he didn't stop for about 200 yards.

They said to Docker, 'Right we're going to have a meeting,' and what they did they was get Docker pissed and hide him in the broom cupboard. So all the press turn up, people down from the national press and everything: 'Well, where is he? He's meant to be here.' Suddenly the broom cupboard opens: 'There's only one Docker Hughes!' and all that, and this bloke runs Twit of the Week in the Daily Star and he had a picture of him in there.

They hold a remembrance race for him. It's like a Docker Hughes Memorial Fund – a horse race, because that's how they got their money for his deposit for the election. It started off with Harry Redknapp, who comes every year to this horse race meeting. You can get a T-shirt of that now, that's how they're raising money for this year's race. A tenner each – a fiver for the T-shirt and a fiver for the fund.

Honfleur Trip and Riot

'THE DEMONSTRATIONS STARTED WITH JUST POMPEY FANS.
WE WERE SUPPORTERS WHO WERE FRUSTRATED AT WHAT
WAS GOING ON AT FRATTON PARK AND WE WANTED
TO AIR OUR VIEWS. BUT NOW THE BIG PROBLEM IS THAT
OTHERS ARE JUMPING ON THE BANDWAGON.'
JOHN WESTWOOD, THE POMPEY BUGLER

The pre-season friendly at Honfleur in France was always going to be a big must-go trip because Pompey have never been in Europe in a proper club competition. The other reason was a high-profile chance to show the board that the Portsmouth fans were unhappy with what was going on around their club at boardroom level. Enter Fareham loyal, remembering the 6.57 antics when Pompey played Le Havre. These are the accounts of Doug, Tim and Chris

FAREHAM LOYAL

Fan Two: *I remember meeting in town, in Fareham and having to get trains over to Pompey. It was early, half-past six in the morning. The ferry left about 8 o'clock but you had to be on the fucking thing by seven, once everyone had sussed out they needed passports to get into France. People didn't have tickets or passports but it got to the stage where, if it hadn't been for the Old Bill just letting people on, no one would have because every time someone went to get on there was a problem with them. Eventually the Old Bill just said, 'Right, well just give us one big passport. Everybody that I know from Fareham went and that's got to be 50 at least from, plus the Pompey lot. There was families there, but you didn't take no notice of them 'cause all around there was geezers, fucking hundreds, everybody who was a geezer went. It was right across the board. It was four hours on the ferry – four hours on the piss, foot passenger, cheap as fucking cheese. Everybody was well tooted up. Lovely Summer's day.*

Fan One: *Got on the ferry, the first thing you did, straight into the bar. There was a few moody £50 notes floating about which went over the bar paid for everyone's day straight away. Straight on the Stella. Any moody money was got rid of on the ferry on the way over there and it was mostly in exchange for French francs 'cause you just wanted to blow it all over there. Then we spent the French francs: bevvies when we were on the boat, the fruit machines, even on the roulette. We knew it was going to be a mad day when at 8 o'clock in the morning you had 300–400 geezers pissed. There was lots of visits to the toilets and things like that early on. Everybody got prepared for getting to France, as you do, as if it was a marching army. It was a great, great excuse for Pompey just to be in Europe.*

Fan Three: *They were shit as a football team, there was no finances in the club and everybody was pissed off. This seemed the perfect excuse to go out and say, 'Look, we've had enough, a bellyful. There was never going to be any football game in France. Everybody knew that weeks before we went. The whole point of going there was to protest against Gregory and his tenure of Portsmouth Football Club, which was disgraceful.*

Fan One*: I feel like it was a little bit – well, the Gregory thing, yes, but it didn't matter whether it was Gregory or not, because it was so close everyone went to make the papers and Pompey were in Europe. The Gregory thing was a great excuse, but it would have happened whether it was a Gregory thing or not. You had 400 or 500 geezers on the boat getting pissed at 8 o'clock, all visiting the toilets, landing in Europe and we still had six hours before the game or something. It was obviously going to be trouble, wasn't it?*

Fan Three*: When we got off the ferry, they held us back. The gendarmes said we could only get on the coach, and they'd laid on coaches four or five at a time. We were left at the end and, as we got on the coach, one of the best comments was 'You weren't so good at your roadblocks in 1939.' Looking at their reaction you have to realise it did not go down well with the frogs. I remember Popey – there was loads of Old Bill and he freaked out 'cause we'd been on the boat six hours. He jumped off the top deck of the ferry into the harbour because he thought they weren't going to let him off. The poor soul just freaked out, just thought, I'm going ashore, and he launched himself off the top deck to swim ashore. They had to fish him out of the harbour. The whole journey was one drama after another. The main objective was to* get as pissed and out of it as we could, have a laugh, a good day out.

Once we actually landed there in Le Havre, the French were seriously worried about what was going to happen. 400 geezers just marched off into Le Havre. What they're used to is a ferryload of Brits coming over and ordering six or seven assortments of cheeses, and now they've ended up with 400 or 500 geezers, out of it at 10 o'clock in the morning, running round their town, everybody planning to hit the main square straight away, all kinds of souls falling asleep, everyone getting involved in the major dramas, hundreds of geezers just singing songs all day long.

We marched off to like the main square, just going through boozers all the way. Well, every European town has a main square, hasn't it? So, you always head for the main square. The only pubs and cafés that were open were the greedy bastards that wanted to take as much money as possible and just hope they didn't get their pubs wrecked. That was a funny thing: loads of Pompey fans going in, ordering a beer and getting an ashtray full of beer, 'cause they're little tiny measures of beer, and seeing all the people's faces – 'A grande beer' ended up with a little ashtray of beer.

Even when we got into the square we were all really pissed and everyone's going, 'They haven't got no boys, Le Havre.' There was a couple of geezers in the square and I went up to this mush, and I started talking French to him. I was like, 'Ou est les garçons pour le battle against Portsmouth?' and all that. Zee's going, 'We can't all speak French. What does that mean?' I said, 'I've just asked them where are the boys of Le Havre to have a fight with us.'

This was still only midday, and the only geezer who

got any kind of pasting was some grocer. Everybody walked past and overturned his fucking apples and his pears and all that, and he gave it the large one – he got a good toeing, bless his heart. I felt sorry for him, I did. You expect to go anywhere in Europe and, if they know that an English club is coming, the local leaders will turn up.

Over the course of the next five hours it was just 500 geezers trying to find alcohol wherever they could. It didn't kick off 'cause there was no one to kick off against apart from the Old Bill and they weren't going to hassle us 'cause we were no problem to anyone apart from ourselves. The thing was, over the course of the day, everybody started making their way to the ground and, in the end, there were too many of us.

Le Havre's ground was out of use or something, so we had to play at Honfleur. They tried to lay on buses but obviously you don't want to travel via the Old Bill 'cause you'll get driven round everywhere. So we tried to go independently. We were trying to hit train stations and everything just to get us to Honfleur. We struggled with that 'cause the Old Bill were running round Le Havre, getting hold of everybody saying, 'No problem, just get on these buses. We want you out of Le Havre. Go to Honfleur.'

Then we heard a rumour that there was a pub called the Southampton bar and obviously all the Pompey fans wanted to try and trash it. So we spent at least 20 minutes or half an hour asking everybody where this Southampton bar was. Somebody finally knew what we were talking about and about 15–20 of us got a cab, with the sole intention of having a big drama in the Southampton bar. We got there, got to this Southampton bar, and they'd changed the name maybe three or four weeks before, so we just got back in the cab and went back to town.

Fan Two: *There were some that made the place. I never made it, drunk as fuck, pissed up in a bar full of fishermen. I started arguing with them because they were French and they couldn't work out what I was on about. Then about four or five French coppers came over, dragged me by my hair and my clothes, threw me in the back of the wagon, booted me on the floor and I was just lying there with boots on top of me. Then they dragged me back to the ferry port and left me there for four hours. I never made it to the ground, but them boys did and they can tell you what happened there.*

Fan One: *On the coaches on the way there even more Pompey had got themselves totally pissed and out of it. When we actually got to the ground we were all stunned. It was like Privet Park, Gosport. It was the crappiest little park you've ever seen in your life. We were stunned that we'd brought 700 fans to Privet Park, Gosport.*

They wanted a tenner to get in, so everyone decided straight away nobody's paying to get in. Fences started getting ripped up, all kinds of drama was going on. We jumped over the other side and the gendarmes got hold of us. The security situation was poor. It was like stewards and the Old Bill, nothing to contain how many we had. Remember, they were stunned at the amount of Pompey that were over there. Definitely stunned. Pompey everywhere, game of football outside the ground, we had a Pompey–Fareham football match, things like that. A tenner to get in – nobody was going to pay that money to get in. They would dart through bushes, tripping up, scrambling through fences, ripping up the bottom of the fence and going through. Everyone was dressed in nice gear as it's sunny but you still went underneath the soil. Pathetic really, just to try and save a tenner. It was just our protest, 'I'm not paying a tenner to get in there. You're taking the piss.' Everybody was scrambling all over the place. The security guards were going berserk. I can't even remember how many Old Bill, probably 30 there at the match, and they were really under pressure. They just couldn't cope with it at all. I don't think hardly anyone paid to get in.

There was a few sort of families that went for the day out to France and were disgusted by the Pompey fans' behaviour. A few people would turn up with picnics and be into the landscape and shit, but that's not what we'd all come for.

When you got in the ground, there was a fence about 5-feet high all the way around, just like a Southern League ground, bit like Havant. The ground was a field with one stand and a little bit of terracing. But the funny thing was, all the Pompey fans have turned up, 'cause it's a game in Europe – Union Jacks, St Georges, thinking it was going to be on telly, and there was nowhere to put them. There were a few loyalist flags, as Pompey's got a big loyalist connection. There was some 'Gregory out' stuff – you've got to remember the politics then– but it was soon lost in everyone's drunken behaviour. There was no way that the Gregory thing was the major influence on the way everyone behaved.

Fan Three: *Everyone was pissed off with Gregory though. At the time we were a big club and we were a joke. Him and the directors were trying to do their best but it wasn't good enough for us, was it? So we seized the opportunity to take this game and get some things across.*

Fan One: *Anyway it was a giggle. The game kicked off and nobody was interested at all. My mate Doug kept trying to throw me on the pitch. Well, I was pissed and I was just like, 'Let's just get the game abandoned. Let's just do it.' Next thing I'm launched on to the pitch and I'm walking round the penalty area, bit confused, not really sure what to do, looking like Liam Gallagher, and everyone's saying, 'Get off the pitch, Liam.' I was like, 'Come on then, everyone, get on the pitch,' and then it just flooded on. Everyone just went, 'Fuck this, it's a load of shit, nobody wants to watch it, nobody's interested in it,' and everyone flooded on the pitch, got the match ball and started kicking it about.*

The players, they just stood still at first. They didn't know what was going on. Especially the French. The Pompey players just started running off the pitch but the Frenchies just stood there going, 'What is going on?' I could speak a bit of French and I could see one of the Frenchie players and all that, and he was saying, 'What's going on?' and I said that, in England, we consider ourselves a big club, but we're being run by a load of idiots who don't want to take us anywhere and we don't feel that it's right for our club and we're just protesting about it. I was quite nice to him, I said it's nothing to do with France, nothing to do with Le Havre, it's to do with our protest at the way our club's being run. And the French player said to me, 'I can see you're a big club with the amount of people you've got here.'

Ten, 15 minutes have gone by and it's been abandoned. They tried to come on and say, 'Stop it, please get off the pitch,' but what you have got to remember is that everybody was out of it, everybody was too far gone. They only had about 30 Old Bill and they just stood on the side of the pitch and watched it because they knew that there was no way they could contain what was happening on the pitch.

If you picture the scene, there was Pompey fans in the centre circle as the players were walking off, actually snorting lines of coke in the centre circle after 10 minutes and that's no exaggeration, that really happened. Everyone then got a bit bored, to be honest with you, but it was a lovely, sunny day. There were announcements by the club, a tannoy telling you to get off the pitch, but in the end they just gave up. A football came on to the pitch and everyone was just kicking it around trying to score goals.

By now it was like everyone was on the pitch, hundreds by this time. It was good, people congaing – there was a giant conga on the pitch. Some people were just sitting down cross-legged in the centre circle, just bored and having a sunbathe. If you picture the scene, there was Union Jacks with 'Gregory Out', there was loyalist Union Jacks, people congaing, people sniffing and getting out of it on the piss – it was a surreal scene. This was a joke. This was a laugh. I saw Paul Walsh, who was on the bench, and I'd been out with him for a drink before and he said, 'What you doing?' I just looked at him. We were so gone, I just looked at him. He went, 'Oh fucking hell,' and took his players off. He was having nothing to do with it. The match was gone, and we were all chuffed with that. Hopefully it was going to make the papers, which is what Pompey wanted to do. Little did we know how much it would make the papers.

There were people coming out saying, 'Can you please get off the pitch?' There was all that going on. 'Get off the pitch, get off the pitch' for about 20 minutes, half an hour. There were definitely people trying to get us off the pitch. And it's funny how, when you're involved in that and you're on the pitch and you get the game abandoned, after a little while, you wonder how many of us wanted to get the whole game abandoned and how many are saying, 'Get off the pitch.' When I got on the coach, everybody was like, 'That's a disgrace.' I was thinking, Nah, nah, surely we all wanted it abandoned.

Fan Three: It's a surreal thing. They laid on loads of coaches to get us away from Honfleur now, to get us back to Le Havre. Everyone got on the coaches 'cause it was a two-bob little town and we just wanted to get back to Le Havre for more drinking, 'cause the boat wasn't leaving till 8 o'clock at night. So, we still had six or seven hours in Le Havre. Everyone regrouped in the middle of the town. We lost Chrissy, 'cause he fell asleep somewhere. I think there was a few like that, fell asleep, mashed.

Fan One: The best bit was the trip back. But I still remember the 50/50 feelings about the pitch invasion. It's weird how after the event, when you get on there and you sober up a little bit, you realise that people are not actually into what you are. There were genuine fans over there and you were like. 'Fucking hell, they don't agree with what we've done.' Yeah, but I felt like the whole idea of going to France was to get Pompey's name in the paper. Whichever way it was, it was to get Pompey in the paper throughout the country. I remember like the Evening Standard *even had it and my dad was living in London at the time and phoned up, he was just like, 'Do you know what you're doing?' Oh I knew it would be in the papers. I was chuffed to bits when he told me it was in the* Evening Standard. *Fantastic.*

The protest was put across by Pompey fans but the Old Bill totally fucking exaggerated the situation 'cause they were fucking useless at trying to get it sorted, simple as that. The Old Bill put the stories in the papers about how bad we were, but there was nothing about the reasons why we'd gone. Sure, we caused upset and so forth but, as per normal, the Old Bill didn't have a fucking clue what they were talking about, didn't see the reason behind the madness and just put down what they fucking thought. We served a purpose, boys, we served a purpose and we did it well and that's what it's all about at the end of the day.

I don't even think the Gregory thing was the main reason. I reckon whoever was in charge, even if it happened today, if we had that match, we'd get it abandoned. But others disagreed, and thought if it hadn't been for Gregory the game wouldn't have been abandoned. I said only if we were top of the league we'd have let them play.

The scene back in Le Havre is that you've 500–600 men who are drunk, starting to sober up, that are on the case. You are in a seaside town, every bar is serving half ashtrays of beer, there's sing-songs going. We've turned up in one pub, and obviously everyone was trying to go down the red-light district. Everyone's looking for women. 'Where's the red-light district? Where's the red-light pub?' I said, and it turns out we were actually in the biggest red-light pub in Le Havre. And I said, 'What do you mean by that?' and someone's pulled a curtain back in the pub and there's two people going at it in the pub, a live sex show. All it was was a dingy little pub with a curtain rail. And as you pulled the rail there was a scabby old black bird, wasn't there? Everyone just cracked up and then one of the birds walked round and all that, and what did you do? The usual – in, out, not impressed, out you go.

But obviously when you find these places, like the red-light places, you're in the local loony place, aren't you? And all of a sudden you've got England's loonies and all the French loonies and, all of a sudden, there's all kinds of banter going on and a right old giggle. We always find that with a pub in Vauxhall, it's always full of low-life, Millwall, south London gypsies, with their half a Guinness.

The ferry left at 8 o'clock. We were just roaming around Le Havre really, not a lot to do, so everyone's heading back to the ferry port, and regrouped there. We got on the ferry, all talking about our stories, having a laugh, who made it to the game, who didn't. Obviously when we got on the ferry we went straight into the disco bar with the DJ.

Fan Two: When the coppers who had handcuffed me to the rail came back, I was uncuffed and was the first on the ferry. The place was empty, the bar was open and the DJ was playing. I've spoken to the DJ who was an English geezer, and he says, 'We'll make sure *everyone has a great evening. The best way to keep all the boys happy is to keep them dancing, keep them full of beer. There'll be no trouble.' I agreed with the fella, I said, 'Yeah, fucking right!' There was English Old Bill on the ferry, I remember that because it dropped us off, went back to England, and came back with them. I spoke to them and said, 'They want to have a drink, know what I mean?' Usual prats of fucking coppers, as soon as we got on they said, 'Close the bar. No music,' and it just kicked off, nobody was having any of that whatsoever. Within half an hour of everyone getting on board, they closed the bar. We were in the bar but they vacated anybody who wasn't to do with us. Even the DJ vacated. He was getting a lot of abuse so he fucked off out of it and the Old Bill left us in there. They virtually shut the doors and we were stuck, 300 geezers left in a bar, no beer, no music – fuck all.*

And that's when it happened. Obviously when the Old Bill had just gone and left us on our own, we were just standing around. Twenty minutes passed and, all of a sudden, people started scurrying behind the bar. And all of a sudden there were a few optics being taken off and then there were cupboards broken into, a few padlocks got broken, some spirit was thrown around. There were fags coming out, so I was straight over there and had 200 fags. No bar staff. We were cut off – one part of the boat was for the families, the other part of the boat was for us lot. They'd turned the music off, and everything was all a bit stuck and then all of a sudden somebody – I think it was Justin – got into the DJ bit and put on a real disco record and started firing CDs all round the dance floor. CD frisbees, weren't they? The DJ machine went to full blast from nothing, absolute silence to the full-monty blast. It was loud, the place was heaving and it just erupted. The bar got ripped to shreds, anything we could have out of the bar was gone. We're talking fruit machines turned on end and people shaking them for a few 50p pieces. There was a lot of money coming out of them machines, I tell you. One fruit machine was being bounced around the dance floor like a domino, with pound coins flying out. I had tears streaming out my eyes from laughing, it was the funniest thing. I tell you what, I had about a one-er out of that machine. I just followed the trail of money coming out as they dragged it across. They wanted to throw it down the stairs but they didn't make it there.

It was so heavy in there that the Old Bill would not come back. Nobody entered that room at all, and we were left to do exactly what we wanted. Two to three hundred geezers, no one behind the bar. If you can picture the scene: you've got people behind the bar breaking into where the spirits are, handing out free spirits and fags; you've got somebody else in the DJ bit handing out George Michael CDs to people, just pinging them around; you've got other people tipping the fruit machines, handing out 50p pieces left, right and centre; and the rest of them are all congoing and singing, jumping all over the cushions and chairs. The cushion seats were getting thrown across the room. It was chaos. Chaos. I had tears streaming down my face.

There was a few people who then turned up and went, 'What's going on?' as they're loaded up with, like, Swatch watches and things from the duty free. I can remember a geezer walking around with one of them Spanish bull's legs, them ham things. Chaos had hit the boat. There were people with Armani perfume just spraying it around the place. The boat got rifled totally, especially the duty free bit. Other people weren't in the bar bit when this happened, but they just wandered in, at the end. I think the police and everybody had just given up. We actually thought it would really come on top, 'cause we thought there were cameras.

In Pompey's firm there are people who will seize that opportunity to thieve as much as possible. There are thieves, real thieves. Any Pompey game away you do see that little firm turn up – coming back from Plymouth '83, remember? I do. They will use the cover of 300 hooligans to go on a thieving spree. There were people there who were doing that, they'd gone to Europe to do that. 'We're going to thieve as much as we can.' You sit there and you think, Jesus Christ, there are cameras on here. We've got to land at Portsmouth, and you can't disperse anywhere. I thought there were cameras on board. I thought there'd be Old Bill checking you when you got off and everything. And when we actually landed, it was six in the morning, it was like a twelve-hour trip or whatever. It had calmed down by then, though, 'cause there was nothing else to wreck, nothing else to thieve, it was a case of everyone sleeping. On the seats, under the seats, everywhere. Danny's room got done, the Portsmouth liaison officer from the police service, rifled his room. But anyone that knew anything knew the Old Bill were going to be waiting at Pompey on the way back. We knew.

No, to be fair, the people with the Swatch watches just held on. I thought when we got off the boat that we were all going to get searched, pulled off to one side, everything like that. When the boat landed, we were all hung over. Everyone's had enough now, 'cause it was a long old day. We walked off the boat, and I think everyone was quiet because we thought, Here we go, going to get the interrogation and that. There must have been 100 Old Bill waiting.

The funny thing was, when the boat stopped, in the sunlight, everyone sobered up and then the Old Bill from the Pompey side all got on and got leery with us. All the other families got let off, but we were on there for an hour after it stopped. While all of this has been going on, Nick D has been asleep underneath the sofa thing, and he's stood up and gone, 'What's going on, what's going on?' and got fucking nicked. He didn't do a thing the whole night. That was funny.

As we got led off there was a complete line of Old Bill either side of the way out and we thought we were going to get led to a room where we would be searched, questioned, names, everything like that. We walked straight out, straight through the harbour bit, no worries at all, giggling. We couldn't believe how easy it was.

Looking forward to Gillingham the following Saturday? Well, they scrapped Gillingham after that. The Old Bill were going to cost too much to police it. What they thought was a 'Gregory Out' campaign, for me, personally, was Pompey in Europe and we wanted to get our name in the paper. All the other clubs have, haven't they?

Yeah, the only other opportunity we've had to go to Europe was Bari, some Anglo-Italian cup competition which a load of us went to. There was probably about 300 of us in Bari on a Wednesday night, but it was a *non-event. We turned up. People didn't even know why we were there. We were there with all our flags and everything, great spread in the paper but … embarrassing.*

The underlying thing about the whole Honfleur thing was it was a laugh and a giggle, a lark. That's all it was. The 'Get Gregory Out' maybe was a part of it for a few people but not me. Personally, I thought it was a sunny summer's day, we were Pompey let loose in France and we were going to cause as much mayhem as we could. Any time I think of that day I have a big smile over my face about all the dramas we got involved in.

I long for the day when Pompey do make it into Europe. I want to go to Madrid on a Wednesday night. When we had that FA Cup semi-final against Liverpool and we went 1–0 up, everyone was dreaming of the Cup Winners' Cup. That was our one little 15 minutes that we could be there. But I'm telling you now, if we ever did get in Europe you could never have a better laugh than that day. No, it was a great day out because it was so easy for us to do. We still talk about it now – it was great, it was funny, there was no real violence. I don't know how many people actually got nicked and charged for what happened that day, but I'm telling you now, a lot of people should be doing a long time for what we got involved in on that day.

Break 4 Love

*'THERE IS NOT THE LEAST SHADOW OF DISCIPLINE,
CARE OR ATTENTION. DISORDERLY SOLDIERS ARE COLLECTED
HERE (THE DOCKYARD), SOME FROM THE SHIPS, OTHERS
FROM THE HOSPITAL, OTHERS WAITING TO EMBARK, DIRTY,
DRUNKEN, INSOLENT SCOUNDRELS IMPROVED BY THE
WICKED NATURE OF THE PLACE WHERE EVERY KIND OF
CORRUPTION IS CARRIED TO EXCESS.'*
GENERAL JAMES WOLFE

B elow are accounts requested by us from people heavily involved in a scene we believe was to have a huge impact on not just the 6.57 crew but also the rest of the football firms nationwide. We make no apologies for featuring them – these events happened and it is their lives.

We had all dabbled with all kinds of drugs right through the eighties. From skinning up and trips, to snorting the lethal pink whizz at the weekends, which inevitably ended up with a cry of 'steam the bouncers' and a gang of wide-eyed teenagers piling into the doormen at different clubs. Nero's (later called 5th Ave, now Time and Envy), Some Place Else (SPECS) and the Mecca (Ritzy's) were some of the victims.

To work the doors in Portsmouth in those days you had to be either brave or stupid as, unlike in other towns, the bouncers are not the chaps. We never mixed with them as they were all either ex-skates or steroid freaks and generally had a dog's life, especially from us. Turnover was high, as they would be individually targeted and picked off, usually at about 3am as they were going to their cars from work. The drugs at that time did not calm the violence in any way, in fact when mixed with alcohol it quite suited it.

A lot of the boys liked a smoke and we would always set up in the first class on the train and get rolling on our journeys to matches up north. Pat always bought along a quality bit of hash, on top of that he was a game fucker too, as were most of the out-of-towners that used to run with us. By the time we would land in enemy territory we would be smashed, and head straight for the nearest boozer. As the smoking became heavier the direction just began to change. We used to have a real laugh stoned, as a few football days in London will verify. Thirty of the lads were walking about, steamed up, in the West End on the way back home from a match up north, when they spotted Marc Almond from Soft Cell, who is probably remembered more for having that stomach pump than his music. He was set upon, half-heartedly, and, while he was rolling about on the floor squealing like a pig, one of our lot took his leather studded hat. He still has it to this day. It will occasionally make an appearance about four in the morning if he's holding a party. A couple of weeks later the victim was Marilyn, another gay singer (and Boy George's sidekick). He was chased to his car by a similar group of 6.57, and locked himself in. He was on morning TV the following week describing his terror as the car was almost turned over. Hysterical.

Another time when we were on our way back from Leeds, Terry Scott, the actor, had got on the train and

the carriage was packed with at least 100 6.57.
Everyone was just chanting his name and he had to
suffer us all the way to Godalming. He had it ripped
out of him all the way and to make matters worse it
was the slow train. But it was all in good fun and he
took it well.

As time moved on and the drug intake got heavier,
the emphasis on match days started to shift to who
was sorting the gear out rather than how many are on
this train, where are we meeting, what to expect
opposition-wise, etc. The days of arranging meetings
with opposing fans and getting into towns early to
avoid the Old Bill were numbered.

We pulled up in Manchester one day for an
afternoon kick-off against City, already having
mullered a huge bag of Thai stick en route. A few of
the younger lot came running over to the motor,
calling us, as they were skirmishing with some Mancs.
We were so stoned that we done the window up and
pissed ourselves laughing. We later got our act
together and had it with them, not leaving until 8
o'clock that night, as a couple of our Zulu mates who
used to come along will testify.

We had a great day out on the gear about this time
in 1988, when Joe Bugner fought Frank Bruno at
White Hart Lane. We had QPR away that day and
nothing really happened apart from Pompey losing
2–1. White Hart Lane was very hostile, with it going
off all over the place, but we just stood on the old
Shelf, skinning up huge spliffs, trying to keep it
together on the trips we had necked earlier. There was
an absolute monster of an Aussie walking about in full
regalia, and no one touched him. It would erupt with
violence in the crowd every few minutes with different

crews and it went off quite badly between Tottenham and West Ham in the Paxton Road End. Before the fight 'celebrity' ringside guests were introduced, and Chris Quinten (aka Brian Tylsley from Coronation Street) was roundly booed as he got in the ring in his dinner suit. He then did a double backflip and landed perfectly arms at each side, v-signs displayed. We had a drink in London with him years later and laughed about it. He was quite a decent bloke.

Another of Bruno's fights was against Tim Witherspoon at Wembley. We didn't have tickets, and were on the 9 o'clock news ramming the gates with a huge tidy bin trying to smash them down, off our heads on acid, with a 50-strong mob. Later on that evening we were outside Stringfellows, abusing the bouncers, when a real gorilla of a doorman, 20 stone, 6ft 6in, came out of the club and squeezed himself into a Hillman Imp. To this day it has to be one of the funniest things ever seen. He looked like the cartoon character Mooncat.

We went to our first Glastonbury in the summer of '86 in a five-year-old Rover 3500, which was chocolate brown with beige leather interior. We thought that motor was the bollocks. One of our lot had blagged it for 100 quid as it was rotting away in a garage somewhere. We had heard good things about Glastonbury and that there were people selling all types of drugs, shouting out loud like they were on a fruit and veg cart in a market. It was unbelievable. One black fella was standing in the alley between two of the fields where all the dealers would congregate, shouting at the top of his voice, 'Black hash, white lightening, speed, Moroccan, African bush.' We couldn't believe how open it all was. We were tripping and continually asked him what he didn't have, but he *didn't find it funny. The music was really good that year, with The Cure playing a blinder in the pouring rain with a really awesome light display. We went home late that night, exhausted, but a few of us had a rush of blood the next day and went back up. It was the day Maradona scored his hand of God goal when Argentina beat us 2–1 in the World Cup quarter-final. The game was meant to be shown live in a big marquee, but it went pear-shaped so we missed it, but they had probably blagged it so people didn't fuck off home. On the same day on a boiling afternoon Simply Red played a wicked two-hour set. Happy days.*

We went up to Grimsby in about '86–'87, not expecting much opposition anyway, and were surprised when 30 of their boys burst into Cleethorpes Pier where a car full of us were having a drink. Instead of reacting, we rolled a couple of huge spliffs and just sat there. You could see them talking between themselves deciding whether or not to steam into us. They didn't in the end. I think our total indifference to the situation put them off a bit. We just didn't give a fuck. We ended up that day absolutely wrecked, sitting at the back of the stand where the Pompey fans were housed and seeing who could start off the most ridiculous seventies football song. It worked big time. No one knew we were taking the piss and all the singers joined in with us. We couldn't stop laughing as long-forgotten tunes were belted out. And to cap it all we won 2–0, which was unusual to say the least, as Pompey rarely won up north.

When we took acid in those days it would go one of two ways – we would either end up round someone's house with the lights off losing the plot to Pink Floyd, or rampaging through Southsea, smashing up clubs and anything else in our path. One such night we caught a geezer and his bird in their Robin Reliant on the seafront having a bit more than a cuddle up. There was about 15 of us tripping out of our heads on some lethal gear called pink dreams. One of the boys had got hold of a bottle of liquid acid and some blotting paper and overdone it. A fella called Tommy got on top of the car and went straight through the roof. The poor couple must have wondered what the hell was going on as a 6ft 3in lunatic was half in and half out of their car with 14 others, pissing themselves laughing, pulling him out. As the bloke got out to remonstrate, Chalky called him a dirty bastard and gave him a slap, which only made it funnier.

Later that night, three of us ended up at a hot-dog van, unsuccessfully trying to get some food, having had a big off at the seedy Bistro club on the way. The Bistro was a real dive, frequented by DHSS types and other low lifes, and that place got all it deserved. We could smash the granny out of anyone at the time but could we order a jumbo with chips? No. There was even a rumour circling that one of the chaps had spiked a local dignitary's drink with a trip in the players' lounge at Fratton Park. Apparently he had gone into mental fits of laughter within about 20 minutes of downing his pint. After being driven off in a Bentley, he had promptly done a U-turn straight back in a taxi for another drink, stumbling about all over the place with a bright red face.

* * *

The main meeting place around the early drug days was a large ground-floor flat in Sedgely Close, which we nicknamed the 'anarchy ranch'. One of our good friend's sisters had emigrated to the Middle East and had mistakenly left him in charge. It ended up as a squat, slap bang in the middle of Somers Town, one of the worst areas in Portsmouth. It was lawless. We all used to drink in a pub close by called the Robert Peel and would then head for Sedgely at closing time. At the weekends a big system would be put outside with reggae music thumping out and the Old Bill could do nothing about it, as we would be 100-strong on party nights. All good lads. Quite a few people had pit bulls then and they would roam freely round the ranch. Red Stripe was the favoured can, but in the Robert Peel we would drink Skol Special, affectionately called 'affray juice'. The ranch was a hive of activity in the day with different little groups dropping in and out. The numerous gangs of hoisters would meet up and go out of town shopping for the day, with others getting up to all sorts of illegal activities. It was a total piss-take all round, hence the anarchy tag, and we knew it couldn't go on forever. We even got a singer round the ranch one day and all had a knees-up singing 'Mrs Robinson'. But when we eventually got fed up with him he went head first through the bedroom window, breaking his arm on the way. Bang out of order, really, but Steve the busker is still a legend to those who were there. We even smashed his guitar over his head, poor fucker. One of the boys even made him a makeshift sling out of a bedsheet to wear up the hospital. We weren't totally heartless.

The ranch would host many fist fights, but rules were laid down and referees appointed. There was good order in the ranks and unwritten rules were obeyed. It really was first-class entertainment and, especially with some of the needle matches, there were some really good tear-ups.

The cozzers eventually shut the ranch down early one morning. Last to leave was ranch stalwart Spider, dressed in battle gear that included Everlast boxing gloves, flying hat and goggles. He was dragged out the back window screaming, 'You'll never take me alive', as the door came crashing in. It was the end of an era. We were gutted.

Around this time we would also go to a pub in the centre of Portsmouth, where bands would play and you could freely smoke draw and score whatever you wanted. We were pally with the punk lot from Nightingale Road, and they had some quality blokes: Nuts, Johnny, Little Bri and Mark Ex spring to mind.

The 6.57 had adopted a local band called the Emptifish and followed them wherever they played. They were pretty good and popular blokes, who seemed to love the raucous partisan following they suddenly had. But the inevitable happened at most of their gigs, and it would go off quite badly with the punky lot that used to follow them around before we were on the scene. One such battle at Reading went on for ages, with us only just coming out on top. The band had a support act called the Shakin' Sharks, involving a couple of known faces, who would mime and fuck about dressed up as the Blues Brothers. A separate book could be written about the Emptifish days.

The football had been calming down for a while as the courts were really getting severe and dawn raids were becoming more frequent. We got them in '86 when we stirred up a hornet's nest on a dodgy estate in Derby, and after Brighton when 70 of us were nicked. The Old Bill tried to make more of it and put the wind up everyone, talking about three- to five-year sentences, although nothing ever happened. But football was starting to lose its edge off the pitch in Portsmouth. Birmingham had come down and taken the piss all round the ground and everyone was getting fed up with it. It was a far cry from the heady days of '83–'84 when we deemed ourselves just about invincible, as top mobs such as Cardiff have verified in black and white. The Old Bill always went for us and not the other fans and we knew it was only a matter of time before we all got hammered in court. The drugs were also distracting people and the next few months finally killed it off for our lot, but no one could have predicted to what extent.

***

We first tried ecstasy early on in 1988. One of the chaps was bringing in some draw from a fella in London, who gave him some MDMA capsules, which looked more like horse tablets they were so big. A few of us were drinking in a boozer and, when five of us necked these monsters, which we had heard made you love everyone. Not us. We went on the rampage that night. After an hour we were buzzing and walking down Albert Road, Southsea, shouting, 'There are new sheriffs in town', and looking for anyone who disagreed. We first hit a bar called Scandals, where nervous bouncers and the owner, Simon, said we couldn't come in. Simon soon went spiralling back down the stairs from a right-hander and the bouncers went running for their lives as the Scandals sign came falling down on them. We then headed for the centre of town and our next victims were the police on duty outside Ritzy's. We met up with some fellas we knew as they were leaving the club and a free for all on plod developed, resulting in numerous arrests. Not a great start to the loved-up world of ecstasy.

***

A few of us went to a Pink Floyd concert at Wembley off our heads one night. What an experience that was. We all agreed on the way home we had never known anything like it. Anyone who has been to a Pink Floyd concert and necked about three good trips and isn't having their food through a straw in a nuthouse will know what I mean. While we were there, two spaced-out birds asked us if we had ever been to an acid house rave in London and recommended them to us. A fella from our way had also been raving (for want of a better word) about the underground clubs up there and how the football firms were mingling together and having a great time dropping Es together. It didn't sound realistic at the time, but after the first trip to London and our second, much better, experience with Es, we were hooked and couldn't think of anything else.

Within a matter of weeks the bug had spread through Pompey and our lot. We went to Unit 4, a really spectacular warehouse do in Battersea, and all of a sudden we had our own area instead of little pockets of us scattered around. A big crew of Pompey dancing and singing along to 'Jibaro' – a song that stands out from Unit 4 – was a sight to see. The numbers were swelling after every night in London and it was catching on. The Es at the time were the *best ever, split Callys, which were so strong even the guttiest pig could only manage two or three. They sent you into orbit. They were fantastic, but came and went very quickly. We were so loved up on them we talked endless bollocks, although we thought it made perfect sense at the time. Everyone used to get the raving horn on them and relationships broke up all over the shop. We would all phone each other up the next day, cringing like mad saying, 'Oh fucking hell. Did I really say that to her?' It was great.*

Appearances changed and in no time at all it was Converse trainers, ripped jeans, tracksuits, there were even waistcoats and iffy cowboy boots floating about. As it progressed, people grew their hair long and some even started wearing ponchos and beads. It was like a re-run of 1967, with everyone chilled out and hippified. However, this time around it was hardened thugs talking about peace and love. It was the second summer of love. In about a three-month period, thousands of pairs of Pasty shoes were sold in Pompey alone, with Kickers also very popular. One shop owner sold thousands of pounds' worth of purple tops and tracksuit bottoms in one day. Other brands of clothing that were everywhere then were Naf Naf, Chevignon and Stone Island, which as everyone knows is the terrace uniform of today, although the emphasis then was more on the Stone Island Marina range of washed-out faded clobber. It was comfy and increasingly baggy, as everyone shed the pounds through too much gear and too many late nights.

* * *

No one gave a fuck, it was madness. It had come from nowhere but things had stagnated and ecstasy seemed to have given everyone a new direction. The amount of drugs being consumed was outrageous. We couldn't have been further away from the violence of a year before if we tried. All the tough talking from the Thatcher government, all the police surveillance, the infiltration of various mobs, the millions of pounds of taxpayers' money spent and the reason for a dramatic decline in violence at football matches across the country was a tiny pill. We would be 40-handed on the dance floor having the time of our lives, and we are talking cream 6.57 who had never been on a dance floor before. Well, only when the fight they were having spilled on to it. Not only that but everyone was embracing total strangers and having in-depth conversations with them. It was bizarre. The very same people who had spent the previous 10 years standing around in nightclubs with a beer bottle in hand waiting for someone to look at them a fraction too long, were now taking centre stage. Every single one of them thought they were the world's best dancer as they poured with sweat with eyes bulging and arms waving to the trance-like beats. Waterloo station changed from being a potential battleground with the likes of Millwall or Chelsea, to a place to change and shower between raves. Now we were mobbing up in considerable numbers not to confront London firms but to socialise with them. It was the strangest turnaround and had to be experienced to be believed.

***

The other main clubs we would visit at that time were The Wag, with Dave Durrell on the decks, on Friday night, called Love, and Saturdays was the star-studded

Prohibition, called Baby Love, also with Durrell. On a Sunday at one club, Kid Batchelor would play 8–1am, Confusion. Word of mouth spread around as places chucked out in the morning. Trade was open all morning but was a bit too gay and sleazy and not for the faint-hearted. Sunday lunchtime a few little gaffs would open, the best one, which the Spurs lot never shut up about, was the Queens Club at Heathrow. One character who seemed to be in every rave we ever went to was Paul, who worked on Oxford Street. He was one of the worst E casualties around. He would explode with excitement when he saw us and never stopped telling us he loved us, while pushing a huge bottle of mystery liquid up our noses, which we called industrial nitrate. The funny thing is none of us had known him from Adam before the rave scene. And have never seen him since.

The A3 was beginning to become a hazy blur as it was back and forth to the capital. Night after night we would drive on auto pilot, with the trees just after Hindhead, that have now been chopped down, creating a smoky tunnel at about six in the morning after a heavy night and no sleep, beat still pounding in your ears. Anyone who has done that drive nutted will know that when they eventually got home and tried to sleep, all they could see going through their head would be road signs: Portsmouth 45 miles, etc. We would never sleep on the way home, even if dog-tired, always keeping an eye on the driver. The classic phrase at the time was 'He ain't blinked since Guildford'. God only knows where the motorway police were, because we made that drive packed in a van or car hundreds of times without a pull. Incredible.

* * *

Dealing was becoming rife between most football firms and attitudes had changed. A lot of the main chaps from all over had decided that there was no money in fighting and it was time to have an earn. A lot of them have never come back to football. A classic story of one of our lot shows the naïvety of the whole situation. One particular fella in south London buying a parcel of gear had a tester of some potent Charlie while making the purchase, and was dropped at a taxi office in Brixton. His cab home was a Mark Four Cortina with reggae pumping out, and red, gold and green visor and mudflaps driven by a Bob Marley lookalike – a rare sight in Pompey. Seventy quid later and after being asked umpteen times by the driver if he liked 'a reefer, mon', he was dropped at the end of the M27, feeling paranoid as fuck, with a holdall full of puff in his hand. The first police car that saw Marley in his Cheech and Chong mobile driving through Portsmouth would have pulled them. He never did a drug pick-up again.

***

Everyone was having a ball: West Ham, Millwall, Spurs, Arsenal, all getting on fine. Chelsea too, although their Boys Own parties, though full of pretty women and playing superb music, were run by a couple of pricks who were definitely up their own arses trying to be too cool. The way they used to get themselves at it on the door was comical, as we all used to get in anyway. We all turned up at a weekender in Bognor and they shit themselves. Mind you, not surprising really as it took thousands of them, some with blades, to see a few hundred of us off in Milton Park in '84 when Pompey had played them. They opened a bar in the West End in the nineties and we were amused to discover our mate Mugger from Tottenham had popped in for a drink and nutted one of them, calling him a pretentious idiot, amongst other things. Mugger was a bit of a handful and one of Spurs' main faces throughout the eighties. We had made good friends with a few Tottenham faces by now through the Wag scene and they were doing warehouse parties over on their patch. We took a coach up to one of their nights and met up with our pals right outside White Hart Lane. To everyone's joy they hopped on board, dished out the goodies and directed us to the warehouse in Edmonton. We had a good night up there and were fascinated to see a huge black geezer standing on his own in the corridor rocking to the beat shouting, 'Bang on three bang on three bang on three.' He was there in a total trance until the Old Bill stopped it at 5am. The same firm ran the hugely successful Ibiza/2001 warehouse raves at King's Cross all the way through '89. They were massive and they had a hell of a run getting 3,000 a fortnight through the door, until they were closed down at the end of the summer.

We were different, however, with Southampton. And not just because of the so-called rivalry between us and them. They were not into it in '88–'89, and have always been a bit slow on the uptake. They were confused by our clothes in '83 when they met some of our lads saying, 'Why the fuck are you wearing that French shit (La Coste) and that gym wear (Tacchini)?' And they still remain the only firm to have ever sported 'taches – south of Sheffield that is. So it's no surprise that they didn't get anything together up there until at least 1992 in the way of rave parties. None of our boys have ever wanted anything to do with them as they have absolutely no respect here. Travelling east along the M27 is not their thing as they have never managed to get much together in Pompey. So it was just as well for them, really, as even at the peak of love and peace they wouldn't have been tolerated here. One of the reasons is that a whole pub took liberties on six of our finest, who still walked out (after being bombarded with glasses and missiles, with no punches thrown). Pompey is a tight-knit city and it hasn't been forgotten. They were prominent at the Manor House in the New Forest but that wasn't until late '92, with most of our lot having left it alone then, apart from a few casualties. So we didn't mix with the Scummers at all, not in business or pleasure. They know who our faces are and we know theirs, but with the exception of some of the younger lot being chummy with Rolfie, we simply don't have it with them.

The local scene was coming along rather well and although some of the organisation was a bit of a mish mash it didn't really matter as the drugs were so potent, you would have had the time of your life stuck in a phone box for the night with a set of drumsticks and a biscuit tin. A couple of the chaps had become pretty good DJs and we had it going on in the town. A few memorable nights include Aldridge's acid boat, the pig farm and the warehouse at Hilsea. Also Amberley Castle was an excellent night. The police first realised they had a problem in our area when they stopped Gordon's warehouse do at Hilsea. The level of abuse and piss-take was high when they stopped it in mid-flow for no reason and as everyone was being searched they were all telling the coppers to go and *fuck themselves. As there were so many people abusing them they were just glad to clear the area. It was on the TV the next morning. We had some mates down from London for that evening, and they bought a pal with them to DJ. Tracey Kirby – the page-three girl was also with them. She was staying at the Queens Hotel in Southsea, so we went back for a party. The DJ who had tried to be paired off with Tracey had had a severe case of premature ejaculation. He said to us, 'I couldn't get it out of my head that she's page 3.' It wouldn't be fair to name the one-minute wonder, so don't worry, your secret's safe with us. Tracey just looked totally embarrassed for him. She was all right and we met her quite a few times after that and in Tenerife when she was on holiday.*

***

There is an old ruin just inside West Sussex where all the punk lot and alternatives would meet up every year and have a chilled-out party. It was known as Racton Ruins. In 1989 we decided to change it and had a full-on rave there attended by 2,000 people. It was a different class. The sight of all our mob hanging off the back of a big Luton van and dancing in the fields was unforgettable. Football was well and truly out the window, although it has to be said not everyone got into drugs. A DJ organised a huge do at Hayling Island with everyone going crazy in the sand dunes. Even the older lot from Navy Arms were there and loving every minute of it. There was this complete nutcase who used to go and he would chop up wood with a huge axe in the mornings and just stomp about keeping the fire going. We would be off our heads exchanging nervous glances. He was harmless, but mad all the same.

Another one the Old Bill tried and failed to stop was just outside Pompey at Denmead. Just as it was about to start they came piling on to the field but everyone surrounded them and they fucked off after a senior copper thought better of starting on us. It was a great do and when the music started a huge cheer went up. Later on in the evening, when we were all buzzing like mental, one of our mates, Eddie, collapsed. So we were immediately running round shouting, 'We'll have a score's worth of what he's had.' He was all right within a couple of minutes and marched on dancing away like it had never happened.

***

Glastonbury '89 was visited by loads of us from Pompey. It was pretty much the same as three years before, apart from the arrests for supplying were up and our numbers had swelled considerably. Hardly suprising, really. None of our lot really went to deal up there as they were far more interested in having some fun. And at the festivals and raves the dealers were more often black guys. This time the weekend was more organised and the landmark Pompey flags were set up in fields, as it was immense and you could really come unstuck trying to find your way back late at night fucked out of your face. Mobile phones were still relatively rare and the size of housebricks, but a few people had the enterprise to pitch up offering the use of them at a pound a minute. The toilets were, as usual, disgusting and you could see a look of horror on people's faces as they came out of the portaloos.

The rave scene had kicked in and The Rhythm Doctor had set up in a field, playing all day and long into the night. They had a big screen set up with a psychedelic slide show that some guy had to do by sleight of hand for effect. He must have done it for 12 hours and how he didn't get cramp is a total mystery. The record 'French Kiss' was being played to death at the time and in the top field Darren Emmerson of Ratpack fame had it going. However, when most of our lot had turned in for the night, with a few stragglers left, a couple of vans of security pulled up and lined everyone up. The women were really distressed. Earlier in the day, some gangs had been steaming through the fields mugging people. It would have been interesting to say the least if they had have come by the Pompey stronghold as we had a good mixture of town and some top Paulsgrove boys.

***

Record sales were booming with loads of new customers out buying 12-inch imports, and 100 different lads must have attempted a spot of DJing. Mostly unsuccessfully. Technics decks were appearing in the most unlikely of households throughout the town. Powerhouse Records was a popular meeting place at the time, as was the clothes shop Swag in the same arcade in Arundel Street, central Portsmouth.

Almost every city in England hosted illegal acid parties in 1989. Most of the more obscure and select nights were run by football faces and the doors were being run by the respective town's football firms. This happened to a certain extent in Pompey, but not as much as it did in the bigger cities as it's always been on top here. The Hampshire authorities were far stricter on licensing and permissions, with the police only too keen to clamp down and enforce the decisions. West Sussex was a much safer haven. The Hampshire Police even had Optica plane spotters out looking for people setting up sound systems and other apparatus out in the sticks. A lot of people wasted a lot of time and money by being thwarted at the last minute by the partypoopers in blue. Crowds gathered at meeting points only to get the call that the police had found the venue. So we all had to find something else to do that evening. Very frustrating.

We were still travelling to London, too. The Downham Tavern was loved by all and the laser show that they used to put on was second to none. On Christmas Eve '88 we took over 100 up to the Tavern on a 12–12 all-dayer. We were even represented on the turntables there by football face Mick Wearn. This was bang in the middle of Millwall territory, run by their top boys, and they were perfectly happy with that. A year before that or two year's after and it would have been a full battle but the vibe then was peace and love, despite the bitter rivalry between the very people dancing together and saying how great the other was. The clubs had even banned each other's fans from their respective grounds for two seasons in the eighties, such was the trouble between the two mobs at the time. One of the first times two clubs got together and said enough is

th firms would laugh and joke about various battles at places like Waterloo and Charing Cross. There was even a heavy ICF presence at the Downham, the Bushwhackers' fiercest rivals, but even that particular powder keg failed to ignite. But the Tavern was *always well run, with most people transfixed by the sounds and lasers and totally off their face. The same crew also ran a sweatbox called Bonnies in Catford, with Tony Wilson on the decks – another cracker. At one of the last Downhams, a few of our younger lot were fronted by some Millwall, but it was an isolated incident, and the main players up there sorted it out. Maybe they were trying to clip our wings as they thought we were taking the piss.*

We also visited a club called Faces which was in the East End, run by the ICF, and although we never had a problem there, it was not as relaxed as the Tavern and there were some pretty nasty-looking characters about. It was always bit moody visiting the toilet at Faces. In the early days there was a corker of a pirate radio station called Centreforce, run by one of the ICF's top boys which was very popular with the ravers, as it would drop hints on where to meet up for the elusive parties. It would also play top rave tunes night after night and gained cult status amongst the underground. Unfortunately it was closed down in 1989, but was great while it lasted and fondly remembered by all.

After whatever help you had to find your venue it would be like finding an oasis in the desert, as you would be that close to giving up your quest and going home. But then wide-eyed people would run up to the doors having found their holy grail. It was particularly satisfying as the parties that survived the police were usually well planned and thought out, which inevitably meant a good sound system and music. More often than not, small exits were used to prevent the police shutting it down, and it could sometimes be a bit of a tight squeeze and rather frantic to get in and out – a health and safety nightmare. The only real problem we used to have was knowing where the fuck we were, as we staggered out in the morning with everything looking so different.

On Monday nights 100 strong would always make their way to Spectrum at Charing Cross: the queue was a pain but worth the wait. As time went on, a coach would ferry us all up, as the drive home was becoming hazardous, with people dropping five and six Es a night. Far too many and very dangerous, but still it went on. We unearthed a little gem of a place right in the middle of Brixton called Barrington Road. The coach drivers would be nervous about stopping there but gentle persuasion and a few quid would sort it out. It's amazing how generous we got when we wanted an extension to our buzz. Inside, the layout was loads of little tunnels and a couple of dance rooms which probably held no more than 150–200 when full. It was set in arches in an old industrial unit under a bridge. We were the only white people there but the crowd were absolutely fine with us all. The DJ Groove Rider would play in one room and Fabio in another. The sounds were really good. We began to notice that the buzz had moved on a bit as menacing-looking blacks would stand round the edge of the dance floor. But, however that sounds, we never had a problem with any of them, and we were very loud. The Tunnel Club was not quite as friendly, and one night we almost got caught up in a massive police raid as the Tunnel was shut once and for all.

New Year's Eve '88–'89 was a great night out and we ended up at a major warehouse rave in Hackney. Even though it was in the middle of East London, we never gave a second thought to what rival firms might *be present, despite the presence of heavy-looking geezers. Things had now changed for the better and it was kicking all night. One of our mates was so off his face, two of his front teeth fell out. God alone knows what he had that night but it really did happen – five of us witnessed it.*

That summer we all used to go congregate at Langtry's, sitting about like one big happy family in the large garden they had out front. Central Park in the middle of town was open by this time and on a Friday it was heaving. A lot of people would come from out of town, which was unusual as strangers had never been that welcome in Portsmouth. The Hayling beach parties had also attracted people from far and wide. We had two good clubs to choose from, and that will never be repeated. A few of the lads had started to disappear to various exotic locations by now, far more interested in getting smashed in the sun with the beat going on than playing cat and mouse on the underground with our local spotters and the Met. Full moon parties in Goa and places like the Backyard Club in Thailand were far more appealing to a lot of people. Much more so than standing on the terraces in the pissing rain, at places like Oxford, under constant observation, with plod filming every move. It was all but over for us by now, it didn't make much sense any more.

It wasn't all love and peace though, as the local police found out after they stopped a rave going on over at a tiny village called Boarhunt in Hampshire. There was a full-scale riot that night. The rave had had a lot of preparation, with time and money spent on a huge marquee along with the Downham Tavern lasers, and top DJs were booked. It was called Manakiss. A restless crowd all ready to party had become increasingly aggressive and the Old Bill got hammered as they tried to stop it. They were chased right out of it and one of their meat wagons was torched and exploded in a ball of fire. Pure mayhem, with a real top mob doing the business. It was all over the national papers. The only thing that kept it off the front pages was the tragic accident when the party boat *Marchioness* had sunk in the River Thames with the loss of over 50 lives. There was a picture of the burned-out police van, much to everyone's amusement, followed by grumblings in Parliament about lawless rave parties, adding more weight to the forthcoming Criminal Justice Bill. If the police had let it go on, they could have avoided any trouble. Nobody got a day in prison for anything that happened that night as it was dark and there was no proof, with any potential police witnesses long gone. For once they took a good hiding. In actual fact they got run ragged and absolutely mullered.

On the same night, some local organisers had put on a boat to cruise round the Solent. It was audacious to say the least, as the flyers advertising it said it was a foxtrot and waltz night. Undercover police were sussed on the boat, and a helicopter even followed. When the boat docked, coaches ferried the crowd over to Boarhunt which poured petrol on to an already fierce flame.

The Monday after the riot, the police questioned Powerhouse records, Swag and even Taboo. The worst the owners had done was to sell tickets, rave wear and records to everyone. They were certainly nothing to do with the violence or the supplying of any narcotics. They were endlessly grilled about the football link.

BREAK 4 LOVE

Our friends in the Midlands were up and running by now and had some huge parties going on. The Zulus have always run things in Birmingham and this continued into the rave days. An old acquaintance of ours who is now doing double life, for what can only be described as a moment of madness and tragedy, ran massive warehouse parties called Time. Tickets would change hands at inflated prices outside, such was the popularity of these events. Top of the DJ bill would be the likes of Sasha and Graeme Park of the Hacienda. Partygoers came from miles around.

The only organisation to match this scale of event in the Midlands was Amnesia, which was run by the Coventry boys, who had 10,000 people at one open-air bash. Although not the most active of football firms, Coventry is a very rough place and the crime centre of the Midlands. Chuff Chuff was born in Birmingham and they put on arguably the best private functions there have ever been to come out of the clubbing scene. They tend to hire out manor houses and run a very tight membership and door policy. They also have such a good reputation that spin-off CDs sell well. We have always had a warm welcome in the Midlands and they are good people up there. The Zulus would have a big presence on the doors at all their parties, but unlike in Pompey, the doormen are the top boys. They use common sense and don't take liberties.

***

Things had just started to change around town and certainly in London. There were complaints about tricky situations encountered in places up there. Deals had started to go wrong all over the place, with people ripping each other off everywhere. Late summer '89 it seemed everyone was robbing everyone. There were loads of issues and arguments kicking off round town and the atmosphere had begun to become tense. It was not as loved-up any more. The second summer of love was over. Killed in no small part by greed and the new drug of choice – cocaine. Because of this it all kind of fizzled out in town in 1990 and although it still went on, the best days had been and gone. The clubs took it over and the freedom of open drug-taking went away as nickings were a plenty and sentences were high.

There was one last epic ballyhoo though, when after much press coverage, 5,000 people danced all night in a Grade I-listed castle on the island. The rave was called Treasure Island and a monster line up of DJs were booked including Fabio, Groove Rider and Colin Faver who, on arrival at the castle, played extra sets free of charge, phoning London to cancel his other bookings. To cap it all the organisers took a six-figure sum on the door giving them a lovely earner, to the Old Bill's dismay.

Words can't be written without mentioning Pete C who was DJing all the way through these times and always played a good set of upfront sounds. Mickey Wearn is also a well-known DJ from the town and still has a good reputation to this day, working under the name Groover Washington.

Ritzy's was shut down in the early nineties after the tragic death of a young lad who had taken an E. It was the end of the most prominent club of our generation in Portsmouth of our generation. It had hosted all sorts of different youth culture, from the *kids' discos on a Monday night in the seventies, when on chuck-out all the different cliques (if they weren't fighting each other) would join up and go skatebashing, a tradition which only calmed down after the Falklands war in 1982. Some of the skates took awful beatings on a Monday night, as gangs of 14- and 16-year-olds do tend to get carried away. There had been different nights for skinheads, mods, punks and, of course, students. It would host bank holiday all-nighters with a jazz funk feel in the early eighties, and it put up with all of us having en masse aggro all the way through that decade. The Clash even played there on the 'Sort it Out' tour of 1979, as did other prominent punk bands such as The Ruts. It has never opened its doors to the clubbers since that tragic death. It's ironic that the rave culture was the last youth fashion to really take the country by storm and unfortunately the drugs that went with it have killed any new ideas or styles that could be adopted. So far it has been the end of the line for anything fresh to hit the streets as everyone seems to have run out of alternatives to enjoy. The E culture shut the doors to Ritzy's and all the memories that went with it.*

Some of the boys are still into the music scene and what goes with it, but not with the same intensity as then. For most of us it was a phase that we went through, and a truly memorable one at that. The feeling of euphoria and the rush of adrenalin was a kind of replacement for the buzz of confrontation at football when everyone used to charge around going ballistic. The actual cry of 'here they are', and the pandemonium that followed, could only be rivalled by a new and untried drug that was to change our lives and direction. Like them or not, drugs are here to stay, but as times have changed, people who still take Es are either youngsters or deemed unfashionable. They are extremely cheap now and nowhere near as potent as they once were as they are tampered with to a dangerous level healthwise.

The favoured tipple today is cocaine, and at most functions attended by the chaps here and in other cities, the toilets are always very busy. It is rife on the England scene too and unlike E it can make a person quite surly and aggressive. It isn't a peace and love drug at all, and no doubt some of the England hoolies are charged up when they go to work. It is a far cry from the days of 'rushing on my second mate' and everyone loving everything.

It has to be remembered that this phenomenon was a brand new experience and took everyone by surprise. There was no precedent or older lot to ask, it just came from nowhere, with the long-term effects still to be seen. Before acid house and raving, clubbing was a sometimes violent experience with slow dances and burger and chips an integral part. The advent of Es turned this on its head and water became the drink of choice. The football crowd were the obvious first exponents of this craze as they were adventurous and thrill seeking, always looking for new adrenalin rushes of some sort. Ecstasy had a huge impact on the football scene in Portsmouth and was without any doubt the major factor in its decline at the end of the eighties.

Where Were You at Fratton Park?

This is not a cheap shot at certain clubs, but some so-called firms have never materialised at our place after we have caused trouble at theirs. The main culprits here seem to be from the Midlands. Aston Villa have never brought a firm to Pompey, although the gauntlet was well and truly laid down in the Cup in '84 at their place. They have played here twice since and nothing. They are now apparently active. Too late, boys. Wolves are also a club who do not travel. They are better off beating up scarfers at Molineux and when we did go up to them in '85 they got the same sort of hiding that Millwall gave them last season. They are another of the Stone Island- and Burberry-clad England mobs we laugh at. We have never rated Wolves in Pompey. They have never been to Fratton Park and they've had plenty of opportunities. To any normal peace-loving football fans who haven't been to Wolves, be a bit careful, they're not fussy about who they attack. Burnley and Sheffield Utd will also agree to this. Derby have also showed very little at ours – they bought about 30–40 boys in '83, got a slap and never returned. We had a right ding-dong at Pear Tree Road with the blacks as we've described, and although we know this wasn't the DLF, we caused havoc in their backyard and nothing was done about it.

Sheffield Utd are another mob who have done little. We have always gone to them in numbers and done well, and it's interesting to see the photos they have taken of the 6.57 coming across the pitch at Fratton. They wouldn't come to the fence that day. We had 500 on the pitch and they didn't want to know. Well, we were hardly going to travel 50 miles to fight a firm who stood at the back of the terrace in awe while we waited on the pitch for them to come and play, were we? This is not really slagging them, because they were always good for a row at their place. They even kidnapped one of our boys in '81 and took him on a pub crawl with his hands tied. It's just a fact that we have never really been troubled by them at home. They have come but not performed. This will really offend die hard Blades, but Wednesday always used to bring a good mob in the late seventies right up to '80–'81. It could even be said that along with Bradford and Huddersfield they were our main games then – the good old Third and Fourth Division days. We do know in these parts, however, that the Blades run Sheffield and always have it their own way with Wednesday who they call 'the Pigs'.

It was amusing to read the BBC police spotters got a kicking in Pompey this season, as they disturbed two blokes doing a phone box over as they walked back to their hotel after the evening match.

This will seem harsh but we are all a bit miffed as to why Lincoln never travelled to Pompey. They were brilliant opposition at Sincil Bank in the late seventies and early eighties. It really isn't fair to disrespect them but they've never turned up at ours. That's not taking anything away from their home turnouts, as when you have the quality of action we had with them it would be wrong to do so. Maybe they just didn't travel in those days so the best compliment they can be given is to say for the size of their city they defended their ground and streets like Trojans and they have the greatest respect in Pompey.

Last and by no means least are our friends from up the road. The internet is awash with stories from Southampton boys describing huge battles when they have been to Fratton Park. Don't be so fucking stupid. They bought a mob of 200 frightened rabbits in the Cup in '84. They must have earned 100 quid each in loose change as they were bombarded with coins, and a big gap in the Milton End was evident where they squeezed along to get out of range. That was our biggest ever firm that day. We had 2,000 on the North Bank alone and they would have got killed. They turned up at ten to three in the old first in '87, and slashed some poor kid who was out with his bird. There was a paltry 150 of them. Well done. The only battles when we have played them at Fratton have been with us and the Old Bill while we tried to get at them. We've always had to go to them. There you are, Scummers, it's in black and white and after much consultation with a lot of the faces, that's being generous. So where were you at Fratton Park?

UNUSUAL METHODS OF TRANSPORT

The favoured ways to travel to away games apart from the 6.57 to Waterloo have been numerous. Southern Self Drive and Mitchells also used to make a fortune out of us. The sky-blue transits were always on the road, as were the classic Luton Vans. We used to travel up the motorway with the shutters open, feet dangling out the back winding up the motorists behind. These were always a good tool for after the game as they would pull up by a rival mob and the shutters would fly open. Ask Villa.

More obscure transport has been a moped to Newport that ended up being put in the back of Fooksie's coach for the trip home as it was fucked – a 50cc bike going up the M4 was a sight for sore eyes and it was a night game. A mob of the lads even left the pub one night and walked to Aldershot, arriving the next morning. That is the same game that their ground was set on fire and everyone was singing, 'Aldershit is burning down'.

A couple of the lads nicked a motor out of a garage in Fareham called to get to the classic Northampton away in '80. It was the promotion game where we took 10,000. It was an old Mini Clubman, with all the wood framework. It even had an eight-track on with Elvis blaring out they picked up a couple of Cosham hitchhikers on the way.

Double-decker and old green army buses have also been used by our firm for away travel and the lengths and means people will go to just to get to a match can at times be ludicrous as well as downright incredible. These are just a few of these instances.

OVERKILL

This book is a walk down memory lane to recap and reflect on the heyday of the 6.57 crew which it is certainly not now in 2004. Although you do get the odd incident, there is no organisation nowadays and not many people go with the sole intention of causing trouble. There is no point and the risks have become too high. We are not looking to compete with the likes of new firms who seem to be popping up all over the place – mainly in the north and Midlands. We have nothing to prove as we earned our reputation the hard way, when fighting was far more important than a Stone Island coat.

Pompey still have a good turn out at England games – the heat is less abroad and it's always a good laugh too. Pompey have just launched a new crackdown on hooliganism called HOOF, Hooligans Out Of Football, what that is all about God only knows, as no one really goes for a row any more. Step forward the newest recruit to the cause, the modern-day spotter. They direct video cameras into faces who are walking up to the ground with their kids for Grimsby at home. Really, is that over the top or what? The most bizarre thing is that they honestly believe he is one of the lads. At least in the days of King and Hiscock, you half knew where you stood. When you get the Sheffield paper expecting 300 Pompey hooligans in town for the whole weekend for a Sky TV game, you wonder what sort of fairyland this new spotter lives in when he picks up the phone.

Yes, we need a police force but they are to serve and protect not for this over-reaction. That's where the money should be spent, sorting that mess out. In a short while the arrest statistics will filter through to the powers that be.

Everybody is looking forward to Premiership football next season. It is also a known fact that there is little trouble in the Premiership due to ticket allocations, and that is that. No doubt if given the chance the spotter will be talking our firm up all over the country when the only allocated seats will be going to the scarfers and a few lads who are happy to leave things in the past.

The game's all but up down here. That brings us around to thinking of the finest and most-missed 6.57 character you're ever likely to meet.

Robin 'Fish' Porter
1961–1994

'My name is Fish
I live in a dish
I ain't got time
To pay my fine'

ROBIN 'FISH' PORTER TO PORTSMOUTH
MAGISTRATES' COURT 1981.

Or 'that crazy facker fash', as he was described by some jock to all of our delight once. He was a legend in Portsmouth, whose name and reputation made him an early hero to every jack-the-lad and potential thug in the town. His exploits gained mythical status in the late seventies which carried on through the whole of the 6.57's most active years. He was without doubt the main face of that era.

When all of us were shaving our heads and running around in the same clothes, he would stick to his trademark long, side-swept hair and brightly coloured jumpers and shirts. He never followed the crowd and even made up his own words and phrases, which everyone copied. 'Rooster', 'coburn', 'lakes', or calling people 'ricky', were all his inventions and they passed quickly into all our conversation. Everything to him was 'skimish' and 'scrannoi', accompanied by his infectious laugh and smile. He had the most outrageous humour ever and could be found in the middle of 50 chanting skinheads pissing himself laughing doing his own mimicked version of seig heil, which he called 'eeking'. But he wasn't being racist, he just found everything a joke. He even renamed London Road, his favourite hang-out, 'the main drag' and would always like to be driven down it when we were out cruising. 'Always stick to the drag' was his cry if you wanted to go the other way.

He was a familiar sight in and around Stamshaw and North End, usually on a nicked bike. You very rarely saw him on the same one twice. But he was Fish, he could do what he wanted. He had celebrity status in the town. Fish never had a bad word to say about anyone, but he was game fucker and would fly in without hesitation at every opportunity. He was someone to aspire to on the terraces and gave a lift to anyone standing next to him. He knew everyone and was a link between the different firms in Portsmouth, which ultimately helped us all to get together the mob that made the name of the 6.57.

He was even on the coach with us when we went to Middlesbrough. Everyone was going, like, 'Middlesbrough have got some boys' and that. We got the coach early in the morning, for this night game in Middlesbrough, I think it was '81, but I'm not quite sure of the season. The coach crashed at Twyford, and Fish smacked his head, but anyway we ended up getting another coach driving up to Middlesbrough, hard shoulder all the way. There was loads of traffic into Middlesbrough. We got there really late, half-past, quarter-past eight, just before half-time. The coach parked up at the wrong side of the ground, straight into the Middlesbrough end, giving it. Imagine Middlesbrough, with about 30 Pompey turning up. We were coming unstuck, but we still stood there and had a go. The Old Bill just escorted us round the ground into Pompey's end, I think we lost 1–0 or something. Who gives a fuck about the result? Yeah, I've got good memories of Fish, fucking mad. He didn't give a fuck about no one, he was the maddest geezer ever. I love him to bits. I wish he was still here.

He'd be up there now, waving us on, going, 'Go on, boys, get in there', the Fish, boys. He loved it. He took the drink, like all of us, but he just took it too far.

A separate book could be written about his football antics but one funny one thing stands out at Plymouth in 1981. There were thousands of us there but he ran on the pitch, picked up the corner flag and, in true Fatima Whitbread style, hurled it into the other thugs, starting the riot that was waiting to happen. Nothing he ever did was normal.

The other thing is still talked about today and that's his now famous reply when asked by the court why he hadn't paid a fine imposed. It was pure classic Fish. No one has had the status he had at that time and he was taken suddenly and far too soon. He had a huge send off by half the town and is still fondly remembered by all of us. RIP, Fish, our first leader.

Fish's Dictionary:
Rooster/Coburn=Cowboy
Lakes=Mental
Ricky=People
Skimish=Drink
Scrannoi=Food

AND FINALLY

And, finally, throughout this book there are references to football violence and major outbreaks of trouble, some serious. Glorifying violence is not what we as authors are about. We have reproduced these stories to show what was a way of life for certain sections of supporters in football.

In what may turn out to be a unique era and time, this was a British youth culture and phenomenon that had its own music, fashion, thrill and a buzz on a scale we are unlikely to experience again.

If anything, the 6.57 crew reflect a collective spirit of what those times were. Their memories of their football-going days were retold from experience. Whether they were the best fighters, mob, firm or whatever, really depends on what side of the fence you saw things. But there's no denying the strength of their tales and that, in their support of their beloved football team, these men gave a whole new meaning to the words 'Play up, Pompey'.

Cass Pennant and Rob Silvester